PLEASANT DREAMS

PLEASANT DREAMS

☆ ☆

Nighttime Meditations
for
Peace of Mind

AMY E. DEAN

Hay House, Inc.
Carson, CA

PLEASANT DREAMS
by Amy E. Dean

Copyright © 1993 by Amy E. Dean

Library of Congress Cataloging-in-Publication Data

Dean, Amy.
   Pleasant dreams : nighttime meditations for peace of mind / by Amy E. Dean.
      p.   cm.
   Includes index.
   ISBN 1-56170-079-7 (pbk.) : $9.00
   1. Meditations. 2. Sleep—Religious aspects. 3. Peace of mind—Religious aspects. I. Title.
BL624.2.D44   1994   93-39153
158'.12—dc20   CIP

Library of Congress Catalog Card No. 93-39153
ISBN: 1-56170-079-7

Internal design by John Vannucci
Typesetting by Freedmen's Organization, Los Angeles, CA 90004

94 95 96 97 98 99   10 9 8 7 6 5 4 3 2 1

First Printing, December 1993

Published and Distributed in the United States by:

Hay House, Inc.
. P.O. Box 6204
Carson, CA 90749-6204

Printed in the United States of America
on Recycled Paper

To Mom and Dad Fowler

INTRODUCTION

Did you know that dropping off to sleep at night, on average, takes most people from five minutes to fourteen minutes? But what happens to this time range when the "normal" stresses you may experience in a day—missed deadlines, rush-hour traffic, conflicts with family members or coworkers, or impossible time constraints—get into bed with you at night? How much does the time increase if you're in the midst of a crisis in your life—the loss of a job, financial problems, the breakup of a relationship or marriage, or the illness or death of a loved one? What happens to the time when your head hits the pillow but can't seem to stop projecting negative messages into your mind? How can you possibly get to sleep when you aren't familiar with stress management techniques, don't know how to let go, rarely place nurturing your mind, body, and spirit first, aren't in touch with your limits, or can't take things one day at a time? Finally, if you're fearful, anxious, lonely, or depressed, getting to sleep will not be the only problem for you—so will staying asleep throughout the night.

What is it about nighttime that can make it so hard to enjoy the benefits of a restful, relaxing, refreshing, and revitalizing sleep? While each dawn may hold new promises and new beginnings—a chance to maybe make everything "right" in your world—the sunset may signal that, once again, you "failed"—you simply didn't have enough time to do all the things you wanted to do, didn't make everything "better," and moved no closer to your goals.

So you may view nighttime as a time in which you must review all of your "daily tapes" and always—ALWAYS—give them a thumbs-down rating. "But I should've . . . could've . . . ought to've . . ." may be the start of negative comments, judgments, and statements you make about yourself, your feelings, your behaviors, your actions, and the result of your actions for the day.

You can continue to spend your nights processing and reprocessing your days, or you can try to make a change. That's what this book is all about: making simple changes in the way you end each day so you can gently ease your mind into a relaxed, peaceful, and accepting state at bedtime.

Each of these nighttime meditations offers practical ideas as well as reminds you of the marvelous tools you have within yourself to help you change your way of thinking so you can increase your peace of mind. As *Tao* teaches:

> "Be still
> And discover your center of peace.
> Throughout nature
> The ten thousand things move along,
> But each returns to its source.
> Returning to center is peace." (*Tao*, 16)

May this book help you view each night as an ending as well as a beginning, and may it always help you find peace of mind, both night and day.

It must be borne in mind that the tragedy of life doesn't lie in not reaching your goal. The tragedy lies in having no goal to reach. It isn't a calamity to die with dreams unfulfilled, but it is a calamity not to dream. It is not a disgrace not to reach the stars, but it is a disgrace to have no stars to reach for.
—*Benjamin E. Mays*

Tonight is the first night of the new year. How would you like it to be different from most of the nights in the previous year? Maybe you'd like to spend more time enjoying pleasant, positive thoughts than filling your mind with obsessive, negative thinking. Perhaps you'd like to set aside time for yourself to relax and unwind. Maybe you'd like to begin meditating. Or perhaps you'd like to feel a little less frantic, a little less stressed.

You can make any desire into a goal for the new year. A goal is simply a change you wish to bring about in an area of your life so you can improve the overall quality of your life. Most goals begin with a desire that springs from a dream: a vision of how you could be, how things could be, or how you could be in tandem with things in your life. But if you don't acknowledge a desire, dream a dream, or create a goal, nothing will change tonight—or any other night this year.

So tonight, resolve to make one of your dreams into a goal. Then make tonight and every night more pleasant and peaceful.

☆

Tonight I'll make one of my new year's resolutions to have a nighttime goal to reach for. I'll dream a dream that can help me create a new vision of how I'd like my nights to be.

You must travel the river, live on it, follow it when there is morning light, and follow it when there is nothing but dark and the banks have blurred into shadows.

—Wil Haygood

Have you ever tried to swim against a current? Even though the safety of shore may be only yards away, the pull of the current may be so strong that you may panic or exhaust yourself in your efforts to go a short distance.

But what happens if you simply relax and go with the flow of the current? While you may drift further down from where you'd ideally like to be, you leave the water without your energy depleted or your peace of mind disrupted.

Tonight you may discover that your weariness is a result of swimming against today's current. Maybe you tried to force changes in people, places, or things. Perhaps you overreacted to situations that were out of your control. Maybe you found it difficult to compromise or be flexible. Or perhaps you tried to force yourself to do things you weren't capable of doing.

Tonight, use the statement "go with the flow" as a reminder to stop moving against the current of life. Whatever happened today is over and done with—and out of your control tonight. Resolving to go with the flow means you'll accept circumstances, yourself, and others without trying to force an outcome or get your way. So relax, take a deep breath, and simply go with the flow.

☆

Tonight I'll be better able to travel the river of my life by accepting the way things happen. I'll respect others as well as myself as I drift calmly and contentedly on the current of life this evening.

*. . . all humans are frightened of their own solitude.
Yet only in solitude can we learn to know ourselves,
learn to handle our own eternity of aloneness.*
—Han Suyin

Loneliness can attack you like a disease. Physically it can drain you like a potent strain of a flu, wearing you down to a point of exhaustion. And, like a long bout with the flu, it can also drain you emotionally, eating away at your ability to think positively so you can't remember a time when you weren't sick and don't trust that you'll ever feel better.

The best antidote to loneliness is to go within yourself in search of companionship. Instead of thinking, "Oh, I haven't a person in the world who cares about me right now," you can think, "I can enjoy this night alone by finding out more about me. Who am I? What are my likes? My dislikes? How do I feel? What's important to me in my life?" Having the opportunity to be quiet with yourself can let the inner voice within you be heard. In such solitude you can nurture your individuality apart from others so you can see just how physically and emotionally strong you can be without the support of others or the need to always have others around.

Tonight, in your solitude, find the serenity that's nestled in the recesses of your mind. When you do, you'll begin to understand that there's really nothing to be afraid of when you're alone. All is well, for *you* are well.

☆

Tonight I'll find my sanity and serenity by letting my own voice guide me. My quiet times away from others can nurture my soul and safeguard my journey through life.

. . . the first sight of the lighthouse set boldly on its outer rock, the flash of a gull, the waiting procession of seaward-bound firs on an island, made me feel solid and definite again, instead of a poor, incoherent being . . . .It was a return to happiness.

—Sarah Orne Jewett

Many people have things that calm them, center them, or bring them inner peace. For some it is the ocean, with its smells, sounds, rhythm, and vastness. For others it is a spectacular sunset, where luminous colors spark each surrounding cloud into an ethereal hue. Still others may have a song that brings them peace and comfort.

What is it that brings you inner peace? Maybe running in the morning, downhill skiing at night, or watching dancing snowflakes in a gentle snowfall can make you feel good inside. Such things are your positive relaxation "fixes." When you haven't been skiing for awhile, for instance, you may have an urge to go again. Just running your hands along your skis or closing your eyes and remembering your last time skiing down a snow-covered mountain can be as reassuring and soothing as the act of skiing itself.

When you do something that brings you inner peace or can close your eyes and remember something you enjoy, you can return to happiness. Tonight, enjoy the reality of one of your positive relaxation fixes or create it clearly in your mind. See what relaxes you, hear it, touch it, experience it, and enjoy it.

☆

Tonight I can feel solid and definite again—a complete, whole, relaxed human being—when I think a pleasant thought or do something that makes me feel peaceful and contented.

Every group has its risk takers, its dancers on thin ice . . . .they are the ones with the finely honed skills, those who dare the most, accomplish the most, fly the highest, have the furthest to fall: the high-wire act in the circus, the pitcher in baseball, novelists among writers, litigators among lawyers . . .
—*Judith Van Gieson*

When you're faced with a choice have you ever thought, "This is an opportunity I shouldn't refuse" and then walk away from it? You may have been too afraid of the consequences of failing in the opportunity, consequences that may include feelings of disappointment, depression, hopelessness, poor self-image, being stuck in the same rut, and so on. Or you may have been afraid of achieving the opportunity because of the pressure to continue to succeed in future opportunities or the need to make changes in your life based upon your success.

Risk taking can be frightening. The worst risk-takers are the people who say, "What do I have to lose?" They have the attitude that if they don't succeed, such failure will validate the negative feelings they may already have about themselves. The best risk-takers are the people who say, "This is what I have to lose, and this is how I'll try to avoid losing it, yet I'll take the risk anyway."

From now on, resolve to take charge of your life by facing your fears and learning from them. Instead of asking, "What am I afraid of?" reassure yourself with the thought, "Whatever fears I have, I can always conquer them."

☆

I may be afraid of trying something new because of unknown consequences. Whenever I face a new challenge, I'll remember that my fears are simply fears of the unknown.

Any concern too small to be turned into a prayer is too small to be made into a burden.

—Corrie ten Boom

Each day you may try to meet your physical needs by eating, sleeping, and exercising. You may strive to meet your intellectual needs by solving problems and expanding your wealth of knowledge. You may attempt to meet your emotional needs by sharing your feelings with others.

But how do you meet your spiritual needs? These needs may include quiet time for meditation, connecting with the wonder and splendor of nature, developing inner peace through relaxation, and asking for spiritual guidance and support through prayer.

Perhaps the only times you meditate are when you're stressed out. Perhaps the only times you take a walk in the woods are when you have no pressing commitments. And perhaps the only times you pray for help are when you're in the middle of a crisis.

It's certainly easy to ignore spiritual needs. They don't cry out for attention like your other needs do; you won't starve if you don't meditate and you won't pull a muscle by not praying. But you also may not be able to handle the stresses in your life so you can relax and unwind at night.

Tonight, think about whether you allow enough time for your spiritual growth. Then set aside five minutes in which you can close your eyes, breathe deeply, and thank your Higher Power for today.

☆

Tonight I'll take time to unwind my spiritual side. Before I fall asleep, I'll give thanks for a natural wonder I saw today or a spiritual gift I was given.

I sometimes give myself admirable advice, but I am incapable of taking it.

—Mary Wortley Montagu

Without self-acceptance, most people see life as a constant struggle. They make war on themselves and others on the job, in their relationships, and at home. They may suffer tremendous emotional ups and downs. They may be plagued by a nagging sense of inadequacy. They may doubt their own capabilities and judgments.

Building self-acceptance means knowing yourself so you can trust that you're the best resource for advice and decision-making. How do you do this? Begin by reprogramming the "mental tapes" inside you that tell you only negative, critical, and demeaning statements about yourself. The next time you "hear" one of your self-critical statements, counter with a positive one. Rather than believe, "I did it wrong again—just like I always do," say aloud, "I can learn and grow from this experience. I'm proud that I made the effort." After this, repeat the following affirmation several times: "I love myself. I accept myself. I trust in my own judgment."

Then distance yourself from any continued attempts at negative "dialoguing" by focusing your full attention on something positive you can do. From this moment on, resolve to play your favorite music, paint, go for a run, plan out your summer garden, or cook your favorite dinner. It's true that what you believe, you create. To believe in yourself, *create* yourself.

☆

To bring a self-accepting end to this day, I'll make a mental list of all the things I appreciate about myself and all the positive things I did in the day.

> *In certain moments a single almost insignificant sorrow may, by association, bring together all the little relics of pain and discomfort, bodily and mental, that we have endured even from infancy.*
> —Samuel Taylor Coleridge

Did you experience something today that returned you to a time in your life that may have been painful, difficult, or seemingly never-ending? The scent of a particular perfume, a song played on the radio, something someone said, the cooking aroma that drifted out of a restaurant you passed by, or a picture in a photo album may have brought you face to face with a memory you may have felt you had effectively dealt with in the past. However, the flood of emotions you may have experienced as a result of that memory trigger could now make you feel unsafe and uncertain—as if that awful time could somehow return to haunt your life tonight.

But now's the time to keep in mind that what's past is past, what's done is done, what's over is over. You never have to go through that exact moment in time again, except as it replays in your mind as a memory. While you can be reminded of what life used to be like for you as a child, of the loss of a loved one, or of a past addiction, what was true for you then isn't true for you right now.

Now pause and savor this present moment and reflect on how far you've come. You can remember the way things used to be, but you can also be thankful for today.

☆

Whenever I experience a sense of déjà vu or history repeating itself, I'll remind myself that I'm a different person in a different place in time. I'll treasure the way life is now rather than tremble at my memories of the past.

It used to be that, if I had a good working day, I thought I was a wonderful person, but otherwise I thought I was a terrible person.

—Byron Janis

How often are you buoyed up by successes and achievements, but deflated by failures and shortcomings? If you've done well or had a good day, you may feel as if you're a good person. But if your day has gone badly, you've made a mistake, or things didn't work out as planned, then your self-image for the evening may be negative and critical.

But no matter what happened today, you're still a good person inside. No one can be wonderful all the time, no day can go exactly as scheduled, no achievements can be made without some disappointments. So a good day on the job, at home, or at school doesn't mean you're good, just as a bad day doesn't mean you're bad.

Look at how you're feeling about yourself at the end of this day. You may not be the person you want to be right now; you may not have acted the way you wanted to act today; you may not have done everything you wanted to do in exactly the way you wanted to do it. But you have the power to change all those things.

From now on, see your self-image as completely separate from your job or your job title, the responsibilities you fulfill as a home manager, or the obligations you have as a student. See yourself as an independent person, not as a subordinate to a group, company, family, or institution.

☆

Tonight I'll look inside myself and be courageous enough to see good. No matter what happened today, I'm still a good person inside.

Sleepless nights.
Diet, mind, conditions
Hold the possibility of correction.
—Deng Ming-Dao

Whenever you feel out of sorts, find it hard to concentrate at the end of a day, or cannot sleep at night, you may struggle unsuccessfully to restore your inner peace. However, your problems may be related to three areas in your life in which you may need to make changes. To find out, ask yourself these questions: "Am I eating right? Am I allowing time for meditation? Do I feel safe in my world?"

First, look at the way you eat. Is your diet rich in nutrients provided by fresh fruits and vegetables, lean meat and fish, and whole grains? Are you drinking plenty of water throughout the day? Are you chewing your food slowly or eating at a time or in a place where you don't feel rushed?

Next, consider how much time you set aside during the day or at the end of the day to still your mind. Ideally it's best to provide at least half an hour for communing with yourself and your Higher Power. Not having this time keeps your mind on the treadmill of the daily grind, always focused on the things you've yet to do.

Finally, roommate hassles, family pressures, and work stresses can contribute to disruption of your inner peace. So keep your home a haven, your relationships stable, and make your work space comfortable. Paying attention to your diet, your quiet times, and your living and working conditions can work wonders on restoring your peace of mind.

☆

Tonight I'll keep in mind that I'm not going to have a deep, relaxing sleep without good food, good thoughts, and good relations.

*We tend not to choose the unknown, which might be
a shock or a disappointment or simply a little difficult
to cope with. And yet it is the unknown with all its disappointments and surprises that is the most enriching.*
—Anne Morrow Lindbergh

Do you have a rigid addiction to the status quo? You do
if you don't like your home, job, or relationship, but are
afraid to change any of those things. You do if you're afraid
to take chances. You do if there's something you'd really like
to do, but you're afraid you'll fail if you try. You do if you're
afraid that if you really care about something or someone,
you'll lose it or the person. You do if you're afraid that if you
make changes in your life, people won't like you.

When you're rigidly addicted to the status quo in your
life—a dead-end job, an uncomfortable living situation, an
unhappy relationship, or an unhealthy pattern of behavior—
you may hang on to a familiar situation year after year, even
though you're miserable. Why? What you may be afraid of
is not knowing what to expect if and when you change: you
fear the great unknown!

Yet no matter how tightly you cling to the familiar, the
only true constant in life is change. Tonight, think back to
the people, places, or things in your life that have changed
over the years. Think of a good thing gained from such
changes. By thinking of change as positive, you'll be more
ready to make a change in your life when you need to.

☆

*From now on, when I think about doing something new in my
life, I won't be afraid. I'll keep in mind that if I try it and don't
like it, I can always try something else. I always have the power
to change the change!*

Anyone can blame; it takes a specialist to praise.
—*Konstantin Stanislavski*

Assessing blame is easy. After all don't you, like most people, know what it's like to fail? You may even feel blameworthy yourself, either from what you were taught in your dysfunctional childhood or because of your low self-esteem. Sometimes you might even enjoy pointing out the failings of others so you don't feel as if you're the only person who has ever been blamed.

But why should you be so begrudging of giving out a little praise now and then? Praise doesn't diminish you in any way. To the contrary, it reflects a spirit of giving to others, of noticing others, and of being sensitive to what others do. True praise is a form of love; oftentimes, when given it can come back to you in kind.

When was the last time you spoke praise that came from your heart? Think about your coworkers or employees, life partner or family members, friends or acquaintances, members of 12-step support groups to which you belong, and others with whom you interact. What things have they done lately that you feel earns praise? Perhaps a coworker offered invaluable help on a project, a life partner called to let you know that he or she would be late for dinner, a child behaved well in a difficult situation, or a recovering person shared a gem of wisdom that helped get you through a trying time. From this moment on, resolve to recognize such actions by rewarding them next time with praise.

☆

I want to become a specialist of praise. That means that I need to seek out occasions for praise as a way of showing love to others.

Strange feelings. . . . Just a sort of unexplained sadness that comes each afternoon when the new day is gone forever and there's nothing ahead but increasing darkness.

—*Robert M. Pirsig*

Just as each day is a new beginning, so too can each evening be a new start. The darkness of a cold winter night doesn't limit you to hibernation; rather, it can present you with a multitude of exhilarating and energizing opportunities. Nighttime can be a time for you to start on a project you've been putting off. Nighttime can be the first night of an adult education class, a bowling league, or a volunteering opportunity. Nighttime can be the time you take a courageous first step in getting to know someone new. Nighttime can be the time to try a new recipe, start reading a good book, or take in a first-run movie.

Each night gives you the chance to recharge yourself after your day's batteries have run down. Each night presents you with endless opportunities to start anew on your goals, your growth, and your interests. Instead of using the time you've been given tonight reflecting on the past events of the day, you can enjoy each moment.

Although the day is done, tomorrow has yet to come. There are plans you can make, places you can go, people you can see, projects you can do. Rest assured that tonight isn't a closing; it's also an opening.

☆

Each night is a new beginning. I'll make light of the darkness at night by enjoying myself in my solitude, with a close friend or companion, or with family members.

Sleeplessness is a desert without vegetation or inhabitants.

—*Jessamyn West*

The effects of sleeplessness are perfectly illustrated in the movie *The Spirit of St. Louis*, starring Jimmy Stewart. Stewart recreated the role of Charles Lindbergh in the cinematic story of Lindbergh's historic trans-Atlantic solo flight. Although Lindbergh faced many obstacles during his epic journey—bad weather, failed instruments, low fuel—probably his most trying moments came when he had to fight off sleep. Watching Stewart painfully fight off the excruciating fatigue Lindbergh must have experienced in his isolated flight provided an excellent picture of the effects of sleep deprivation.

The emotional and physical effects of sleep loss have long been studied and are greatly documented. Minor effects can range from irritability and loss of appetite to, over time, mental depression and hallucinations. So getting plenty of rest is as much a part of your physical health as it is your mental health.

Tonight, respect your need for sleep. Don't put off getting into bed so you can fold another load of laundry or finish cleaning out a closet. Those projects will be there tomorrow, but your sleep time won't. Unless you're crossing the Atlantic Ocean on a solo flight, nothing else is so important that you need to deprive yourself of a good night's sleep.

☆

I'll prioritize my evening's activities by placing sleep time at the top of my list. Tonight I'll be certain to get my sleep so tomorrow doesn't feel like I'm plodding my way across an endless desert.

We should think seriously before we slam doors, be-fore we burn bridges, before we saw off the limb on which we find ourselves sitting.

—*Richard L. Evans*

Did you have a difficult day today? Maybe people disap-pointed you. Perhaps events or circumstances upset you. How did you respond to such things?

Anger may have been your first—and only—response to such frustrating, trying, and disappointing times. Unfor-tunately, acting upon that anger without thinking—hastily saying things you later regretted, making short-sighted de-cisions, or even slamming a door in someone's face—may have done considerable damage. Sometimes a slammed door won't open again. Sometimes people you insult or snap at will back off. Sometimes decisions made in anger and haste can't be changed—or may take considerable time and effort to undo.

Angry moments don't have to erupt into fiery volcanoes. If you can learn to sit with your anger awhile until you're calmer and more rational—perhaps by counting slowly to ten, calling for a five-minute time-out, or going for a walk in the fresh air—you can avoid shameful, regretful results.

From now on, let the dust settle from the anger of the day and tempers cool. Resolve to deal with the effects of your anger calmly and rationally. Keep in mind that it's a wise and mature person who can let time help put things back in perspective.

☆

Tonight I'll use the time I've been given away from the anger-producing situations of the day to chill out. I'll take a deep breath and let rest heal the sores of anger I may have inflicted today.

When things are bad, we take comfort in the thought that they could always be worse. And when they are, we find hope in the thought that things are so bad they have to get better.

—*Malcolm S. Forbes*

What's the worst possible thing that has happened to you recently? Maybe you were laid off from your job. Perhaps a close friend or loved one revealed that he or she has a serious illness. Maybe you've been faced with a difficult issue or crisis in therapy or in your life. Or perhaps a recent loss—the death of a family member, the ending of a long-term relationship, or a divorce—has left you feeling hopeless and alone.

Any loss or difficulty can put you in distress. There's often little anyone can say or do to comfort you or make life easier. Sympathy from those who care can help, but it doesn't provide lasting solace or the answers you might like to have. At times like this you may feel like a baby who can't get to sleep when he or she's too tired. What you want is for things to get better; what you need is patience to get you through to the time when things *do* get better.

Tonight, seek comfort from a spiritual resource. As written in Psalm 77, "When I was in distress, I sought the Lord; At night I stretched out untired hands . . ." Ask your Higher Power for help in making the transition from today's restlessness and distress to tonight's restfulness and peace.

☆

Tonight I'll trust that my Higher Power will lead me through even the most difficult circumstances and the most trying times. All I have to do is pray for comfort.

Give us to go blithely on our business this day, bring us to our resting beds weary and content and undishonored, and grant us in the end the gift of sleep.
                              Robert Louis Stevenson

Tonight your reward for everything you did during the day is sleep. To make your sleep more peaceful and relaxing and filled with pleasant thoughts, set aside a few minutes to gently close your mind to the day's events.

Before you turn off the lights, visualize walking down a pleasant, nature-filled path. Each step you take moves you farther away from the day's activities and the many tasks you did or left undone. Look around you as you walk. Breathe deeply. See lakes and mountains and hear the soothing sounds of a babbling brook; watch the rise and fall of gentle ocean waves that reflect a glorious sunset; breathe deeply of the humid air in a tropical rain forest while being serenaded by an orchestra of jungle sounds. In the inner sanctuary you create in your mind, nothing is important—nothing except peace of mind and the hours ahead in which your mind will be gently stilled.

As you reach the end of your nature walk, you may feel the tensions and pressures of the day fall from your shoulders. Your body may feel lighter. Your lips may be turned upwards to form a gentle smile. You may feel a yawn building in your chest. Now tell yourself, "Today has been good. I can close my eyes and let the reward of sleep drift over me."

☆

My day has been good. I've done well. Tonight I'm satisfied and ready to let sleep overtake me.

Love is a great thing, a good above all others, which alone maketh every burden light. Love is watchful, and whilst sleeping, still keeps watch; though fatigued, it is not weary; though pressed, it is not forced.
— *Thomas À. Kempis*

Love isn't just a word you say or write. Love is the way you present yourself to the world: the face you put on, the clothes you wear, the way you walk and move—your very heart and soul. If you're not made up of love, you'll reflect this to others and feel it within yourself. Inside your chest will be a heart, but one that's heavy and cold and made of stone.

Love isn't just a feeling. Love is a truth filled with forgiveness and kindness. It's a gift that's bursting with generosity and honesty. Love is the willingness to serve and protect, to cherish and respect, to honor and be strong. You don't have to be in love to feel love; you simply need to embody it. That means that while you might not have feelings of love for everyone you meet, you can love them nonetheless.

Have you loved those around you today? Have you shown them that you accept them and love them just the way they are? Have you given this love freely and willingly, with no expectation to be returned in kind?

From now on, consider that you can love more people in your life than you're in love with. To do so, see love as separate from the feelings of falling in love. Love is really part of everything and everybody.

☆

Do I acknowledge the goodness, wisdom, beauty, and love in another in the same way I'd like this person to acknowledge such things in me? Tonight I'll reflect love to another so I can feel the love within myself.

Tension is a habit. Relaxing is a habit. And bad habits can be broken, good habits formed.
                                              —William James

Are you aware of how you vent your nervousness about events yet to come? Nail biting, pacing, deep sighing, and hand wringing are some of the more harmless things you may do that indicate nervous tension. There are other more harmful indicators, however, such as using drugs, alcohol, caffeine, sugar, tobacco, sex, or food to cope with frayed nerves.

You may be so obsessed about an upcoming happening that you're not even aware of the things you do when you're tense. Maybe you have to give a presentation at work tomorrow, face a big test in school, want to talk with your life partner about an intimate issue, need to confront someone in order to work through a conflict, or have party plans days from now. Are you unable to relax and go to sleep because you're caught up in a whirlwind of tension and anxiety? Do you want a drink or a cigarette? Are you biting your nails or jiggling your foot?

Right now, replace a bad habit with a good one. Instead of biting your nails, clutch a seashell, smooth stone, or soothing crystal in your hand. Instead of reaching for a cigarette, take slow, deep breaths. By using positive replacements for bad habits, you can release nervous energy in less self-damaging ways.

☆

What are some of the bad habits I fall back on when I'm faced with a stressful or tense situation? I'll use a good habit now to replace a bad one so I can let go of my anxiety and go to sleep.

*Intimacy happens in moments. The mistake we make
is in wanting it all the time.*

—*JoAnn Magdoff*

Have you noticed how people you care for seem to move
from job to job or neighborhood to neighborhood, how intimate relationships don't always last too long, and how old
friendships sometimes die out? You may feel that feelings of
intimacy you share with other people change more frequently than you'd like. Those enjoyable coffee breaks at
work, nice dinners with friends, pleasant evenings with loved
ones, or intimate conversations with your best friend are
sometimes lost when things change in your life or the lives
of those you love.

But as you think back tonight on wonderful times of connection, laughter, and lightness you've experienced, keep in
mind two important sentiments. First, "Sometimes good
things have to come to an end." And second, "Special, intimate moments can come again."

What that means is that warm, loving feelings you felt with
loved ones in the past don't have to go away forever or can't be
replicated with someone else. You just need to be patient and
trust that although time and distance can disconnect you from
some people, such things can also reconnect you with others.

Tonight, delight in the memory of shared laughter, relax
with the echoes of casual chatter, and feel comforted by your
memories of physical touches and embraces.

☆

*From time to time I know I'll experience pleasurable intimacy
with those I love. Tonight I'll treasure the pleasure not as an investment for the future, but as an enrichment of the present
moment.*

I think the purpose in life is to be useful, to be respon-
sible, to be compassionate . . . to count, to stand for
something, to have made some difference that you
lived at all.

—*Leo Rosten*

A student at a preparatory school had just completed his assignment for a "Death and Dying" class. The assignment was to write an essay detailing how he'd like to be remembered at his funeral. A few days after he had completed the assignment, the young man was killed in an automobile accident. At his funeral, his essay was read and his family members, students, teachers, and members of the community followed his wishes to the letter.

Whether you're in good health, are growing old, or are battling cancer, AIDS, or another life-threatening disease, focus on the good things in your life you've accomplished so far, the good qualities you have, and the positive ways in which you've contributed to your life and the lives of others.

Then, from this moment on, change your view on the meaning and purpose of life from that of a constant struggle to achieve happiness, fame, wealth, or material rewards to a life dedicated to giving, to guiding others, and to promoting good in your community. How well you live your life in the future begins in the present.

☆

What do I think is my purpose in life? Tonight I'll think about
what I can mean to my life, not what my life should mean to me.

I have but one lamp by which my feet are guided, and that is the lamp of experience.

—Patrick Henry

Think about what it would be like to walk through the woods at night without a flashlight. You'd be at the mercy of every root, stump, rock, and hole. Although you may be so familiar with the woods that you could take the same path in daylight without a problem, without the guidance of a light at night it would be like walking the path blindfolded—and for the very first time.

Your daily experiences often teach you the right paths to take so you may have few problems getting to where you want to go during the daylight hours. You may know the right route to take to work so you avoid traffic tie-ups. You may know the right people to call in order to get a job done quickly and efficiently. You may know the best places to eat lunch, the greatest places to shop for bargains, and the right time to leave your office for the commute home.

But at night, you may not have such a firm base of experience to follow when you're having a hard time. Even though some of your past difficulties may have taught you to trust in the slogan, "And this, too, shall pass," you may not know how to get through feelings of fear, sadness, doubt, anxiety, and insecurity. Yet there are many flashlights you can use to light your path tonight. Reach out to a friend or loved one who will listen to how you're feeling and reassure you that all is well.

☆

Tonight I can choose to stumble in the dark alone or I can walk easily with the light provided by others I know and trust.

There are two things to aim at in life: first, to get what you want; and, after that, to enjoy it. Only the wisest of mankind can achieve the second.
—*Logan Pearsall Smith*

Twenty-five centuries ago—long before there were compact disc players, luxury cars, high-paying salaried jobs, summer homes, pleasure boats, and elegant mansions—Chinese philosopher Lao Tzu realized the dangers of excess. For individuals, he said, excess can cause sensory overload, imbalance, and disease.

Are your home, your garage, your dresser drawers and closets, your rooms, and your calendars impossibly cluttered with all the things you want? Take a look around you tonight and mentally inventory all the material things you've accumulated. Now ask yourself, "Do I enjoy these things? Do they bring me happiness?"

You live in the richest nation in the world, yet you may be chronically unhappy. Your life may be filled with things to prove you've gotten what you want from life. But how much do they *really* matter?

Getting rid of things you no longer need or use can help you discover what you do have and what you really want. Focus on one area in your home and resolve to go through it in the near future. Make it a rule to discard anything you no longer use or need. Releasing old possessions not only creates greater order in your life, but also circulates new energy in yourself.

☆

I'll make it a goal to bring things I don't use any more to my favorite charity. Recycling what I no longer need can bring someone else happiness, so everyone benefits.

. . . she looked around and found there were no monsters, only shifting shadows from the play of moonlight through the trees outside the window.

—Lisa Alther

How often were you told as a child that your bedtime fears were the result of an overactive imagination? So your parents might not have let you watch scary movies at night and may have tucked you into bed with your favorite stuffed animal, placed a nightlight in your room, or left your bedroom door slightly ajar.

But now, as an adult, your nighttime imagination may still run wild to such an extent that your realities become distorted. You may begin to imagine things that really aren't real. For example, an unreturned telephone call may signal that you've done something to upset a friend, who now hates you. A boss's coldness during the day may lead you to believe that tomorrow you'll be laid off. Or your partner's disinterest in sex may hint that he or she is cheating on you. Instead of seeing what really exists, you let your imagination take over. Minor inconveniences become major catastrophes; small sounds become amplified into "things that go bump in the night."

Tonight there's nothing to fear except the thoughts that run wild in your mind. You can chase them away by remembering to look at things as they really are, not as you imagine them to be. Tonight, don't let darkness cloud your thoughts; use your mind to see clearly.

☆

Tonight can be as real as today. I'll remember that at night realities can become distorted, like the "monsters" that are really shadows dancing on my window in the moonlight.

Lost, yesterday, somewhere between sunrise and sunset, two golden hours, each set with sixty diamond minutes. No reward is offered, for they are gone forever.

—*Horace Mann*

As you reflect on the day, were there moments you felt that you wasted? Was there a chunk of time you idled away because you were bored, depressed, or restless? Did you putter when you could have produced? Did you spend your evening in front of the television because you couldn't motivate yourself to do anything else? Did you devote an incredible amount of time taking care of the needs of others and allow little or no time to take care of your own needs? Did you become entangled in a pointless disagreement with a loved one? Did you think about all the things you *could have done*, but instead did the things you felt you *should do*?

Those moments are gone now. You can never get them back. But what you can do from now on is become more conscious about wasting your precious moments in the future. Make up your mind tonight not to waste any more time. You can give to others, but not to the extent that it infringes on your time. You can walk away from an argument. You can venture out to a movie in the evening or spend time conversing with friends. While the time you've already wasted is gone, there's a great deal of fresh, unused time yet to come. Tonight, resolve to make every future minute count.

☆

I won't waste any more of the precious moments in my life. Tonight I'll make the most of the rest of today and resolve to make the most of every minute given to me in the future.

*It wasn't until late in life that I discovered how easy
it is to say, "I don't know."*
                              —W. Somerset Maugham

In her book *The Tao of Inner Peace*, Diane Dreher tells the
story of a midwestern farm boy who was the only one in his
family to go to college. Al went to a State University, then
earned a graduate fellowship to a fancy Eastern school.
There, Al often felt embarrassed when his classmates asked
if he had read this or that learned book. He would remain
quiet as his classmates discussed theories and authors he
didn't know. But one day, he decided to tell the truth. "No,
I haven't read that book," he responded when asked. "Could
you tell me more about it?"

Were there times today that you felt embarrassed,
ashamed, or guilty that you didn't know something others
were discussing? Did you remain quiet, or did you answer
the way Al did?

The next time you face an area of ignorance in your life—
on the job, with your family or friends, or with your
children—don't be afraid to admit, "I don't know." Ask for
more information. Such honesty can provide you with the
opportunity to learn. It can foster closeness with others who
are often more than happy to enlighten. It can gain the
respect of others who might be afraid to admit limitations in
knowledge. And it can bring you peace of mind in remov-
ing the strain of defensiveness or egoism. As the Tao teaches,
"Those who know they do not know gain wisdom."

☆

*From now on, I won't hide behind the shame of not knowing.
Instead, I'll step to the front of the line to show I'm eager to want
to find out.*

People who fly into a rage always make a bad landing.
—Will Rogers

Do you storm around the house at night filled with anger because things didn't go your way at work today? Does your anger sometimes make you explode at your pets, your children, or your partner so they give you a wide berth? Does your anger keep you up at night as you rehash the anger-producing scenarios in your head?

Anger is an emotion that can easily escalate from resentment to rage. At its peak, anger can ignite explosively into verbal tirades or physical contact. At times when anger gets this hot, it can be almost impossible for you to act or think clearly or effectively.

De-escalating such intense anger requires that you first take a break from the anger, then work through the anger. Taking a break involves a two-step process of saying out loud, "I'm beginning to feel angry and I want to take a time-out," and then leaving the situation for the time you need to cool down.

To then work through the anger, try doing something physical so you can wind down before you try to go to sleep. Sing along with a cassette tape of your favorite music. Take a walk or run the vacuum cleaner for awhile. Doing such things can discharge some of the angry tension in your body and take your mind away from the situation or person who sparked the anger. Releasing the anger in healthy ways can bring you peace of mind tonight.

☆

Tonight, if I'm still troubled by anger, I'll close my eyes and see myself excelling at a sport, running a marathon, or racing a slalom course down a snow-covered mountain. Then I'll leave my anger there and return home to my soft, soothing bed.

Whether you realize it or not, there are no boundaries,
but until you realize it, you cannot manifest it. The
limitations that each one of us has are defined in the
ways we use our minds.

—*John Daido Loori*

In 1982 mountain climber Hugh Herr and his partner
Jeffrey Batzer reached the top of Odell's Gully on Mount
Washington and decided to push for the summit. They
immediately stumbled into a blinding blizzard. Herr and Batzer survived three nights in gale-force winds and below-
freezing temperatures. Although they came out of the ordeal
alive, Batzer ended up losing one leg; Herr lost both.

Doctors warned Herr about the limitations he would have
to accept. Instead, Herr designed artificial limbs that enabled
him to continue climbing. He invented a more comfortable
socket for leg prostheses. And he became an advocate of
technical solutions to physical disabilities.

As you reflect on the day, think about ways in which you
might have limited yourself. Maybe you refused an invitation to try something new. Perhaps you were given an opportunity to work on a challenging project, but didn't accept
the challenge. Or maybe you heard about a career opportunity, but hesitated to take the next step.

Today Herr's dream is to design legs to enable those who
are physically challenged to run marathons. Tonight your
dream can be to conquer one of your limiting attitudes so
you can treat it as an illusion.

Limitations are walls I erect where walls have never existed.
Tonight I'll step up to one of these walls and work up the courage
to tear it down.

When you worry, you go over the same ground end-
lessly and come out the same place you started.
                                    —*Harold B. Walker*

The sole inhabitant of a small island often has one confined and very limited space in which to move. When you
worry, you're like that island inhabitant. Worry keeps your
mind confined to one set of thoughts—a child who's out long
past curfew, information you couldn't gather in time to finish a project today, an ailing parent or loved one, a financial
problem, or the future. Worry keeps your body in a constant
state of tension and anxiety. Even though you may believe
that your worrying is helping you to work towards a solution,
in actuality all you're really doing is dwelling on the futility
of the problem. You're like the island inhabitant who spends
day and night pacing the same path—and going nowhere.

It's only when you're released from worry that you can see
solutions clearly or begin to make changes. To free yourself
now from worry's constraints, ask, "What can I do to change
this situation?" What you may discover is that there's nothing you *can* do. And if there's nothing you can do, then continuing to worry is simply a waste of your time.

So focus instead on relaxing thoughts so you can sleep in
peace. Such thoughts will be like the wind in the sails of a
rescue boat that takes you off your remote island of worry
and moves you towards the mainland of living in the
moment.

☆

For as long as I'm worrying, I'm stuck in either a past that has
gone by or a future that has yet to happen. Tonight I'll stay in
the present by paying attention to my need for serenity and sleep.

Surely this must be an ancient proverb: If the situation is killing you, get the hell out.

—Hugh Prather

You may shake your head in disbelief at people who stay in uncomfortable, violent, or even life-threatening situations. Yet you may be experiencing similar emotional or physical pain in a difficult situation in your life. Perhaps you dislike your job so much that you feel tired and run down every night. Maybe your intimate relationship makes you so unhappy that you can't seem to concentrate on anything else. Maybe your son or daughter has an alcohol or drug problem that keeps you up at night, worried sick. Or perhaps you're sick or injured but continue to push yourself to make it through the daily grind.

Imagine that whatever situation you're in is like wearing a pair of tight, uncomfortable shoes. Obviously you want to take the shoes off. But how?

Start now by asking, "Are there situations in my life that are causing me physical and emotional distress?" Identify these "shoes," then think of one resource before you turn out the lights that can help you "remove" the shoes tomorrow. You can resolve to make an appointment the next day with a career counselor. You can decide to schedule a time with your partner to sit down and talk about where you're going in your relationship. You can find out where the nearest support group meetings are. Then you can close your eyes and go to sleep.

☆

Tonight I'll take the first step to remove myself from an uncomfortable situation that's disrupting my peace of mind. Knowing what I can do tomorrow will help me to get a good night's sleep tonight.

At last, deathly tiredness drained him of all apprehension; so might a man fall asleep half-an-hour before he was to be woken by a firing squad.
—Nadine Gordimer

Have you ever voiced complaints such as "I'm so tired I can't even see straight," "I'm so tired I'm dead on my feet," or "I feel like I could sleep for months"? Such statements are often made by those who believe in the adage, "If I don't do it, it won't get done." What this means is that it may be so hard for you to share the burden of your responsibilities that you may take the hard road in life—one that's unpaved and needs a four-wheel drive vehicle to negotiate it—rather than the smooth, paved highway you share with others.

It doesn't matter whether you're a single parent of many children, a graduate school student, a business owner, a community leader—or a common, ordinary person. Overextending yourself isn't limited to one particular job or role in life. The effects of overextension are felt by anyone who believes that in order to get things done, they must be done in the right way—your way—and by the right person—you.

There's nothing more wearing to the body, mind, and soul than trying to do everything. But in the play called "Life," remember that you have just one small role—you're not the director, the set designer, the lighting technician, playwright, producer, press agent, and publicist. You're just a person.

☆

Tonight I'll remember that I wasn't put on this earth to carry the world on my shoulders. I can learn to rest without always feeling obligated to others.

February can be lovely if you know what to do with it. . . . February is the perfect time to read all those books that have been piling up. . . . February is for being a kid again, for sticking out the tip of the tongue and catching snowflakes, for warming your hands with a mug of scalding cocoa made from scratch . . .
                                                    —*Joanna Kavanagh*

The Chinese word *tzu jan* means "natural sciences" as well as "living in harmony with nature." When you're tuned in to the cycles of nature, you can be more sensitive to your energy flow. This means living in harmony with the natural seasons—spring, summer, winter, and fall—as well as living in harmony with your natural cycles. As in nature, you have cycles in your life where your energies go through renewal (spring), high output and drive (summer), decline (fall), and exhaustion (winter). Respecting these cycles means avoiding being driven and compulsive when you're not and refraining from exhausting yourself by pushing yourself beyond your capabilities. It means honoring your energies, not fighting them.

Because February is a winter month, your energies may run low or wan more quickly than in other seasons. So think of February as a month for meditation and introspection—a month for tuning out the world and hibernating for awhile.

Tonight, don't fight your energy cycle. Rest your mind when you're tired. The things you need to think about will still be there when you have more energy and insight.

☆

Tonight I'll take a break from pushing myself into an inappropriate energy cycle. I'll rest and honor this energy rather than fight it.

What would you do if you were stuck in one place and every day was the same and nothing mattered?
   —*Bill Murray, in* Groundhog Day

In the film *Groundhog Day*, an obnoxious and egocentric television weatherman, played by Bill Murray, gets stuck in a time-warp fantasy. While covering the Groundhog Day festivities in Punxsutawney, Pennsylvania, Murray discovers there's no tomorrow. Instead, he keeps waking up the next morning to discover that it's still February 2nd. He's doomed to relive the day until he gets it right.

For most people, that's how midlife feels. Midlife can be a time when you're through with studying, building your career, beginning your family, and making a home. Midlife then becomes a "maintenance stage," where you direct your energy into getting through each day. Like Murray's character, you may feel trapped and depressed as you face each new day that looks just like the one before it.

But tonight, think about this: You can change your world and each day in it, but only by first changing yourself. When the outline of your life is pretty clear—as it is in midlife—then what you need to do is strive to make the most of what you have. Ponder a small "repair" or improvement you can make in yourself or in your life. Even small changes can help you appreciate that the commitments of midlife—the work you do, the family you've created, and the things that interest you—can be exciting.

☆

Making the most of what I have doesn't mean going through the motions or doing only what I need to just to get by. It means becoming a more active, lively participant in my life—not a sleepwalker.

Never let your head hang down. Never give up and sit down and grieve. Find another way.

—*Sachel Paige*

When children are tired they make their feelings very clear. They just stop, sit down and—no matter where they are—start to cry.

As an adult, you may sometimes feel like that child, ready to sit down and give up. Rushing around the house every evening helping others by doing endless loads of laundry, cooking, or picking up the same things over and over again or bringing work home and trying to get through it when all you'd really like to do is soak in a hot tub and go to bed can sometimes reduce you to tears.

But while tears may release some of your tension and frustration, they don't relieve the burdens in your life. Instead of giving in to tears and feeling like giving up, try to find more productive ways of handling your responsibilities. Make up your mind that from now on, you will ask for help. There may be others at home or in your family who can take some responsibility for meals, family care, and household duties. You can also rearrange your schedule so you're not doing too much at one time and not enough at other times. Instead of feeling like giving up under the pressure of your responsibilities, resolve in the day light to think about some solutions. Remember, nothing is cast in stone—unless you want it to be.

☆

Why do I have to try to take care of everything? Who gave me the title of "super woman" or "super man"? I'm ready to look at the reality of what I'm capable of handling rather than the fantasy.

People are lonely because they build walls instead of bridges.

           —Joseph Newton

Remember building snow forts when you were a kid? The best time to do so was after a deep, wet snowfall. Then you'd roll and pack the sticky snow into a big snow wall. As you crouched behind the wall, you'd mass-produce snowballs to use in battle. If you built the best snow fort, you usually won the battle, for your wall afforded you the best protection.

Are you still hiding behind your snow fort as an adult? You may have a wall inside you that you began to build in childhood to protect you from the hurt and pain of your dysfunctional home. As you grew older, you may have fortified the wall whenever you were hurt again. You might not even realize it now, but you may have such a strong, high wall in front of you that even the nicest, kindest, gentlest people can't get over it and get to know you.

You may feel protected behind your wall, but you may also feel lonely. To feel less lonely, you need to make a little crawl space to let others in. You don't have to completely tear down your walls, but you can think about one person you might like to let in. Over time, you may learn that by letting one person in at a time, you may feel less protected—but you can also feel less lonely.

☆

Walls are built to keep people out. Yet I can still be safe if I let one or two people in who have earned the right to get through my wall of protection.

It is true that as we take two steps forward in our journey, we may take one or more steps backward. But when one has faith that the spring thaw will arrive, the winter winds seem to lose some of their punch.
—*Robert L. Veninga*

Pain, illness, sadness, depression, grief, separation, and other difficulties can sometimes feel so overpowering and all-encompassing that they seem to take on a life of their own. At times you may feel as if you're never going to get through a tough time or get over a painful loss. One crisis is sometimes all it takes to make you feel that time has stood still—and things will never again be the same.

That's when you need to take a look outside your window and remember that the trees, now bare, will soon bud. The ground, now frozen and snow-covered, will soon thaw. The bulbs you planted last fall, now dormant, will soon break through the ground and blossom. The robins will return from their winter vacation, along with the summer songbirds.

Tonight, if you have faith that the spring renewal will arrive and the winter winds will soon die out, then you can also have faith that you'll get through this time of crisis. One day it may feel as if the dark clouds have been lifted; another day they may return. But nothing ever lasts forever. Nothing ever continues with the same intensity with which it began. Just as there are endings, so too are there beginnings. You need to believe that you can move on from one place to the next—with patience, time, and trust.

☆

One moment I may smile, the next moment tears may fall. Tonight I'll trust that both are part of the process of recognizing an ending and getting ready for a new beginning.

Won't God protect his chosen ones who pray to him day and night? Won't he be concerned for them?
—*Luke 18:7*

There's a story often told in spiritual circles about an old woman who lived in the center of town in Moorefield, West Virginia, during the Civil War. Because the town was so close to the border in the battle between the states, one day it would be controlled by Union troops, the next day the Confederates.

One evening several enemy soliders forced their way into the woman's home and demanded they be given dinner. They tramped noisily about her small home, placed their muddy boots and soiled clothing on her furniture, and helped themselves to many of her cherished possessions as she cooked for them. When the food was ready and she had joined the soldiers at the table, she announced to them: "It's my custom to pray before my evening meal. I hope you won't mind." Then she bowed her head and gave thanks for her home and health, the food on her table, her good neighbors and other members of the community, and the guests with whom she was to share her evening meal. While she was praying she heard the sounds of the men moving. When she said, "Amen" and looked up, the men had left.

Tonight, when you feel as if your enemies have gotten the better of you, when you feel overwhelmed with fear or anxiety, or when you face dangers or difficulties in your life, reach out to a Higher Power through your prayers. Nothing can harm you as long as your Higher Power is near.

☆

Tonight I'll reach out for the invisible power provided by spiritual strength. I'll pray to my Higher Power for protection, guidance, hope, and serenity.

I'm too busy. I can barely see the numbers on my calendar for all the meetings, talks, appointments, programs, deadlines and classes penciled into . . . [the] little squares.

—Linda Weltner

Self-inflicted stress is the voluntary creation of too much to do in too little time. It usually begins simply and innocently enough, with an offer on your part to "help out." What happens next is like a snowball rolling downhill. "Help out" turns into "support" which turns into "share" which turns into "organize" which finally turns into "single-handedly manage." By the time the snowball reaches the base of the hill, you may find yourself assuming responsibilities that go well beyond your initial offer to help.

Yet rather than cease to offer help at night when you've already spent most of your day overwhelmed, you may actually jump at the next opportunity to lend a hand! Why? Perhaps it makes you feel good. Maybe you enjoy keeping busy. Or perhaps you like to help others. But what you may not realize is that the real reasons for your giving nature could be unhealthy. You may help others because you want them to like you. You may like being busy because you're afraid of unstructured time. You may feel good only when you're in charge or in control of a number of projects.

From this moment on, resolve to say "No" when it's appropriate—and say "Yes" to doing something special just for you.

☆

If I can't set aside one evening a week out of seven to do something I want to do for me, then I'm too busy. I'll look forward to letting go of my responsibilities to one group so I can be more responsible to me.

. . . you must have faith in yourself—faith that you can determine what must be done to solve the problem . . . and faith that you will be able to take the appropriate action.

—Marsha Sinetar

How would your life be different if, from this moment on, you made up your mind to *do* things instead of just *try* to do them? How would your actions be different if you eliminated the word "try" from your vocabulary and inserted the word "can"? Instead of saying, "I'll try to stick to an exercise program" you could say, "I *can* stick to an exercise program." Rather than say, "I'll try to set aside time to spend with my family" you could say "I *can* set aside time to spend with my family."

Wouldn't your life be filled with potentials rather than possibilities, intentions rather than insecurities, and results rather than repeated attempts? The difference between believing you can try and believing you *can* is the difference between having doubt in your abilities and faith in yourself.

How do you foster faith in yourself—faith that you *can* do something? You start by tackling simple things. Bake a cake, not a souffle. Jog three blocks, not three miles. Enroll in one evening class, not a few. Read one self-help book, not a library. And do meditation or yoga so you become familiar with it, not so you can teach it.

☆

I can set a small, easily attainable goal for something I've always wanted to do. Rather than focus on the end result, I'll concentrate on simply beginning.

Blessed is the person who is too busy to worry in the daytime and too sleepy to worry at night.
　　　　　　　　　　　　　　　　　　　—Leo Aikman

Your reward for today's activities will be sleep. Although your body and mind may crave this slumber, it may take some time to "turn off" stressful thoughts so you can relax your body.

To release energy from your body and fill your mind with pleasant thoughts, set aside some time before going to bed for sleep-inducing meditation. Sit or lie down in a comfortable position and close your eyes. In your mind, picture yourself walking down thickly carpeted stairs as you count slowly backwards from ten. With each step, imagine that you're descending closer to a lush forest glen. When you reach the last step, look around you. Perhaps you see a sparkling stream that reflects a shimmering full moon. Maybe there are distant mountains capped by a night sky decorated with twinkling stars. Perhaps the gentle hoot of an owl, the low "grumps" of bull frogs, and the tender sounds of crickets fill the night air.

Now shift your attention to your breathing. As you inhale, imagine clear, fresh air going into your lungs. Bring the air slowly and deeply into your abdomen. Then release the air in a slow, steady exhalation, feeling your abdomen sink. Imagine your breath as a gentle breeze that barely stirs the leaves on the forest trees. Breathe in, breathe out. Fall asleep.

☆

Tonight I'll envision a peaceful, calming world where the only thing that matters is a good night's sleep. My mind relaxes and fills with the gentle sound of my own breathing.

I have wept in the night
For the shortness of sight
That to somebody's need made me blind;
But I have never yet
Felt a tinge of regret
For being a little too kind.

—Anonymous

You have only to open an evening newspaper or turn on the evening news to be deluged by all the unkindnesses in the world. Natural disasters destroy and kill. People murder, rape, and steal. Governments oppress and torture. People discriminate against others. Hate crimes abound. Children and animals are abused.

But when you set aside the paper or turn off the evening news and take a look at your own life, are unkindnesses just as prevalent? Did you speak harsh words to a coworker or family member? Did you cut someone off in traffic or cut ahead of someone in a supermarket line? Were you impatient with a physically challenged person? Were you nasty to a friend who was lonely and wanted to talk?

Kindness is like a beautiful flowering plant. Pay attention to it, water it, nourish it, and it will flourish. Show it no kindness, and it will close up its beauty and die. From now on, take time to look at all the flowers around you and ask, "Who is it who hasn't received my kind attention?"

☆

Rather than regret the unkind things I've done or said to others in the past, I can instead offer kind words and act in loving ways towards the "flowers" in my life in the present. I'll cultivate my "garden" with kindness and watch it grow.

"The road, wrote Cervantes, "is always better than the inn." Those who settle on fame or fortune as the inn, and having arrived, call it quits, miss the whole point of life. Realistically, there is no inn, no ultimate point of arrival. It is the road now and forever . . .

—Leonard E. Read

Do you sometimes think, "Once I land that promotion, all my financial troubles will be over," "Once my spouse and I move out of state, we're going to get along much better," or "Once I meet the right person, I'll be happy"? Yet when you finally attain such things, do you really become financially stable, satisfied in your marriage, and truly happy?

Believing that a person, place, or thing will give you everything you want from life is like believing that you're going to win the state lottery and live happily ever after. First of all, the odds of winning are quite slim. But even if you did get all that money, it wouldn't make you a better person, restore your health, repair relationships that have fallen apart, rewrite your unhapppy childhood, or help you find what you want in life. People, places, and things don't give you the answers or provide you with what you need. You have to do that for yourself.

Keep in mind that you must journey on the road of life and find your own way. While you may meet some wonderful people, see some magnificent places, and enjoy other exciting stopping points on your journey, ultimately what matters are the things you discover along the way.

☆

I shouldn't expect that somehow all my wants and needs are going to be taken care of, without any effort on my part. To get what I want and need, I have to find them myself.

So every faithful heart shall pray to Thee in the hour of anxiety, when great floods threaten. Thou art a refuge to me from distress so that it cannot touch me . . .

—Psalm 32

Right now it may be difficult for you to relax and look forward to a good night's sleep. Your mind and body may be filled with anxiety about something that's about to happen. You may be so obsessed with this upcoming event that you're like a time traveler—someone who exists not in the present moment, but in some future time.

Maybe tomorrow is opening day for your new business, your first day at a new job, or the day when you'll be trying something new. Or maybe you're anxious about plans that will be taking place a few days or a few weeks from now— a party, a family get-together, a trip, a college reunion.

Your mind may be spinning in a whirlwind of tension and anxiety and your muscles may be tight as you obsess over these things to come. To stay in the present so you can relax and get a good night's sleep, ask for help. Pray to your Higher Power to help you let go of your nervousness. Say, "Higher Power, grant me the serenity tonight to stay in the present moment. I cannot change or do anything about tomorrow. Let it come when it will. Until then, help me to relax my mind and body now."

☆

Is an upcoming event causing me a great deal of anxiety tonight? I'll pray for help in staying focused in the present so I can be calm and serene.

*The most beautiful discovery true friends make is that
they can grow separately without growing apart.*
—*Elisabeth Foley*

Too often when you're in a close friendship or intimate
relationship you may think that you each have to be like
twins—to dress alike, think alike, talk alike, and act alike.
Individuality can be threatening to two people who harmonize well with one another, for they may feel that taking
separate paths may eventually force them apart or in some
way damage the peaceful resonance in their relationship.

Yet time spent apart, with others or alone, is not only essential to both people in any relationship, but also strengthening for the relationship. Healthy relationships are made of
two individuals, not one. And even though the relationship
may be based on common points of interest, the two individuals still need to maintain a variety of friendships and
outside interests.

Since one person can never satisfy all your needs, it's important that you consider what's an appropriate and healthy
balance between "separate time" and "together time" with
a close friend or intimate partner. Remember that separation
from one another can be encouraged, supported, and
respected—and not be a source of stress or a threat to your
desire to be together.

☆

*When I'm ready, I'll discuss with someone close to me the time
I need to spend alone or with others. I'll encourage this person
to do the same. Such discussion will help us to connect, rather
than disconnect.*

Between them whom there is hearty truth, there is love.

—*Henry David Thoreau*

Every February 14th millions of Americans send valentines to people they love. How did this tradition start? One theory is that people began sending love notes on Valentine's Day in the late Middle Ages. Medieval Europeans believed that birds began to mate on February 14 and wished to emulate them. This belief was widespread in England—it was mentioned in Chaucer's writing in the 1400s—and crossed the Atlantic to America. The first paper valentines date back to the 16th century; enterprising Yankees soon were making good money—selling valentines. In fact Esther A. Howland, who produced the first commercial American valentines in the 1840s, sold $5,000 worth—when that amount was a lot of money.

But how true is love when it's expressed by someone else's words and your signature on a two-dollar greeting card, a box of chocolates, a bouquet of flowers, or dinner at a fancy restaurant? To show you care, keep your actions simple. Compose a poem that comes from the heart. Do something unexpected and special. Share a hug. Expressing your love in such truthful ways can make your feelings that much more meaningful.

☆

I won't let Valentine's Day customs dictate how I show or express my love to someone dear to me. I'll convey my love through things I want to do, not things I ought to do.

*We ought to hear at least one little song every day,
read a good poem, see a first-rate painting, and if possible speak a few sensible words.*

—Johann Wolfgang Von Goethe

At the end of each day, do you feel as if you ever really
accomplish anything? While things may often go according
to schedule—you arrive at your appointments on time, the
carpooling goes smoothly, the stores aren't overly crowded,
the materials you need for your project arrive as scheduled,
your plane departs and lands on time, the service people
show up when they say they will—you may still feel as if
your days lack in substance. Maybe that's because even
though you did all the things you *had* to do in a day, you
didn't get an opportunity to do anything you really *wanted*
to do. So you may approach your evenings with the same
sense of obligation and duty as you strive to do the things
you have to do instead of things you want to do.

Tonight, resolve to do something different—something out
of the routine—at least one evening a week. That means you
can set aside time to reread a favorite book. You can play a
CD that's been collecting dust. You can call a friend or write
a letter. You can prepare a special dessert or take a hot, luxurious bath. Even the smallest of changes in your nightly
routine can help you unwind, center yourself, be more
relaxed, and get a better night's sleep.

☆

*A little variation is healthy! From now on, I'll opt for a change
of pace rather than go through the motions of the same old
nightly routine.*

The ebb and flow of will is like the movements of the tides. . . . If you cease your vain struggles and lamentations long enough to look away from the personal self . . . we realize life is going well with us after all.
—Charles B. Newcomb

Everything in nature changes. You can trust that the sun and moon will rise and set, the tide will ebb and flow, and the seasons will change. Because you can trust that such things will happen, you can also trust that they're part of a natural rhythm. So you don't get up every morning and worry whether the sun will rise or stand on a beach at low tide, concerned that the waves won't return to shore. Without your doing anything, nature takes care of itself.

So it is with people. Everyone laughs and cries. Everyone works and plays. Everyone is born and dies. Just as nature has its natural flow, so too do people.

There are also natural rhythms in your life: one that leads you to awaken—the flow rhythm—and one that guides you to sleep—the ebb rhythm. Tonight your natural ebb rhythm —which is expressed by physical fatigue, mental exhaustion, and the desire for closure—can lead you to peace and relaxation. If you can go with that flow and trust it—just like you trust everything in nature—you'll experience calmness and the chance to revitalize yourself for tomorrow. Now is the time to follow your natural rhythm and sleep in peace.

☆

Can I rest tonight in quietness? Can I trust that my natural flow will calm my mind, spirit, and body? Tonight, I'll just let go.

For the happiest life, days should be rigorously planned, nights left open to chance.
—*Mignon McLaughlin*

How spontaneous are you? Would you call yourself a more rigid person or someone who's more flexible? If the plans you had made for tonight, tomorrow, or sometime in the near future suddenly changed, would the change be easy or difficult for you to handle?

If you're more rigid, change can be very hard to deal with. You may feel anger, resentment, hurt, sadness, or frustration when a friend calls to cancel an engagement, someone isn't ready on time or is late picking you up, or a snowstorm or something else out of your control interrupts your plans. You may even find that you're so rigid at times that you can't take a different route to work or park in a different lot; sit in a different seat in a group meeting; or stay somewhere new on vacation.

Rigidity is something that's built up over time. That means it needs to be loosened up over time. Making little changes in your routines or patterns can help you deal with the little changes in your life. By gradually learning to accept smaller changes, you'll be better able to learn how to deal with the bigger ones. Tonight, make a small change in tomorrow's schedule. Then, each night, make another minor change so you can develop flexibility over time.

☆

To become more flexible on a daily basis, I'll begin to make slow and gentle changes. Starting tonight, I'll learn to change from rigidity to spontaneity and flexibility.

. . . If we want to keep living with ourselves, we must keep on trying, trying, trying.
—Robert J. White, M.D.

Tonight you may feel as if you failed in some way today. Maybe you didn't meet a deadline. Perhaps a professor gave you a low grade on a paper, saying it wasn't at all like your usual work. Maybe you did something that let a child or loved one down in some way.

You may have felt you did your best at the time. But now you may regret that you could've done more, done it better, or tried harder. You may now be telling yourself, "If only I had _____, then things would be different now."

But some things may well be beyond your control. Maybe you weren't given enough time to complete a complicated job. Perhaps the library research materials you needed for your paper weren't available. Maybe another commitment prevented you from attending an event that was important to a loved one.

Tonight, don't expect that you'll be able to do everything right so that everyone will be happy. Some things are out of your control. Even the most skilled surgeon loses patients despite the surgeon's skill, a top-notch operating room team, and the best medical technology.

Tonight, recognize that even though you probably always strive to do your best, the outcome of your efforts will always be out of your control. Accept this limitation, but keep on trying.

☆

I'll resolve to keep trying to do my best, even when that isn't good enough for others. What's most important is that I make the effort and keep moving forward.

Only in quiet waters, things mirror themselves un-distorted. Only in a quiet mind is adequate perception of the world.

—*Hands Margolis*

Meditation is the process of emptying your mind from stressful thoughts so you can experience physical relaxation and inner peace. It's a way to open yourself up to "communicate" not only with your "inner self," but also with a spiritual "guide" such as Higher Power. In making this contact you gain knowledge, inspiration, and guidance about the people, places, and things in your life so you can handle them more calmly and effectively.

How do you meditate? There are no hard and fast rules. Some people sit in a quiet, candlelit room, their eyes closed; some listen to soothing music, recorded nature sounds, or a guided meditation tape; some chant one word; others use running, cross-country skiing, or walking as a chance to meditate.

To begin meditating, select a place where you won't be interrupted and an appointed time each night; in that way, you become "conditioned" to calm and still your mind in this space and at that time. When stressful thoughts occur, simply let them float through your consciousness. Don't pay close attention to them; let them drift gently in and out of your mind. Keep your breathing steady, your body relaxed, and your thoughts stilled, and you'll know what it's like to experience a quiet mind.

☆

Tonight I'll visualize that my mind is as stilled as the surface of a tiny pond on a sunny, windless summer day. There's nothing to disturb the surface of the water; there's nothing to disturb the depths of my mind.

*Human beings are like tea bags. You don't know your
own strength until you get into hot water.*

—Bruce Laingen

Bruce Laingen was one of the many hostages held in Iran.
During his 444 days of internment, he stayed level-headed
and optimistic throughout his trying time by using positive
thinking about himself and his circumstances.

How often do you think, "I'm really good at such-and-
such" or "I'm proud of the things I've accomplished in my
life"? How willing are you to point out your pleasant physical qualities—for example, "I have really beautiful blue
eyes," "I look really good in this outfit," or "I like my new
hair style"? How often do you focus on the positive elements,
not the negative ones, in the things you do or say—for example, "I'm getting much better at not interrupting others
when they're speaking," "I'm glad I was able to remain calm
when my parents criticized me," or "I've stopped smoking
now for almost three days"?

Positive self-talk can help you see that you have many
wonderful qualities—even on the difficult nights when it
might be hard to see anything good about yourself. You can
make tonight a positive one by saying, "I'm a wonderful person who has many talents and abilities." What you may find
is that having a positive dialogue with yourself can make you
feel more peaceful and accepting of who you are.

☆

*I'll end the day by saying at least three positive statements about
myself: one about my physical appearance, one about how I
interact with others, and one about something I'm doing just for
myself.*

Every generation finds it hard to hear what its children need—because its own childhood is still ringing in its ears.
—*Ellen Goodman*

Do you ever say to your children, "You'd better appreciate everything I do for you. I certainly never got the attention, all the nice things, or treated as well as you get treated when I was growing up." You may think back to when you were a child and remember the hurt, sadness, pain, or fear over having to endure an experience of parental dysfunction or emotional, physical, or sexual abuse. Your thoughts may then drift to the present and your children's blasé attitude towards the efforts you make so they won't have to go through what you went through as a child. "Why can't they see how much better I'm making things for them than they were for me?" you may wonder.

But treating your children in ways designed to make up for your own unhappy childhood isn't giving them what they really need—your time and attention in the present. Showering children with material goods you never had doesn't teach them the value of money. Never raising your voice doesn't show them boundaries or teach them right from wrong. Always being there for them doesn't give them room to grow.

From now on, try hard to hear what your children need right now. Maybe it's a shoulder to cry on, a reassurance that they're okay, or reading aloud a favorite bedtime story. You don't have to make up for your lost childhood with your children; you simply have to let them be.

☆

Sometimes I raise my children with my own parents or past childhood experiences in mind. To create a healthy childhood for my children, I need to let them guide me as well.

*We have gone from "Early to bed, early to rise, makes a
man healthy, wealthy, and wise" to "Late to bed, early
to rise, leads me to addiction, affliction, and demise."*
—Gary E. Hurst, Mike Kachura, and Larry D. Sides

Workaholism is the inability to separate your personal life
from your professional life. When you're a workaholic, you
have a tendency to overidentify with your job in ways that
make it hard to walk away from it—even at the end of an exhausting or long work day. How do you do this?

First, when you perform well on the job, do you feel ecstatic? Second, when you perform poorly on the job, do you
feel like a complete failure? Third, is work your number one
priority? Fourth, do you feel more yourself when you're
working than at any other time? And fifth, do you find it hard
to relax on vacations?

A workaholic is someone who isn't comfortable with time
away from work. Workaholics love labor-saving devices such
as car phones, faxes, laptop computers, and dictaphones not
because they save time, but because they're tools that enable
the workaholic to continue to work even after the long work-
day is over.

In order to recover from an addiction to work, be willing to
set aside time for doing absolutely nothing. Don't bring work
home at night and don't cut into sleep time to be the first at
the office. Give your mind and body a chance to recuperate
from work by creating adequate rest time for yourself.

☆

*I know I work hard at work. But can I also work hard at not
working hard? Resting tonight will not only give me the proper
perspective I'll need for tomorrow, but also the chance to
recharge today's depleted batteries.*

As we feel for ourselves, we must also feel for all forms of life . . .
                                                            —*Greenpeace*

In the 1950s the World Health Organization used the pesticide dieldrin to eliminate malaria in northern Borneo. Initially the project seemed to be a great success because the mosquitos and malaria disappeared. But researchers soon discovered that the dieldrin also killed wasps and other insects that ate caterpillars that fed on the villagers' thatched roofs. Sickness spread because typhus-infested fleas lived on rats and rat populations were out of control because cats had died from eating lizards that had eaten poisoned insects.

What this story illustrates is that in order for peace to exist between individuals and nature, the interconnectedness between the two needs to be honored. Any action can have far-reaching effects unless the balance is respected.

So, too, is it with you. Your actions can create cause and effect patterns. Making a change in yourself or your life, for example, can impact on those around you who have to adapt to the change. If you decide to go back to school at night because it would be wonderful for you, remember that others may not be as happy when they have to shoulder responsibilities you can no longer perform.

Strive to create harmony not only in your own life, but also in the lives of those around you. What you do for yourself *can* have far-reaching effects upon others.

Peace of mind results not just from inner balance and harmony but also balance and harmony with life around me. I'll strive to be understanding and respectful not only of my needs, but also the needs of those around me.

The world is full of people looking for spectacular happiness while they snub contentment.

—Doug Larson

Anyone who has gone to Disneyland or Disneyworld knows that the ride with the longest lines is "Space Mountain." This roller coaster type ride is the number one attraction because it promises its riders speed, excitement, and thrills. Those who complete the ride bound out of their seats talking excitedly about the adventure with other riders or those who are waiting for them.

On the other side of the park is "It's a Small World." This ride is totally different from "Space Mountain." Riders are taken on a pleasant journey to foreign lands as they hear children of different nationalities sing the theme song. When the ride is over, most disembark with relaxed smiles on their faces.

The difference between the two rides is like the difference between contentment and spectacular happiness. One is enjoyable while the other is ecstatic. It's only natural to want to experience the upward lifts of ecstacy rather than nice and pleasurable meanderings. But, in your life, when you equate happiness with emotional highs and unhappiness with emotional lows, then you may be uncomfortable without the "space mountains" in your life.

That's why it's important to accept that life doesn't always have to be a roller coaster ride. You can feel contentment, cheerfulness, serenity, and peace—and still be happy.

☆

Do I try to keep going from emotional high to emotional high in my life so I can find happiness? Let me accept that happiness isn't always so dramatic. Happiness can be simple and gentle, too.

When you aim for perfection, you discover it's a moving target.

—George Fisher

Do you believe you must be unfailingly competent and almost perfect in everything you undertake? Do you believe in the existence of perfect love and a perfect relationship? Do you believe that your worth as a person depends on how perfectly you achieve the things you do?

Such perfectionistic thoughts are unrealistic. A more rational assessment of your worth depends on your capacity to be fully human and alive. Belief in a perfect partner and perfect love often results in unhappiness and resentment in the search for the "perfect fit." And believing you must always be perfect can make you hesitant to try anything for fear of failure.

Promoting realistic thinking, rather than perfectionistic thinking, is one way to get through this. Whenever you find yourself thinking about one of your beliefs about perfectionism—for example, "I should be able to do everything perfectly," ask yourself, "Is there any rational support for this idea?" Discovering that your ideas of perfection are of your own creation—rather than the way things really are—can help you let go of your need to always hit the mark right on the bullseye.

☆

From now on I'll lower the perfectionistic expectations I have of myself. I'll tell myself that I'm going to try to do my best. My best effort—not the perfect effort—is what counts.

Dawn is a shimmering of the horizon.
Dusk is a settling of the sky.

—Tao

Sunrise and sunset together represent the measure of a day. When the sun rises, the moon sets; when the moon rises, the sun sets. Without such alternation, a day would have no beginning as well as no end.

So, too, are there cycles in your life. There are endings as well as beginnings. A layoff from a job means the end of your time with that particular company, but it also signals the beginning of your employment elsewhere. The termination of a long-term relationship means the end of your time with that particular person, but it also signals the beginning of your time spent with someone else. An illness or injury means the end of the way you've lived life up until that point, but it also signals the beginning of a new, healing way of living.

It's a sign of wisdom to not only be able to recognize such cycles of life when they occur, but also to accept them. Without such acceptance, your energy stays focused soley on what you've lost and you remain riveted to the same spot. To live and grow, you must be in motion.

Tonight, remember that you can never go back to the past nor will the past become the present—even if the past was only yesterday or just this morning. To live in the present, accept that everything you do from this moment on must be clean, fresh, and new.

A pile of sawdust that gathers under woodworking can never go back to its previous form. To accept the present, I must begin to work with new pieces of wood and make new piles of sawdust.

If a man had as many ideas during the day as he does when he has insomnia, he'd make a fortune.
—*Griff Niblack*

Have you ever wondered why you're sometimes more awake at night than during the day? From the moment you arise in the morning until it's time to go to bed, you may feel as if you're trying to negotiate through a vast sea of thick pea soup. Your body may physically feel heavy while your mind seems lost in a fog.

But the moment your head hits the pillow, you may feel as if you're sailing free on a shining sea. Your body may physically feel energized while your mind spills out thoughts and ideas like an active newswire machine. Perhaps you're excited about an upcoming trip or vacation. Maybe you're anticipating seeing old friends again. Perhaps you're in the process of house hunting or have just moved into a new home. Or maybe you're thinking about leaving your job and going off on your own to start a new business. After the burden of thinking about other people, places, and things is relieved at the end of the day and you've had a chance to wind down, it's only natural that such future thinking can leave little time for you to get some sleep.

Rather than stay up all night thinking, tonight tell yourself what you'd like to dream about before you go to sleep. In that way, you can teach yourself to dream your own exciting dreams—but while you're asleep!

☆

What will I dream tonight? Before I go to sleep, I'll close my eyes and visualize a dream. In this dream, I'll see myself doing whatever I want to do and being whoever I want to be.

We should have much peace if we would not busy ourselves with the sayings and doings of others.
—*Thomas À. Kempis*

Have you built your life around the person you love, the family you've created, the profession you've trained for, a cause you're committed to, or the desires of your parents? Then you may be a "should-based" person—someone who tries to please a partner "because I should," someone who takes care of a family "because I should," someone who places job first "because I should," someone who spends hours volunteering "because I should," or someone who does what your parents want you do to "because I should."

While you may be in a relationship, you're not your relationship. While you may have a family, you're not your family. While you may have a profession, you're not your profession. While you may be devoted to a cause, you're not your cause. And while you may have parents, you're not a child anymore.

Submerging yourself into a role others want you to have, thinking only of others first, using something or someone else as your center, or acting from a basis of "should" rather than "want" can make you tense, unfocused, and out of touch with what you want in your life.

From this moment on, resolve to stop trying to please others. Ask, "What do *I* want to do?" Then strive to do it—with or without the approval of others.

☆

When I affirm my right to choose, I'm able to live my own life. I'll begin to make choices that start with these three words: "I choose to . . ."

Were it possible for us to see further than our knowledge reaches, perhaps we would endure our sadnesses with greater confidence than our joys.
—*Rainer Maria Rilke*

When Henry David Thoreau was at his retreat on Walden Pond, he wrote of a life lesson he attained after enduring a stretch of rainy spring days. At first, as he watched the rain, he expressed his dissatisfaction that he was housebound but his happiness at seeing the bean seeds he had recently planted being watered. As the rain continued he observed that even if the seeds rotted in the ground, the rain " . . . will still be good for the grass on the uplands, and being good for the grass, it would be good for me."

In moments of sadness, the seeds of new growth are often planted. You may cry because you know you're dying. But the person you are now will soon become transformed into someone new—a soul who has moved on to a different plane in the universe. You may cry because someone you love is dying. But the person he or she is now will become someone new to you after they're gone—a beloved who has left you with endless memories and reasons to smile. Or you may cry because you feel sad, overwhelmed, frustrated, scared, or alone. But such tears will cleanse your soul and leave you refreshed.

Tonight, think of your tears as that gentle spring rain Thoreau witnessed years ago. The tears you shed now need to fall so new stirrings of growth can happen within you.

☆

Tonight I'll remember that sadness and joy are one with the life process. Without one, the other cannot exist.

The man who removes a mountain begins by carrying away small stones.

—*Chinese proverb*

Author Joseph Conrad wrote a lengthy and intense novel and struggled repeatedly with the language. Because his native tongue was Polish, the task of working out precise English words and phrases in his story was very difficult for him. When he finally completed the book, he didn't write "The End." Instead, he scrawled a single word across the last page. It wasn't "finished" or "complete." Conrad wrote the word "victory." And that became the title of his novel, *Victory!*

Ask any writer who has completed a book how he or she did it, and the answer will often be "One page at a time" or even "One word at a time." No author can sit down in front of the typewriter or word processor and expect to complete a novel for publication without months of dedicated writing, laborious rewriting, and then meticuous review of galley proofs from the publisher. The mountainous task of writing a novel can only be conquered by taking many small steps.

So, too, it is with the goals you want to reach in your life. Tonight, rest assured that you will soon attain your goals—but only by taking one step at a time!

☆

My "victory" tonight will be a continued commitment to working on a project or goal that's important to me. I'll keep in mind that the bigger the task, the more steps I'll need to take.

"And this, too, shall pass away." How much it expresses! How chastening in the hour of pride! How consoling in the depths of affliction! "And this, too, shall pass away."

—*Abraham Lincoln*

Sometimes when you're in a dark hour, you may believe time has suddenly stopped. It may feel like days since your children have behaved well, even though it may only be hours. It may feel like months since you were laid off from your job, even though it may only be days. It may feel like years since your relationship ended, even though it may only be a few months. Now you may feel that from this moment on, you'll always be in pain or you'll always feel sad, empty, hopeless, depressed, lost, and lonely. "From here on," you may say, "this is how it's always going to be—minute after minute of pain."

But you can reassure yourself tonight with the thought that while time passes quickly when you're enjoying yourself, when you're in the midst of a difficult time every hour can seem like two. This present hour will not endure. Pain passes, just as pleasure does. Nothing really stays the same; nothing ever stands still.

All you need to do right now is endure this moment. It, too, shall pass. You need to call upon your strength, patience, faith, and truth that this moment—and the feelings of this moment—will not go on forever. Time passes, and so will the pain.

☆

Tonight I need help remembering that this, too, shall pass. I'll ask my Higher Power, through prayers and meditation, to help me get through this time.

Why do some people always see beautiful skies and grass and lovely flowers and incredible human beings, while others are hard-pressed to find anything or any place that is beautiful?

—Leo Buscaglia

Do you wonder why a stranger who passed you on your morning walk commented, "Nice morning, isn't it?" Do you find it hard to believe that the smiling secretary in your department comes to work every day in a good mood? Do you feel uncomfortable with warm welcomes, unexpected hugs, or positive people?

You may wonder how anyone can always be so happy. "After all," you may say, "no one would be happy if they had the kind of day I always seem to have!" That may be why you snap at coworkers, make sarcastic comments to store managers, scream at drivers who share the road with you, or complain to others about your day when they arrive home.

It may be hard to break the pattern of seeing only negative things. It takes work to think of things in a more positive way, for this may be a way of thinking that's strange and unfamiliar to you.

Tonight, instead of lying awake remembering all the negative things that happened today, sift through the events until you find one positive thing. Focus on this positive point and let yourself enjoy the nice feelings it evokes.

☆

Tonight I'll try to emulate a positive person. I'll think back over my day and focus on something nice that happened to me or that I shared with someone.

Holding onto anger is like grasping a hot coal with the intent of throwing it at someone else—you are the one who gets burned.

—Buddha

Do you remember a time in the past when you felt anger towards a lover, child, sibling, parent, coworker, or friend, but didn't get it out at the time? Instead of working out the anger then, you may have ignored it or tried to cover it up—like placing a band-aid on a wound. But covering up the anger didn't "cure" it or make it better—it just hid it. So today you may still be holding onto that past unresolved anger. And the longer you continue to go without expressing this anger, the angrier you may end up feeling.

Unresolved anger is like a bright red neon light that constantly flashes in your mind. Try as you might to ignore it, you can't. Attempt to shut it off, and you won't succeed. Soon the anger may overtake your life, casting its fiery red glow over everything and everybody you come in contact with so you feel angry most of the time.

Unless you know how to get rid of your angry feelings and bring yourself back into balance, anger can dominate you and color everything you come into contact with.

Tonight, ask your Higher Power to help you let go of anger that's left over from the past. That may not be easy, for you may want to hold onto it almost as much as you'd like to let it go. But with practice, you can learn to conquer an anger that burns hot inside you.

☆

I'm tired of holding onto past anger. Tonight I'll stop seeing red everywhere I look and color my world with soothing, relaxing colors.

You want to spend time with your kids and yet how can you do that and work and do the work of the family and make sure your child gets the sleep he needs.

—Arnold L. Stolberg

When many of today's parents were growing up, mothers often didn't work. Dinner—once a true family meal, with everyone in the family sitting down together at the table—was usually at six sharp. Children were often in their rooms doing homework by seven and were in bed with lights out by eight. But those patterns don't work anymore.

Today's society places tremendous demands on parents. Not only do they have to maintain their family, but they also have to maintain a job and a household, provide emotional and material caretaking, and address each family member's individual needs. What this often creates is a very "nonfriendly-family" evening environment for children and parents. Mealtimes are often eaten late or dinner seatings are staggered; children sometimes don't get to bed until nine in order to spend time with parents.

How can you change this? From now on, instead of children going to bed later at night, get everyone to bed earlier so they can get up earlier and share a family breakfast. Encourage children to cut back on extracurricular activities so they can structure some of their afternoons around doing homework. Then cut back or drop your habit of taking work home so you can spend "family-friendly" evening time with your children.

☆

From this moment on, I'll think of ways to alter "evening crunch" time. I'll make shared play time and time for a good night's sleep the important priorities for both adults and children.

The practice of deception was so constant with her that it got to be a kind of truth.

—Louise Erdrich

Picture in your mind a calm lake, its surface like glass reflecting the sky and the full trees along its edge. A short distance from shore a group of geese float smoothly along the surface. With their long necks extended gracefully, they barely create a ripple on the surface of the lake.

You may take in this scene and marvel at how serene it is. But is it really? What you don't see, below the surface of the water, is a flurry of webbed feet furiously churning. What you're unable to feel is the strong pull of a current that courses through the deep part of the lake. This visualization can teach you a lesson: Things are not always as they seem.

So, too, it may be with you. Your smiling face may not reflect your broken heart. Your efficiency as a worker may not reflect the nervous approval-seeker you are inside. Your responsible adult image may not reflect the hurting, angry child within. And your sleeping face may not reflect the terrible nightmares you dream.

Are you like the smoothly-floating geese because you try not to let anyone see your struggles? Tonight, think about letting go of your deceptions soon and letting someone in. Resolve to be honest and show the emotions that exist under the surface.

☆

Keeping up appearances isn't helping me out—or letting anyone in to help me. So keeping up appearances is really for the birds!

Rest is not a matter of doing absolutely nothing. Rest is repair.

—*Daniel W. Josselyn*

When do you allow yourself time to rest? When you're sick? When your muscles are so sore it hurts to move? When several sleepless nights catch up to you?

If you're like most people, you probably don't set aside time for rest until your body cries out for it. But by getting into the habit of listening to your body, you can "tune in" to the messages your body gives you that signal a need for rest. Tight muscles, a backache, a slight headache, stiff shoulders, tired eyes, and poor concentration are just a few rest-related messages.

To take a rest doesn't mean to do nothing. It simply means slowing your pace, becoming less active, and easing some of your tension. Lying down for a few moments is resting, as well as going out to a movie, reading a good book, watching television, listening to music, or talking to friends.

Rest allows the body time to release tension and return to a more normal, balanced state. And when you're well rested, you're often more energized. As the Chinese explain the lesson of the tortoise, which knows when to withdraw into itself and when to restore its energy: "The tortoise is good at nurturing energy, so it can survive a century without food."

☆

To nurture my life energy, I need to make time tonight to withdraw from the hustle and bustle of the world and rest so I can get a good night's rest. Doing so can increase my emotional, physical, and spiritual strength.

When we inhale, the air comes into the inner world.
When we exhale, the air goes out to the outer world.
The inner world is limitless, and the outer world is also
limitless. We say "inner world" or "outer world," but
actually there is just one whole world.

—Zen philosophy

The yin and yang life force is central to Eastern philosophy. This philosophy explains that yin is a phase of repose and relaxation while yang is the phrase of activity; all of life emerges from the harmonious synthesis of these two forces. You need both moments of reflection and introspection for your actions to have purpose and meaning, as well as moments of action so your thoughts can take form.

Western philosophy, on the other hand, proposes a choice: action or repose. Most Americans prefer yang over yin, as evidenced through acceptance of the Puritan work ethic, by burning the candle at both ends, and by equating a successful day with the quantity—not the quality—of tasks completed.

Yet without a balance of yin and yang in your life, you will bounce from one extreme to the other—going from times of overwork to periods of exhaustion and collapse. Tonight, visualize your yin and yang on opposite sides of a scale. Bring them into balance by breathing deeply and imagining that your life is filled with peace and harmony.

☆

Balancing my yin and yang isn't based on choosing between one or the other. Instead, it means I need to avoid extremes on either side so I can create a harmonic balance between activity and inactivity.

You must have long-range goals to keep you from being frustrated by short-range failures.
                              —Major General Charles C. Noble

Many of today's inventions—the automobile, the telephone, the electric lightbulb, computers, or airplanes—weren't created overnight or even on the first try. The first models didn't always work as intended; sometimes even the thousandth prototype broke down. But inventors continued the process of reworking and revising until they found what *did* work. What motivated them was keeping their long-range goals in mind.

How many times have you started on a project, goal, or making a change in your life only to abandon it after a short time? You may have decided that it wasn't what you wanted or there wasn't enough time to achieve what you wanted to achieve. Instead of following through, you usually gave up just when it was getting challenging and difficult.

Yet each project, goal, or change you'd like to achieve can only be done by persistence and dedication. As Richard L. Evans says, "It is a matter of first beginning—and then following through." You don't have to give up an endeavor just because the hard work has begun. Instead of looking down the road at where you want to be, simply look at this moment. If you take one small step towards what you want, then you'll be one step closer to what you'd like to achieve down the road.

☆

A long-range goal is like a flashlight and the short-range goals are like the batteries I need to light my path. I may have to change my short-range goals from time to time, but they'll only help me to stay focused on my long-range goal.

When you have power over yourself, circumstance has no power over you. Your inner weather is at your command.

—*Olga Rosmanith*

Do you ever find yourself saying or thinking things like, "I'm going to fail," "I'm too nervous to handle this," "I know that person doesn't like me," or "I can't do this"? Such thoughts are "stress thoughts." They're often based on a fearful or anxious interpretation of an incident. Stress-thought thinking also impacts upon your body so you respond in anxious ways—your palms may be sweaty, you may feel shaky inside, and your breathing may be quick and shallow.

"Stress-coping thoughts," on the other hand, act as tranquilizers that can mentally and physically calm you so you can overwhelm and then push aside feelings of panic and fear. Stress-coping thoughts tell your mind there's no need for mental or physical arousal so you can relax.

How do you encourage stress-coping thoughts rather than stress thoughts? In the midst of any stressful situation tonight, say or think a series of statements such as: "Stay calm . . . everything's okay . . . you've handled this before . . . relax and take a deep breath . . . it's a totally safe situation . . . take it step by step and don't rush . . . I can always ask for help if I need it" . . . and so on. Tonight, the more attention you pay to creating and keeping such stress-coping thoughts in mind, the less impact stress thoughts can have on you.

☆

How I feel inside is always in my control. Tonight I'm the one who can plant the seeds of stress in my mind and body—or the seeds of serenity.

> *. . . each cycle of the tide is valid; each cycle of the*
> *wave is valid; each cycle of a relationship is valid.*
> —Anne Morrow Lindbergh

Any photograph or painting will show you a moment frozen in time. Forever after the places in the pictures remain the same, the people never grow old, the objects remain fresh and new, and the action never progresses.

Yet in day-to-day living, there's no such thing as "still life." Nothing stays the same from one minute to the next. Many things in your life have cycles—one of them is your intimate relationship. You may not like change in your relationship, for you may think that any variation from the norm somehow threatens the relationship. Any fluctuation in your happiness together may mean pain, loss, or rejection. You may even be frightened to have change occur during a relationship's dark moments of disconnection, disagreement, and discord. What might happen, you might wonder, if things don't get better? What guarantee is there that you'll still be together after you make the changes?

Yet change is a valid measurement of growth and time. It is as natural a rhythm as the ebb and flow of the ocean, the change of the seasons, the waxing and waning of the moon, and the rise and set of the sun.

Tonight, rest assured that your relationship is only right when it has a rhythm to it. Savor the good times and the bad as part of the natural cycle that can bring you closer together.

☆

Tonight I'll keep in mind that sometimes motion can bring two people together instead of pull them apart. Just as the ocean waters recede and return, but never diminish in power, so too can my relationship be strengthened by change.

Laughing . . . stirs up the blood, expands the chest, electrifies the nerves, clears away the cobwebs from the brain, and gives the whole system a cleansing rehabilitation.

—*Anonymous*

Did you know that a large corporation once hired the Muppets to present a program explaining the company's restructuring and the possible layoff of employees? Or that a prison uses cartoon therapy to help angry inmates deal with the loss of their freedom? Did you know that a doctor in New York teaches patients to juggle in order to take their minds off their illness? Or that many hospitals show patients comedy videotapes to help reduce their pain?

Humor is one of the few things you can use to deal with a high-stress situation that you can't escape. Humor can instantly take you away, if only for a few moments, from your troubles and makes them easier to bear. But unless you allow yourself to see the humorous things in life, you'll have a difficult time experiencing this delightful release.

From now on, find ways to add more humor to your life. Watch reruns of your favorite comedy sitcoms—"The Three Stooges" or "Dick Van Dyke" on cable television. Rent a comedy video. Read a joke book or flip through a book of cartoons. Finding humor first in the media may help you to find humor in some of your real-life situations.

☆

I don't need to be a comedian in order to be able to laugh. All I have to do is want to see the other side of life—the humorous side.

When we hate our enemies, we give them power over us—power over our sleep, our appetites, and our unhappiness. Our hate is not hurting them at all, but it is turning our days and nights into hellish turmoil.

—Dale Carnegie

"That person really burns me up!" you may grumble all the way home from work, while you're eating dinner, during every commercial break as you watch television, while you're brushing your teeth, and then when you're changing into your pajamas. Even as you shut out your bedside light, the image of that person may remain seared in your brain. Try as you might to let go of that person, the strong intensity of your negative feeling won't let you let go.

Hate is such a strong feeling. Often it can become an obsession. You may hold onto it dearly, never wanting to forget your hatred for others, as you painstakingly use your valuable time and energy to commit their appearance, the sound of their voice, what they wear, and their actions or behaviors to memory.

Yet spending your precious nights nurturing a strong dislike for a coworker, boss, teacher, parent, former lover, or even a complete stranger is a waste of time and energy. Instead of making one person your focus tonight, think instead of all the people you hold near and dear to you. Visualize the faces of those who give you strength, happiness, and comfort, and let those be the images you have in your mind as you fall asleep.

☆

Why am I wasting my time thinking about one person who has aggravated me? Instead of seeing one face I dislike in the crowd, I'll see many I like.

*If you are lonely when you are alone, you are in bad
company.*

—Jean-Paul Sartre

Imagine for a moment that you have no plans for tomorrow. There's no job you have to get up for, no classes to attend, no errands to run, no family meals to prepare, no housecleaning to do, and no one who needs your time and attention. Initially you might think such a situation is great. But how comfortable are you being totally alone for that amount of time, with no place to go and no one to spend it with? Think back to the last time you had to be alone. Were you content to sit comfortably with yourself, enjoying the pleasure of your company? Or was your first instinct to turn on the television or pick up the telephone so you could escape being with you?

While you live in a world with others and need to feel connected with them, you also need to feel connected with yourself. When you like who you are, it doesn't matter whether you're with others or alone. Both times are enjoyable. But when you don't like yourself, you crave time with others and dread time alone.

From this moment on, resolve to become more comfortable being by yourself. Don't be afraid to set aside time to be alone. Then, when you're in that "alone space," simply feel what it's like to be with you.

☆

*Why would I not like to spend time with myself? Alone time is
one of the best ways to help build a wonderful relationship with
myself.*

Patience! The windmill never strays in search of the wind.

—Andy J. Sklivis

Being laid up with an illness or injury can be frustrating. Hobbling along the sidelines when your basketball team is playing in the league finals, staring at a racquetball racket you won't be using at the club for weeks, watching others prepare meals or do the laundry for you, or having to cancel plans for a pleasant walk on a spring-like evening because you're feeling under the weather can sometimes make you feel even worse.

Although the healing process may seem slow, every day your broken leg, sprained ankle, bad back, stomach virus, or bout with the flu gets better. Each day you may feel a little stronger, a little more capable of functioning at full capacity. So wanting to speed up the process of healing will only leave you feeling frustrated and helpless. That's when patience can truly become a virtue. Patience requires acceptance of your current condition and trust that it *will* change.

Developing patience is simply a matter of focusing your attention on something other than your injury or illness. Tonight, make up your mind to be more patient tomorrow. Even though you can't help your team on the court, you can cheer from the sidelines. You can read a book on racquetball to sharpen your strategy. You can enjoy being pampered for a short time. And you can trust that there will be other pleasant evenings for a walk.

☆

I don't mind helping others out when they're injured or ill. So tonight I'll take the same advice I'd give to others: "Rest and relax so you can recuperate."

You let your kids stay up late so you'll have some time together. You take your daughter to a restaurant you can't stand because you don't want to have a fight. . . . You agree to the third bedtime story, even though you're so exhausted you could scream.
—*Barbara F. Meltz*

Would you call yourself a "guilty" working parent? To find out, ask yourself the following questions. Do you allow your children to do things you wouldn't let them do if you were a full-time parent, such as staying up past their bedtime, not making them pick up their rooms, or letting them invite friends over whenever they want? Do you push yourself beyond your physical and mental limits so you feel like you've given something to your children? Do you justify the concessions you make by saying, "I'm away all day. How can I say 'No'?"

While most working mothers and fathers feel guilt from time to time over the office-home imbalance, it's important to distinguish between healthy guilt—"I shouldn't have stayed so late at the office" or "My child's play was much more important than the conference I attended"—and the guilt that can eat you up—"I'm such a bad parent. I'm ruining my children's life!"

Tonight, before you go to sleep, decide to sit down with your children soon and find out the time they'd like to spend with you. Then close your eyes and rest assured that you can compromise between your work schedule and your children's expectations so you both can feel satisfied.

☆

I need to develop healthy guilt. In the light of day, I'll be more conscious about my time away from home and come up with ways to devote more hours to my children or others.

Unless each day can be looked upon by an individual as one in which he has some fun, some joy, some real satisfaction, that day is a loss.
—*Dwight D. Eisenhower*

So many things may seem to loom over you from time to time. There may be an addiction to alcohol or drugs, food, or people that seems to require your constant attention. There may be fears that fill your anxious mind—fears about expressing love, feeling feelings, being alone, being abandoned or rejected, or of failing. There may be miseries of childhood that don't seem to go away or present-day unhappinesses—an unfulfilling relationship, a family illness, or dissatisfaction with your life. Sometimes the world in general may seem like a place that's filled with people and events that are tragic or frightening.

At such times it may be hard to see anything that's good or experience anything that's enjoyable. Yet nothing has absolute power over you and how you feel if you have the power to think positively. As Charles Fletcher Lummis says, "I am bigger than anything that can happen to me. All these things, sorrow, misfortune, and suffering are outside my door. I am in the house and I have the key."

Tonight, as you reflect on your day, let in positive feelings and "lock out" the negative ones. You can then feel safe and secure that this day was one filled with value and meaning.

☆

The only thing in this life that can eliminate a negative day is a positive outlook. Tonight I'll be positive and look back on this day as one that was filled with enjoyment and fulfillment.

Is this not life's purpose—
to know that you belong,
that you are safe and eternal,
to know that in your spirit reality
you are already one with God?
—Emmanuel

It has been said that in order to feel that you're truly one with your spirituality, you need to study a dozen years under the guidance of a good spiritual teacher. While you may protest that such time is too much, isn't it a considerably shorter period of time than what you'd need to become a good musician, a skilled athlete, or a successful artist? And isn't it much shorter period of time than it would take for you to collect your pension?

The need to feel like you spiritually "belong"—to feel connected with a Higher Power, nature, humanity, or the universe—can sometimes become an obsession. Like a starving person who constantly dwells on the thought of food, a spiritually hungry person can only think of connection to the world of the spirit.

Yet you have been and always will be spiritually connected with the world. You don't need to have had an "awakening," a near-death experience, be a regular church-goer, or even a student of a spiritual teacher. All you simply have to do to feel spiritually connected is to live the entire course of your life well. Tonight, recognize that you're spiritual simply because you're alive.

☆

Tonight I don't need to search for spiritual enlightenment. I just need to open my eyes and look around me at the loving support I can give to other people and receive from them. That is spiritual enlightenment.

Men go abroad to wonder at the heights of mountains, at the huge waves of the sea, at the long courses of the rivers, at the vast compass of the ocean, at the circular motions of the stars; and they pass by themselves without wondering.

—St. Augustine

Do you know that native palm trees grow in Arizona—not on the desert, but on the shady side of a mountain? Jutting majestically out from the granite sides of a 2500-foot canyon in the Kofa Mountains of Arizona are the only native palm trees in the entire state. How do the tropical plants live year after year in the dark, almost perpendicular sides of the narrow gorge? How can they flourish when the sun reaches them only two hours in a day? Botanists who have studied this incredible phenomenon have concluded that the stone walls of the canyon reflect enough light and store enough warmth throughout the day to enable the trees to survive in the seemingly uninhabitable environment.

You probably don't have to stray far from your own backyard at this time of year to see some similarly miraculous wonders. There may be tiny green shoots from buried bulbs pushing their way through a pile of snow. Awakened insects may buzz sluggishly in the warm sunshine. The returning robins may seranade you with evening songs—even when temperatures are near freezing.

From now on, appreciate the joy of discovering nature's beauty near your home. You may be surprised by the number of wonderful things you've never noticed before.

☆

Spring is a time for everything and everybody to come alive after the harshness and bleakness of winter. Tonight I'll appreciate my own growth as well as the natural growth around me.

With history piling up so fast, almost every day is the anniversary of something awful.
—*Joe Brainard*

Which do you remember: the anniversary of a painful time or the anniversary of a wonderful time? You may be more aware of the dates of terrible events in your life—when you got laid off from work, when your relationship ended, or when a parent died—rather than the wonderful events—when you landed your job, when you began dating a wonderful person, and when your parents got married. The media often helps to perpetuate this habit of remembrance of awful events by reminding you of important dates in history like the anniversary of President John F. Kennedy's assassination (instead of his birthday) or the bombing of Pearl Harbor (instead of when the war ended).

Perhaps from this moment on you could start a calendar of positive anniversaries in your life. You could include the first time you fell in love, a wonderful day spent with a parent, the day you earned your degree, the day you stopped smoking or drinking, the day your promotion came through, a romantic time spent with your partner, or a day when your child said, "I love you."

Keeping such a calendar and adding to it over time can give you a record of wonderful memories you can commemorate each year. Then you'll be able to look at *every* day as the anniversary of something wonderful rather than something awful.

☆

What special thing happened to me this day in my history? Tonight I'll reminisce about the good times in my life and mentally add them to the "Happy Anniversary" calendar I'm creating.

Starting over begins when you say to yourself that what's finished is finished.

—Marian Christy

Are you the type of person who hates to start over, or are you willing to make changes and accept new responsibilities?

When Eleanor Roosevelt was first lady, she traveled extensively as the eyes and ears of her husband. She kept President Roosevelt informed of people's problems throughout the Depression. During World War II, her efforts spanned the globe as she visited with soldiers and heads of state.

But in 1945, after FDR's death, Eleanor's time of service to the citizens of the United States ended. As she faced the dilemma of what to do next in her life, she was asked by President Truman to be a delegate to the United Nations. At first she hesitated, wondering if she could make the transition from former First Lady. She accepted, and by 1946 had become chair of the United Nations Human Rights Commission. In 1952, when President Eisenhower failed to reappoint her as a delegate, she accepted this change and began working as a U.N. volunteer. Nearly a decade later, she returned as a delegate when President Kennedy reappointed her.

Tonight, think about how difficult it must have been for Eleanor to make the numerous transitions in her life. How can you be more like her—ready to let go of a former way of doing things so you can accept whatever new role has been created for you?

☆

I can be stubborn and inflexible about letting go of what's over and done with, or I can be open-minded and willing to move on. Tonight I'll remember that these options are part of every choice I need to make.

It is universally admitted that there is a natural heal-
ing power resident in the body . . . .Many people have
learned to relax and keep quiet like the animals, giv-
ing nature a free opportunity to heal their maladies.
                                        —Horatio W. Dresser

Do you know people who rarely get sick, even from a sore throat or the bug everyone seems to have? Then there are those you know who always seem to be sick, getting one cold after another or having a perpetual headache.

You may notice that those who rarely get sick make their wellness a priority. They eat nutritious foods, exercise on a regular basis, allow time each night for a good night's sleep, and strive to maintain a positive outlook. As a result, these people often remain physically, emotionally, and spiritually healthy—even when they're going through a difficult time.

To take the first step towards such wellness, strive to reduce or eliminate any self-destructive health habits you may have that can impact on your overall well-being. Instead of late-night snacking on highly caloric or salty foods, sub-stitute fresh fruit, skim milk or cottage cheese, or a lightly buttered slice of whole grain bread. Stop physical or men-tal work when you become fatigued—not when you can't see straight or are ready to drop. And get to bed at a reason-able hour—one that will give you sufficient time to recover from the labors of the day.

☆

Tonight I'll take the first step towards wellness. I'll strengthen the
healing powers within me through relaxation and by treating my
body with respect.

In Maine we have a saying that there's no point in speaking unless you can improve on silence.
    —*Edmund Muskie*

The noise of modern life can make it hard for you to hear yourself think. Radios drone in your car or home, while piped-in music follows you from work to the grocery store to the shopping mall. Television settles comfortably into your living room with other people's lives, false words, fictitious storylines, and blaring consumer messages.

Many people hide behind such noise, unwilling to face themselves or the silence. Yet turning on the radio or television the minute you get home from work and keeping it on until you go to bed makes it less likely that you'll meditate, write a letter to a friend, work creatively, or pay attention to your own thoughts.

The next time you automatically turn on the radio or television at night, ask yourself why. If you choose to really watch or listen to a program—and not just have it on for background noise—then leave it on. But if you're not going to watch, turn it off.

From now on, resolve to make silent periods in your evening an important part of your day. While these times may feel uncomfortable and strange at first, over time you may find that you revel in the lack of "junk words" that invade your senses. Giving space to "precious words" can be much more entertaining than any sitcom.

☆

Can I learn to enjoy my periods of silence? I'd rather have the real companionship of myself than the artificial companionship of a radio or a television show.

Fear imprisons, faith liberates; fear paralyzes, faith empowers; fear disheartens, faith encourages; fear sickens, faith heals; fear makes useless, faith makes serviceable.

—*Harry Emerson Fosdick*

It has been said that the opposite of fear is faith. But how can you change your fears into faith if you have little or no faith? How do you start having faith?

An old story once told by Chuang Tzu describes a man who was so afraid of his own shadow and the sound of his footsteps that he ran away from them. But the more he ran, the louder the footsteps sounded and the more swiftly his shadow raced after him. The man's fears soon grew into panic, and he ran faster and faster until he finally died of exhaustion. What the man didn't realize is that if he had only stopped running and rested under the shade of a tree, the shadow would have disappeared and the footsteps would have ceased.

Your fears are like shadows and footsteps; your faith is like resting under the shade of the tree. One torments you; the other comforts you. Once you recognize your fears, you can take away some of the power they have over you. Such recognition can help you deal with the source of most fears—fear of the unknown—so you can have faith that you'll be able to work through your fears.

What do I fear and why do I fear it? I know over time, I can develop faith-filled alternatives to my worst fears so I can deal with them.

It takes two people to have a marriage, but only one is necessary to change it. We end up feeling helpless in our marriages because we can't control our partners. The truth is that we need only learn to control ourselves.

—*Melvyn Kinder and Connell Cowan*

In any relationship there's often mutual work that needs to be done by both partners to identify, confront, and then come up with solutions to issues that may affect the relationship.

But if you're unhappy with your relationship a good deal of the time or are threatened by the interests and achievements of your partner, then you may need to do some work on yourself. Making personal changes such as dieting to improve self-acceptance of your body image, going to a therapist to discuss issues that affect how you feel about yourself, spending time alone to get to know yourself, developing a new interest that will broaden your horizons, or dealing with an addiction can bring about healthy changes in yourself that can positively affect your relationship.

The best relationships are those in which both people are happy with themselves first, and then with each other. Tonight, consider how important it is that you abandon the desire to change your partner. From this moment on, use your time wisely to focus instead on the changes you can make in yourself. You may then be amazed at how your relationship improves!

☆

Tonight I'll use this affirmation to help improve the quality of my intimate relationship: "I love (my partner) because I love myself."

. . . there are hundreds of tasks we feel we must accomplish in the day, but if we do not take them one at a time and let them pass through the day slowly and evenly, as do the grains of sand passing through the narrow neck of the hourglass, then we are bound to break our own physical and mental structure.

—Ted Bengermino

Your physical and mental states at bedtime are important. If you're tense, edgy, or feel a sense of failure and defeat from the day's efforts, your sleep will probably be restless and unsatisfying. Instead of mentally winding down from the day or feeling physically at peace when you close your eyes, you may still feel there are things you ought to get done.

But what difference does it make if a few things are left undone tonight? Will they matter ten years from now? Nothing is ever so important that it has to be accomplished right now. Nothing is ever so critical that your whole world will come crashing in if it's not immediately attended to. Nothing is ever so earth-shattering that your life will be on the line if it's not resolved this very minute.

Tonight, put the day to rest. Take a deep breath, then slowly release the air as you relax your shoulders. Breathe in again as you squeeze your hands into tight fists, then release your breath and open your hands. Feel the difference in your shoulders and hands now that you've released the tension of the day. Do the same with your mind; take in a deep breath, then release all the chatter in your head.

☆

I'm ready to relax into a peaceful, restful sleep. Tonight I'll loosen the day's tension from my body as well as from my mind.

*You want me to succeed so much. Could you under-
stand if I failed? . . . Could you love me if I failed?*
                                    —*Sister Mary Paul*

What is it that you fear the most about striving for success?
You might say that you're most afraid of failure. But when
you really think about it, chances are you're not so much
afraid of letting yourself down as you are letting others
down—losing their admiration, respect, or even their love.

When you don't feel good about who you are on the inside, you may expect outside things—a job, salary, home,
material possessions, fancy car, or an advanced degree—to
earn you love, rewards, and approval from those who you're
trying to impress with your success.

Tonight you need to recognize that you're a success—with
or without the externals. No matter what you've done or
what you're doing, you're a success. If you've set out to do
something today and have fallen short of your expected success, you haven't lost the admiration, respect, or love of those
around you who really matter. Those people will love you
whether you succeed or fail because they love you for who
you are and believe in the "inner" you.

Tonight, think about those people who love you and believe in *you*—not for what you do, where you live, how you
dress, what your salary is, or what kind of car you drive. Be
grateful for them, for their love will always be there for you,
rain or shine.

☆

*Tonight I'll recognize that the greatest success I've achieved is
having people in my life who love me for who I am. Because of
them, I am a success!*

*To get peace, if you want it, make for yourselves nests
of pleasant thoughts.*

—*John Ruskin*

A bird builds its nest by first searching for the perfect twigs,
pieces of string, weeds, and pieces of paper. Then it patiently
interweaves these materials until its nest achieves the right
shape, size, depth, and warmth. Once completed, the bird
stops its nest-building and spends its time nestled comfortably in its home.

To be at peace with yourself, you first need to construct
your own nest. This nest could be an apartment, the home
you've always dreamed of, or a quiet room. But your nest
doesn't always have to be a place. Your nest can be created
from intangible things that bring you peace: freedom from
negative thinking or codependency, for example, a daily hug
from a loved one, or time set aside for enjoyment and
relaxation.

Without such comforting "nests" in your life, peace can be
difficult to achieve. From now on, you can start to "build"
your nest by attending a helpful support group, rearranging
your schedule to set aside precious moments just for yourself, by communicating to your partner things he or she can
do to make you feel comforted, or by spending time with
positive people and doing enjoyable activities. Such things
can help you create a comforting nest of pleasantness.

☆

*Before I go to bed tonight, I'll close my eyes and think a pleasant
thought. Maybe it will focus on world peace, peace to loved ones,
or peace to myself. But my one thought can create a nest of
peace somewhere in my world.*

When the friendly lights go out, there is a light by which the heart sees.

—*Olga Rosmanith*

Coming home at night to an unlit house or apartment can be frightening. As you frantically grope for the light switch, you may stumble over tables and chairs that seem to have shifted position in the dark. Yet once the lights go on, you may feel an instantaneous burst of relief as you're once again able to view your familiar surroundings and get your bearings.

You don't always need bright lights to help you find your way in the dark. Sometimes you may feel in the dark emotionally or spiritually. That's when faith in a Higher Power that watches over you at all times can provide you with an inner light. This light burns as brightly as your belief. If you're filled with fear, doubt, and insecurity, then your light will dim and fade and you'll stumble in your inner darkness. But if you're filled with faith, hope, and trust, your light will shine bright and your inner footing will be secure.

Tonight, remember that you're the lighter of your internal lamp. Help it to burn brightly by reciting a favorite prayer, reading a familiar passage from a spiritual text, or by offering up a prayer when you're afraid of the darkness in your life. Tending to and trusting the light within you will take away the power of the night to frighten you.

☆

Do I have a panicked need to run from the darkness in my life? Tonight I'll create an eternal nightlight that will be there for me always, to light my path through my darkness and ease my fears.

There are times when silence has the loudest voice.
—Leroy Brownlow

Indian spiritual leader Ghandi sought out periods of silence by setting aside a day of silence a week. No matter what happened on that day or who came to visit, he would spend the day quietly, communicating to others only in writing.

Could you maintain an entire day of silence? How about a few hours? A few minutes? If you're like most people, you gravitate towards activity, idle conversation, and noise rather than towards inactivity, meaningful but limited communication, and silence.

How can you seek the silence? Establish regular periods of meditation where you sit quietly with yourself. Use slow, conscious breathing to focus your energy, slow your mind down, and help you "go within"—to places deep beneath the noise and surface clatter. After meditation, you'll emerge renewed and refreshed, your tension gone, and your heart and mind at peace.

Tonight, begin meditating before you go to sleep by setting aside as little as fifteen minutes. Over time, you may wish to extend that period to suit your needs. Some people meditate first thing each morning; others do it at the end of the day. Beginning and ending each day with meditation is ideal, but the important thing is to meditate regularly so you can feel the strength in the silence.

☆

Tonight, as I meditate, I'll keep in mind the recommendations of Louise Hay: to sit quietly, empty my mind of its clutter, and then mentally ask myself, "What is it that I need to know?"

*This is a delicious evening, when the whole body is
one sense, and imbibes delight through every pore.*
—*Henry David Thoreau*

The natural beauty of the night can be spectacular. Sometimes there's a bright, full moon that glows ethereal white
against an ink-black night sky liberally sprinkled with sparkling stars. Perhaps you see this image reflected on the shimmering waters of a country lake. Or you may see it in a warm
rain puddle on the side of a city street as you marvel at the
magical kingdom of colors created by the twinkling city
lights.

If you can use your senses to the fullest, there's much
beauty you can find at night. Open your eyes to the sil-
houettes of the trees and buildings around you and the
shadows that dance in the glow of streetlights. Listen to bullfrogs croaking, crickets chirping, or the wind howling.
Breathe deeply of the cool, clean air and take in the aromas
of spring growth. Imagine the feeling of the evening on your
face as it gently caresses you. Open your mouth and mentally taste the delicate flavors of countless raindrops.

Tonight, take a "mental" walk through a peaceful natural
surrounding. Appreciate the sensual beauty of the evening
by using all your senses. Let the night touch you in a way
that brings you contentment and enjoyment. Then, let everything you've seen, smelled, heard, touched, and tasted lull
you into a soothing sleep.

*I'll be as grateful for the night as well as the day. Tonight I'll go
for a short "mental hike" and let the night air soak into every
pore, cleansing me and comforting me.*

If I had my life to live over, I would start barefoot earlier in the spring and stay that way later in the fall. I would go to more dances. I would ride more merry-go-rounds. I would pick more daisies.

—Nadine Stair

You can never relive any part of your life—not even the last five minutes. But what you can do right now is begin to live your life in the way in which you've always wanted to live it.

Each evening, whether you're conscious of it or not, you have a choice. You can choose to continue to do things the way you've always done them—eating dinner in front of the television, gabbing on the telephone for hours, or working—to feel the way you've always felt—angry, lonely, or sullen—and to behave in ways you've always behaved—snapping at those you live with, being rigid and structured, or refusing invitations to do things you normally don't do. *Or you can choose to change.*

In change comes the possibility of being able to feel differently, to act in new ways, and to try new things. You can decide to live like a person who hops merry-go-rounds, picks daisies, and dances. You can be anxious and worried, or you can be bright and positive. You can sit in the front of the television, or you can get up and get moving. You can rigidly stick to your evening schedule, or you can be spontaneous. *It's your choice.*

☆

From this moment on, I want to live my life in the way I would if I had to live it over. I can take a risk, take a chance, and take a journey on a different path.

It takes more than a soft pillow to insure sound sleep.
—Anonymous

You may find that your mind is the most difficult part of your body to relax. From your toes to your fingertips, you may find you can easily make each muscle grow heavy with relaxation. But when it comes to the muscle that exists above your neck, you may find your head so loaded with facts and fantasies, fancies and feelings that the signal "Relax and go to sleep" gets blocked.

If you were to open the top of your head, you might see slips of paper with messages written on them crammed into the small space. What messages might you find tonight? On one slip of paper you might find the word "guilt." Perhaps you feel guilty about yelling at your child this morning. On another slip of paper you might read, "overwhelmed." Maybe you're feeling overwhelmed by the number of projects you have to juggle at your job. On other slips of paper you might find "anger," "stress," "jealousy," "fear"—or countless other messages.

All these pieces of paper do is clog the channels that can connect you with relaxation, contentment, and serenity. When these channels are clogged, even the most comfortable bed and the softest pillow won't give you a peaceful sleep.

To make the most of your bed time tonight, visualize yourself gradually emptying your mind of each slip of paper. As you do, be sure to place each paper where it belongs—in the trash.

☆

Tonight I'll do a little "head cleaning" before I go to bed. I'll remove all the unwanted messages from my mind and replace them with one brief message: sleep!

. . . President and Mrs. Benjamin Harrison were so intimidated by the newfangled electricity installed in the White House they didn't dare touch the switches. . . . If there were no servants around to turn off the lights when the Harrisons went to bed, they slept with them on.
—Jane Goodsell

Have you ever woken up the next morning from a difficult night's sleep and laughed at how silly your fearful imaginings were? Maybe a window rattling in the wind replicated the sound of a burglar trying to break in. Perhaps a howling dog conjured up the image of a werewolf. Or maybe a nightmare that seemed so real harmlessly dissolved from your mind like the crystals of sugar in your cup of coffee.

You can't expect every night's sleep to be peace-filled and mellow 366 days a year for your entire life; there will inevitably be some turbulence from time to time. Work difficulties, family pressures, meals eaten late at night, energy cycles, and other circumstances can make some nights very rough.

Learning to laugh at a terrible night's sleep or a bad dream is one of the best ways to lighten them up. Tonight, be prepared to handle nighttime difficulties with humor. If you wake up from a nightmare you can say, "Take that dream back, please. That's not what I ordered for tonight." Or if you've spent several minutes tossing and turning, you could say, "I refuse to be intimidated any more by real life. I'm now switching to the Fantasy Channel."

☆

I can handle any nighttime anxieties with the ease of a stand-up comedian facing a hostile audience. Statements such as "Take this nightmare—please!" and "I'm still waiting to be slept off my feet" can chase my fears away.

The vision must be followed by the venture. It is not enough to stare up the steps—we must step up the stairs.

—*Vance Havner*

In American society aging is often thought of as an entirely negative experience. Most people are so hooked on youth that they haven't recognized that inexperience and great reserves of physical stamina aren't always virtues; rather, knowing what you're doing, where you're going, and the steps you want to take to get there are the real strengths.

Maturity can give you a chance to do many new things, to develop yourself in new ways, and to set your sights on more distant goals. Just because aging can physically erode your body and slow up your pace doesn't mean that your mind is similarly eroded or your faith and determination is fading.

Tonight, find great security in the knowledge that you've still got many more goals you can set and attain—no matter what your age. Think of at least one vital, challenging interest that you'd like to enjoy now or when you retire. Maybe you'd like to learn how to fly an airplane, do more creative writing, go back to college, or travel to a foreign country. Visualize yourself enjoying this interest as you keep in mind the belief that anything's possible!

☆

Tonight I'll remember that wisdom isn't part of the biological process of aging. I have to take steps to acquire it as I bravely venture out into a world that can help me create new challenges and set new goals.

My world is composed of takers and givers. The takers may eat better but the givers sleep better.
—Byron Frederick

It may not be hard to see how self-centered actions and attitudes can negatively impact upon other people. Riding roughshod over others in order to get where you want or what you want—regardless of their needs and feelings—can cause them pain and misery.

But are you also aware that your own self-centeredness can seriously affect the way you treat yourself? Ralph Waldo Emerson once said, "The selfish man suffers more from his selfishness than he from whom that selfishness withholds some important benefit." As you work your way up the corporate ladder, for instance, haven't you deprived yourself of the comfort of an intimate relationship, the connection with family and friends, times of pleasure and enjoyment, and periods of rest and relaxation? Driving yourself relentlessly may certainly earn you greater financial rewards to put expensive foods on your table, but how well do you sleep at night?

Treating yourself harshly and with disdain as you pursue your own self-seeking goals can deplete you mentally, physically, and spiritually. Tonight, resolve to be a giver to yourself in the future. That means you need to reward your day-by-day determination with at least one kind and patient act towards yourself.

☆

My self-centeredness often prevents me from behaving thoughtfully and generously towards myself. From now on I'll strive to be a beneficiary of my actions, not a victim.

*Do not lose your inward peace for anything what-
soever, even if your whole world seems upset.*
—*Saint Frances de Sales*

Your days may be filled with tense people, hectic sched-
ules, or frustrating events. You may live and interact with a
variety of stressful situations and negative people. But just
because the environment around you is like a battlefield or
the people in it make you so uncomfortable that you view
them as the "enemy" doesn't mean you have to prepare for
battle tonight or lie awake at night fearing those who seem
to be against you. Whatever is happening outside you is
someone else's issue, not yours. What *is* your issue, however,
is how you control your inner peace.

You can transform the world within and around you
merely by transforming your attitude about it. You can do
this anywhere, anytime—day or night—to regain your peace
of mind. How? First, slowly inhale by taking a deep breath
into your abdomen. Exhale completely, visualizing all the
negative energies within you and around you—the jumble
of conflicts, confrontations, and crises—being released in
your expelled breath.

Then focus on each issue that's impacting on your inner
peace. Hold one issue at a time in your mind for a few moments to get a clear picture of it. Then say out loud, "This
is *not* my energy." "Cleanse" your mind of the issue, then
say, "I am now at peace with this issue."

☆

*Tonight I'll release the negative energies that can "pollute" my
mind and body. Restoring my inner self can calm me no matter what's going on around me.*

*Where will I be five years from now? I delight in not
knowing. That's one of the greatest things about life—
its wonderful surprises.*

—Marlo Thomas

The elderly man who had just turned 98 was asked what
his next goal was. "To live to tomorrow," he replied. How
would you live your life tonight if your only goal was to live
to tomorrow?

Some people set complex goals that require years of hard
work before they can be achieved. Others create grandoise
goals they feel will "guarantee" them success, happiness, and
meaning in their lives. Still others set goal after goal, achieving one goal and then immediately setting another without
ever taking the time to reflect on the ground they've gained
or reward themselves for their accomplishments. And there
are those who set goals that put them in the position of burning the candle at both ends as they strive for more and more.

Like the elderly man's desire to simply live to see another
day, the best goals you can make are ones that are simple,
uncomplicated, and easy-to-achieve. From this moment on,
resolve to set a simple goal in the evening—to sit down for
a half-hour and read the paper, to listen to a new CD from
start to finish, to catch up on your letter writing, or to take
a long walk. Then you can go to bed with a satisfied feeling,
knowing that you reached your goal for the night.

☆

*I won't complicate any night by creating a complex, long-range
goal that needs to be achieved. Instead I'll enjoy a sense of accomplishment from attaining a simple, rewarding goal.*

And if your friend does evil to you, say to him, "I forgive you for what you did to me, but how can I forgive you for what you did to yourself?"

—*Nietzsche*

Following the acquittal verdict in the Rodney King police brutality case of April 1992, inner-city residents took to the streets of Los Angeles to try to balance the scales of justice. But in the process legal justice—as well as human justice— were ignored. Racial hatred erupted into rioting, looting, and senseless killing. Instead of achieving justice, the actions of the protestors destroyed stores that provided them with basic necessities and ruined their neighborhoods. Not only did innocent people suffer; so, too, did the ones who incited the violence.

Are you aware of the consequences of your behaviors? There's an old maxim that teaches that when you harm someone else, you're really harming yourself. So words you may speak in anger not only hurt the listener, but also can come back to hurt you when you lose your friendship, damage a good working relationship, alienate a client, or cause a loved one to back away from you.

Tonight, decide to become more sensitive to the consequences of your behaviors. Strive to avoid behaviors or attitudes that can later cause you to feel guilt, remorse, or pain. And learn to count to ten *before* you act explosively or slide into a hostile state of mind.

☆

Tonight I'll keep in mind what can happen to me when I'm angry, unkind, or hurtful to others. So I'll treat everyone in the same way I'd like to be treated.

When you have shut the doors, and darkened your room, remember never to say that you are alone; for God is within, and your genius is within, and what need have they of light to see what you are doing?
—*Epictetus*

Are you so afraid to be alone at night that you comfort yourself in ways you think are childish? As an adult, you may feel very secretive about the things you use to help you feel safe at night so you can fall asleep. Maybe you have a night light in your bedroom. Perhaps you have a baseball bat or golf club hidden under your bed. Maybe you fall asleep to music or with the television on. Or you might hug a stuffed animal tightly to your chest after you turn out the lights. Each of these nighttime rituals is designed to make you feel safer and less alone in the dark.

Yet you're never alone—especially at night. The methods you use to fall peacefully asleep may be helpful, but what may be more comforting would be to remember that there are always three angels that guard your sleep.

The first angel is your Higher Power—a belief in something greater than yourself. The second is the positive feeling you have inside that believes in you. And the third is the gentle, hopeful spirit inside you that helps you to trust that there will always be a tomorrow.

Tonight, fall asleep in peace. Trust that you're never alone. Your three guardian angels are always watching over you—day and night.

☆

I may not know that my guardian angels are there for me during the day, but I'm certain they're there for me at night. With them watching over me, I'm never alone.

Know what you want to do, hold the thought firmly,
and do every day what should be done, and every
sunset will see you that much nearer the goal.
—*Elbert Hubbard*

Every good story has a beginning, a middle, and an ending. The beginning is like your morning, full of newness, promise, and hope. This morning was your introduction to a new day—a chance to meet new people and to have new experiences.

The middle of the story is how your day progressed. It includes all the actions and events, the dialogues and the locales, and the conflicts and confrontations of the day. The middle may have been dull and boring or it could have raced along at a fast pace. But no matter how it unfolded, you may have gotten to know the characters in your story a little better or learned a little more about yourself.

The ending of the story is this evening. Although not all of it has been written, you may have already found resolutions to the conflicts and compromises for the confrontations in the middle of the story, as well as logical endings to some of the events that started at the beginning of the story.

Now you need to write the story's conclusion. You can add more conflict, confrontation, and events, or you can end with a feeling of hope, gratitude, and peace. How will you complete your story—with an ending that demands a sequel, or with a happy ending?

☆

As I "write" the ending to my story tonight, I'll tie up all the loose
ends from the beginning and middle so I can close the "book"
on today with a satisfied, contented sigh.

There are people who learn, who are open to what happens around them, who listen, who hear the lessons. . . . The question to ask is not whether you are a success or a failure, but whether you are a learner or a nonlearner.

—*Carole Hyatt and Linda Gottlieb*

In your mind is a multitude of stored memories, knowledge, and skills. Some of these are the result of living and learning, but most are information given to us by others. Teachers give you much in the way of factual knowledge. Your family may instruct you in morals. Your friends may show you different personalities and lifestyles. Your children may reflect what you've taught them and give you their view of the world. Such people are often the greatest sources for your storehouse of information.

That's why Harry Emerson Fosdick has said: "Life is like a library owned by an author. In it are a few books which he wrote himself, but most of them were written for him." All the information you have is valuable to your growth and maturity. Every person you meet, each place you visit, and every thing you try contributes to your library of knowledge and experience. From time to time others may borrow from what's on your "shelves," but you need to keep your shelves stocked with fresh material each day. In that way you can be open and willing to listen and hear the lessons of life that are being given to you.

☆

Life and the people in it can provide me with valuable classroom experience, but only if I'm willing to learn. Tonight I'll seek out a "teacher" and be an interested "student."

For it is not physical solitude that actually separates one from other men, not physical isolation, but spiritual isolation.

—Anne Morrow Lindbergh

Have you ever marveled at the balance of a tripod or a three-legged stool? Like a four-legged animal that loses a leg and must adapt to being slightly off-balance, the three legs can only work together to support a camera or a person when they are carefully positioned.

You're like that three-legged stool, for you need to balance your mental, physical, and spiritual energies in order to create appropriate self-support and connection with the world around you. If you spend too much time at work tasks, using only your mental concentration, then you won't have time to be able to exercise your body or explore your spirituality. If you spend too much time performing physical labors or exercising your body, your mind and spirituality will suffer. And if you feel that a week-long spiritual retreat will bring your life into greater balance, what you may find is that your spirituality receives attention but the needs of your mind and body are ignored. Blocking out any one of these three aspects can isolate you from yourself—and others.

Tonight, pay attention to your mental needs, your physical needs, and your emotional needs. When these three components are in balance in your life, you'll not only be able to feel connected with yourself, but also with those around you.

☆

Tonight I won't shortchange the importance of my mental, physical, or spiritual growth. I'll pay attention to each of these areas so I don't upset the balance in my life.

Expecting the world to treat you fairly because you are a good person is a little like expecting the bull not to attack you because you're a vegetarian.
—Dennis Wholey

One of life's hard lessons is that not everyone lives by the Golden Rule of doing unto others the way you'd want them to do unto you. So just because you're honest at work doesn't mean your boss and coworkers or the service people you use will be honest with you. Just because you're devoted to your lover doesn't mean your lover won't cheat on you or feel the way you do. Just because you do everything for your kids doesn't mean they'll appreciate you or won't get into trouble. And just because you're a success doesn't mean your parents will stop criticizing you or your spouse won't feel threatened.

The standards by which you treat others will not necessarily come back in kind. So how can you maintain inner peace tonight when the positive energy, selflessness, openness, and honesty you may try to bring into your home, work environment, and relationships is met with anger, deception, tension, conflict, and confrontation?

First, keep in mind that everyone will behave in ways that are right for them, no matter what you do. Then, rather than spend your time trying to change their behaviors, feel good about your own actions. Be proud of your honesty, the selfless love you offer, your determination to be a good parent, and the level of caring you have for yourself.

☆

I don't have to be rewarded by others in order to feel that I'm a good person. Tonight I'll rest assured that I've done my best, treated others well, and taken care of myself at the same time.

*The two words "peace" and "tranquility" are worth
a thousand pieces of gold.*

—Chinese proverb

Are you in touch with your inner self? Your inner self is
the part of you that makes you aware of your need for rest,
relaxation, peace, tranquility, a slower pace, or a new
perspective.

If you're like most people, you're probably more in touch
with your outer self—the active part of you that ignores your
inner needs and urges you to always keep moving, always
be thinking, always be striving as it deals with problems and
hassles, the pressures of failure and success, completing
projects and errands, and handling unfinished business and
accomplishments.

Getting in touch with your inner self through meditation
can help you balance activity with inactivity so you can re-
juvenate and recharge the depleted energy of your outer self.
How do you meditate? Meditation needs only a quiet, peaceful place (a cozy room in your home or a favorite spot outdoors), a comfortable position (sitting cross-legged or lying
down), an object to dwell on (a word such as "peace," a lit
candle, a crystal, or a specific thought or feeling such as "love
for my partner"), and a still mind. Having a still mind—one
that's free of activity and chatter—can put you in touch with
your inner self so you're more aware of your thoughts, per-
ceptions, and feelings—yet feel totally at peace.

☆

*Tonight I'll enrich my life by meditating to get in touch with my
inner "needs." I'll try to get an accurate picture of my outer self
so I can make changes that will bring me inner peace and
tranquility.*

'Tis pitiful the things by which we are rich or poor—a matter of coins, coats and carpets, a little more or less stone, wood or paint, the fashion of a cloak or hat....
—Ralph Waldo Emerson

It may be hard to see the richness in life tonight—by a midnight deadline, you have to complete your taxes and make a check out to the government. You may feel anger at having to give to a government that seems to ignore your needs, frightened at the loss of some of the security your hard-earned tax dollars could have provided, anxious about how you'll pay the bills at the end of the month, or resigned at how little control you seem to have over your money.

This is when you need to step back from the issues created by money and material possessions and instead focus on the creative forces of life around you. Birds are flying somewhere in the world right now. There are nests of eggs with a parent patiently maintaining their warmth. Somewhere there are farmers plowing, children playing, musicians creating, teachers teaching. You are part of it all.

Now focus on your own life. There are many gifts in it that have no material value nor can they ever be purchased or sold. Your health. Your friends. A pressed flower from a romantic night. A child. A lover. Your parents. Special places you've visited. Your creative talents. Your happiness.

Tonight, focus not on what you have to give away, but what you've been given. Those things are far more precious than any amount of money.

☆

Tonight I'll trust that the things that make me rich are not in my wallet or my checking account. They're in my heart, in my home, and in my life.

A hug is a perfect gift—one size fits all, and nobody minds if you exchange it.

—*Ivern Ball*

Do you fear the intimacy of friendships? A hug, a touch, or a friend's gentle nudge may sometimes make you feel uncomfortable. Perhaps you were physically or sexually abused in your childhood or were brought up in a childhood home by parents who weren't physically or emotionally demonstrative. Maybe you believe that any physical contact between two people always signals a sexual overture—and you don't feel "that way" about your friend. Perhaps you were involved in an abusive relationship as an adult. Or maybe you have a low sense of self-esteem that leads you to mistrust that such warm, physical feelings are real. "What can this person possibly mean by hugging me?" you might question as your friend's arms encircle you while your arms remain stiff by your sides.

The only way to feel comfortable with a friend's physical expressions of love and caring is to simply experience them. Allow yourself to receive hugs; you'll find they don't hurt, and they don't mean someone wants you sexually. Hugs just mean that someone likes you and wants to show you that.

From this moment on, be willing to accept a hug that's offered to you or give one to a friend. Through such an exchange you'll learn to not only trust the hugs, but also to feel the wonderful love that encircles you each time you receive one.

☆

In the past I know I've feared physical expressions in my friendships. I'll conquer that fear by being ready to give a hug to someone I care about. Maybe I'll even get a hug, too!

Life has taught me to think, but thinking has not taught me to live.

—*Aleksandr Ivanovich Herzen*

When your problems and dilemmas become tormenting obsessions, then you're doing too much thinking about them. But oftentimes your thinking doesn't start out to be so all-consuming. Perhaps you're faced with a situation that needs your mental concentration: your job, your schedule, your marriage, a living situation, a personal growth issue, your children, or any other situation. You set aside time to deal with the situation, sit down, and *think*.

You may begin by trying to organize your thoughts. You may then try to look for connections, solutions, next steps. You might go off on a tangent or begin a thought with "*What if . . .*" so you can follow that where it goes. You may try to anticipate how something you might do will affect yourself or others. You may attempt to anticipate outcomes. Your mind may drift off to thinking about unrelated matters. Before you know it, several minutes have gone by and you can't *stop* yourself from thinking.

To prevent this moment from turning into a "Thinking Night," realize that your mind can process enormous amounts of information, but *is* limited. Rather than rely solely upon your intellectual powers to help you "think" your way through the dilemmas of life, allow some room for spiritual solutions. Sometimes your most perplexing or troubling situations can be solved without your input!

☆

Tonight I'll set a time limit before I go to sleep for thinking about a particular situation. When this time limit is up, I'll ask my Higher Power for help in finding a solution so I can sleep peacefully.

We have loved the stars too fondly to be fearful of the night.
— *Inscription in crypt of Alleghany Observatory, University of Pittsburgh*

Do you love your work or hobbies with such intensity that you almost become a different person when you're involved with them? Perhaps you wake up every morning energized to go to work or retire at night looking forward to the next work day. Maybe you have a wonderful relationship with your life partner because you both eagerly look forward to evenings when you can share a common interest—watching old movies, going bowling, or adding to a collection. Or perhaps your voice becomes animated, your eyes light up, and you feel good all over whenever you get to talk about your hobby, interest, or career.

If you don't love some *thing* in your life with passionate intensity, then you're missing out on an emotional experience that can drive you, motivate you, and challenge you to learn and grow. By pursuing an enjoyable activity, you can often learn that you have a great deal of skill, talent, and patience that you never knew you had. Developing these positive abilities can enable you to feel more pleasure than you've ever experienced.

Tonight, think about something in your life that makes you feel great. If you can't find something that already exists, then think about what would bring you such pleasure.

☆

What do I love to do? I'll appreciate a job, hobby, or spending time with a person who helps me to feel mentally stimulated, physically challenged, or spiritually connected.

That is happiness; to be dissolved into something complete and great. When it comes to one, it comes as naturally as sleep.

—*Willa Cather*

After a hectic day, how easy is it for you to switch gears and relax? Because your free time is often in short supply, it may be hard to slow down your pace, not feel frantic and tense, and enjoy simple pleasures.

There are many things you can do to make a swift and effective transition from work time to leisure time. Begin by "de-stressing" while traveling home at the end of the day. Listen to relaxing music in the car or use progressive muscle relaxation—alternately tense and relax your muscles from head to toe as you breathe deeply—or read a novel or your favorite magazine on the bus or train.

Before you begin your evening, make a list of all the things you feel you have to accomplish the next day. Then tell yourself there's nothing you can do about them now so you won't use valuable time in the present dwelling on them.

Finally, regularly do something that signifies your busy day is over. Change into comfortable clothes, brew a cup of your favorite noncaffeinated beverage, exercise, or take a hot bath. The particular "ritual" you do isn't as important as choosing an activity that becomes a "cue" that will help you relax and unwind at the end of the day.

☆

From this moment on I'll set aside my worries about tomorrow and my tensions from today. When I can relax during my time away from work and obligations, I'll be much happier.

Everything one records contains a grain of hope, no matter how deeply it may come from despair.
                                        —*Elias Canetti*

Do you keep a journal or diary? How often do you add to it? On a daily basis? Whenever you're going through a crisis or a particularly difficult time? Or only when you have a few free moments when you're not doing something else—something more urgent?

Getting into the habit of writing regularly in a journal can accelerate your growth, take some of the fear out of making changes or taking risks, make the impact of goal-setting and achieving more significant in your life, reacquaint you with yourself, and help you bring closure to a day. Writing about your thoughts, feelings, and actions can help get you into the habit of taking a personal inventory—looking at yourself to see where work is needed—so you can correct your "wrongs" and promote your "rights." Through regular journaling, you can also develop a solid and practical awareness of what works and what doesn't work in your life. You can then apply this knowledge in situations and interactions as they occur. If, for example, you feel as if you're about to "fall apart," you can take a few minutes to write about your emotions, the reasons for them, and how you can quiet them.

Before you go to sleep tonight, resolve to purchase a journal in the near future. Then be ready to contribute to the journal on a regular basis.

☆

The personal progress I can make by journaling can help me to learn and grow. Tonight I'll make a commitment to create an on-going record of my past, present, and future.

I may be in an uncomfortable situation but it is necessary in order for me to grow.

—*Anonymous*

When the sister of a young man who was brutally murdered finally faced the killer in court nearly a decade after the crime, she told him in a trembling voice, "Where ever my brother is today, he may be able to forgive you for what you've done to him. But I can't. *I can't forgive you!*"

When Los Angeles exploded in rioting in April 1992, one black store owner shouted at looters who were invading his business: "What you're doing just isn't right. *It isn't right!*"

Whenever a 16-year-old girl had to endure a chemotherapy treatment for her cancer, she would lie on her back and feel emotionally and physically spent. "I don't think I can make it," she would cry out. "*I just can't make it!*"

It would be wonderful if no one had to face sad times, stiff challenges, and major disappointments. But how you endure such tragic experiences can present you with opportunities for growth. You can choose to sit and moan, "Life isn't fair to me," and stay stuck in negatively viewing your trials. Or you can lose your self-centeredness and discover the truth in what John Milton says, "The mind is its own place, and in itself—Can make a heaven of hell, a hell of heaven."

Tonight, stop eulogizing the negativity in the difficulties you must face. Think instead about all the things you *do* have, you *can* do, and you *can* change.

☆

Tonight I'll build tributes in my life so I can count my blessings—and not my bitternesses.

People go deeper than sleep. You get in touch with the place where you're free of thought. And yet you're alert.
—Tom Stiles

The new exercise of choice for many people has become yoga. Yoga is an ancient form of physical and mental fitness that combines long, measured breaths with slow, gentle body movements—bending, stretching, balancing, reaching, and flexing. There's no rushing in performing yoga "postures" or movements, nor is there a "no pain, no gain" philosophy to the exercise. You don't need pricey equipment or attire. You also don't have to already *be* in shape in order to *get* in shape. Yoga trains you to be both physically and mentally supple; in effect, yoga exercises your body and mind. As a 63-year-old woman who has been regularly practicing yoga on a daily basis comments, "Yoga keeps one focused and calm. I do think it keeps me sane."

Because people at all levels of physical proficiency can benefit, yoga is rapidly becoming a popular course offering at adult education programs, health clubs, and through private instruction. Yoga can also help those who experience chronic discomfort—from arthritis, back problems, asthma and emphysema, or colitis—because it eases the mental and physical fixation on a certain part of the body or on a particular discomfort.

Tonight, consider yoga or another exercise program that can help you experience physical relaxation as well as increase your peace of mind.

☆

Exercise will not only keep me physically healthy, but will also keep me mentally healthy by relieving depression, anxieties, or phobias that can keep me up at night.

*Never give up then, for that is just the place and time
that the tide will turn.*

—*Harriet Beecher Stowe*

Have you ever sustained an injury that immobilized you
for awhile? Maybe you strained your back, sprained an ankle, or broke an arm or a leg. What your doctor probably told
you was to move the injured area as little as possible so it
could heal. Whenever you went against doctor's orders, you
probably paid the price: you may have felt pain, added more
time to your recovery, or reinjured yourself.

But what do you do when you experience an emotional
pain—a job loss, the illness of a child, separation or termination of a relationship, or the loss of a loved one? Maybe
you stay in bed—night and day. Perhaps you don't eat or
sleep. Maybe you overload your schedule with things to do
so you don't have time to feel the pain. Or perhaps you become physically ill.

Being immobilized won't heal emotional pain. Not taking
care of yourself won't make a bad situation better. Working
yourself to the point of physical or mental exhaustion doesn't
ease emotional distress. And making yourself ill only
depletes your already low reserves of energy.

Tonight, the best way to deal with any emotional difficulty
is to feel and face the pain. Pray, if you can put your feelings
into words. Or, if you can't, offer up wordless prayers expressed by your tears, groans, or sighs.

☆

*Tonight I'll trust that relief to my emotional pain will eventually
come. In the meantime, even if I don't know what I ought to pray
for, I can pray with wordless expression of my feelings.*

If only we wanted to be happy, it would be easy; but we want to be happier than other people, which is difficult, since we think them happier than they are.
—*Montesquieu*

Too often people place their happiness outside themselves. This often leads to endless distress as they search for something more, something bigger, something better.

Take, for example, the adult who makes up her mind to be happier than her parents. So today she owns her own company, drives an expensive car, and has two beautiful properties—considerably more than her parents ever had. But she works over 16 hours a day, suffers from an ulcer and chronic fatigue, has had two bad marriages, and is so busy transacting business that she doesn't have time to enjoy the properties she owns. Is she really happy?

There's an old story about a man who approached Buddha to ask the learned man for the secret of happiness. Buddha asked the man, "Did you eat breakfast?"

"Yes," the man replied, confused at the question.

"Did you wash your bowl?" Buddha pursued.

"Yes, yes," the man snapped, a bit impatient.

"Did you do a good job?" Buddha asked, then turned away.

It was then that the man realized that true happiness could only be found by living in the present moment, attending to what he needed to do, and then enjoying it.

☆

Happiness can come from the smallest actions. As I prepare for sleep tonight, I'll keep my focus on the present and find joy in the purpose and order in my nightly routine.

The greatest gift is the passion for reading. It is cheap, it consoles, it distracts, it excites, it gives you knowledge of the world and experience of a wide kind. It is a moral illumination.

—Elizabeth Hardwick

Do you remember as a child how you would beg your parents to read you the same bedtime story? The characters and action in that particular story often relaxed you so you could drift off to sleep. As you grew older, do you remember escaping into the world created by comic books, fiction, and biographies of those you admired? Perhaps you begged to stay up a few minutes longer to find out what happened next or continued to read by flashlight under the canopy created by a blanket draped over your head.

When was the last time you sat down for a few hours to read a book for pleasure? If you think about it, you may discover that most of your reading has been work-related or quick scannings of newspaper and magazine articles snatched in idle moments between necessary activities.

Tonight, resolve to set aside time in the future to borrow a book from your local library, browse a bookstore for a book you've always wanted to read, or locate the book you wanted to read on last year's vacation but couldn't get to. Then be like the child who once loved to read: dive excitedly into the world created by the book, become emotionally involved with the characters, and devour the book from cover to cover.

☆

When was the last time I experienced "a good read"? I'll look forward to spending at least one night a week with a hot cup of tea, soothing background music, a comfortable chair or the support of a few pillows, and a good book.

Nothing in life is more remarkable than the unnecessary anxiety which we endure, and generally occasion ourselves.

—Benjamin Disraeli

According to a Hilton Hotels survey, the average American has to reset seven clocks—not including wrist watches—whenever Daylight Savings Time occurs. Time expert Dr. John Robinson says that this proves that Americans are obsessed with time. In fact, research shows that 14 percent of women and 21 percent of men feel naked, half dressed, or "like they're missing something" when they forget to wear a watch.

Putting real or imaginary time constraints on yourself can create a major source of time-related anxiety in your life. Do you own several watches or keep a clock in every room of your home? Are you either obsessively late or compulsively early for appointments? Do you put continual time constraints on yourself—for example, do you think or say, "In fifteen minutes, I'll have all the dishes done," "When I make that telephone call, I won't talk for more than ten minutes," or "I'm only going to get five hours sleep tonight"?

From this moment on, resolve to take off your wrist watch or pull your eyes away from clock-watching. Instead, take whatever time you need to complete a task, to talk on the telephone, or to do whatever it is you'd like to do. You can allow yourself as much time—or as little time—as you want.

☆

I know that there's nothing more peaceful than a mind that isn't regulated or restricted. I'll stop timing myself and start enjoying myself.

I only went out for a walk, and finally concluded to stay out till sundown, for going out, I found, was really going in.

—John Muir

Recognizing your oneness with nature can expand your horizon, give you a deeper sense of self, and help you move below the brittle surface of life to experience the soft undersides of nature.

There are many ways to "go out into nature." Physically you can camp, hike, bird watch, or work in your garden. Sensually you can smell the richness of the soil, feel the rigid spine of a discarded bird feather, see droplets of moisture on leaves, hear the songbirds bidding *adieu* to the day, and taste the first fresh herbs of the season. Spiritually you can get close to living, growing things.

Right now, take a deep breath and feel your connection with the natural wonders around you. Appreciate the harmony nature has with the world and the process of growth in all living things. Feel how the natural world readies itself for a good night's sleep. Then tuck yourself comfortably in for the night in the same way. Say, "I am one with nature. I honor its growth and its vitality, as I honor mine. I respect it, as I respect myself. Each day I learn more about it, as I learn more about myself. And so my life is peaceful and harmonious with nature."

☆

Tonight I'll feel how the rhythms of my body interact with the natural rhythms around me. I'll believe that I'm one with nature.

*I was not looking for my dreams to interpret my life,
but rather for my life to interpret my dreams.*
—Susan Sontag

Have you ever dreamed of owning the perfect home or achieving wonderful awards? In 1970 when Peter Chan moved his family to their new home in Oregon, others who had seen his property couldn't understand why Chan had spent money on a yard filled with hard clay soil and large stones. But Chan saw his yard not as a problem but as an opportunity to fulfill a dream. He envisioned a breathtaking garden; today, his beautiful gardens have won awards and have been featured in magazines and on national television. How did he use real life to interpret his dream? He enriched the clay soil with compost and used the stones that were viewed as "troublesome" to form pleasant pathways between the raised beds of his vegetable garden.

You may have dreams of your own—some more ambitious than Chan's, others equally so, and a few that are rather simple and easy-to-achieve. But there's much to learn from Chan's philosophy, which echoes that of many Chinese gardeners: "*Use what you have wisely.*"

Tonight, think about a dream you have. Consider the resources you'll need to achieve the dream. Then ask, "What do I have in my own life right now—materially and creatively—that can help contribute to making this dream possible?"

Just as a city dweller can create an indoor garden to grow fresh fruits and vegetables, so too can I create a "growing garden" out of any one of my dreams. All I need to achieve it is time, determination, and a willingness to make it happen.

The best thing scientists could do to improve sleep would be to invent a system for not thinking.
                                        —Wilse Webb

Do you know that it's often the quality, not the quantity, of your sleep that can leave you feeling out of sorts the next day? Going to bed earlier so you can snooze longer at night is not necessarily the best solution to combatting the daytime drowsiness or early-morning fatigue that needs to be chased away with mega-doses of caffeine. In fact, sleep studies have shown that many of the realities of modern life—stress overload, a poor diet, a noisy environment, and chronic worrying—can lead to shallow, fragmented sleep.

But there are ways to "turn off" daytime thinking so you can "turn on" better sleep at night. First, complete your work, school, or family obligations at least two or three hours before going to bed. Use the "free time" for stress-free thinking—read a book, play a game, talk on the telephone with a friend, write a personal letter—or for thought-calming activities—meditate, take a hot bath, do a hobby, or watch a favorite movie or television show.

If you do these things and still find that you can't turn your mind off and continue to toss and turn in bed, get out of bed, go to another room, and write down the things that are bothering you. Then do a quiet, calming activity until you're finally drowsy.

☆

Even though I may be tired in the afternoon or when I get home after work, I'll stop drinking caffeine after 2:00 P.M. I'd rather not suffer from insomnia or wake up tomorrow after another night of poor-quality sleep.

Real generosity toward the future consists in giving all to what is present.

—*Albert Camus*

Tonight you've reached the last day of another month and the eve of a new one. Some people like to think of month's-ends as times to review progress, face up to shortcomings, acknowledge assets, and reward gains. You, too, may like to think that, starting tonight, there are things you'd like to change in the future.

So tonight you may want to take a few moments to think of one thing you'd like to do this week, in the next month, or over your summer vacation. You can resolve to make an effort to stick to the New Year's resolution you made to diet, exercise, or make a personal change. You can develop faith that next month you'll find a different job, meet someone new and fall in love, or locate the perfect home.

Wanting to change is great; it's certainly an essential component to increasing your enjoyment in life. But tonight remember that change is best undertaken one day at a time. So it's more productive to think about what you want to do right now on April 30 at bedtime—get ready for bed—rather than in the days, weeks, or months to come.

Remember, you don't have to wait until the end of a month or even a day to make a new beginning. But you do need to make each change *one day at a time*.

If I resolve tonight to make everything in my life better tomorrow, I'm avoiding the time I've been given today. What if tomorrow never comes? Tonight I'll make the most of any new beginning now.

Be aware of yourself and validate your experience. Pay attention to your world, what's happening, and why.
—*Alexandra G. Kaplan*

Imagine you have the opportunity to take a trip across the United States. You can stop wherever you'd like, spend however long you want at any location, and have no set timetable. Are you going to focus solely on reaching your destination of the opposite coast and simply drive there? Or are you going to let go of the need to arrive anywhere at any particular time and enjoy the scenery, the people you meet along the way, and the places in which you linger?

Every evening you have the opportunity to go on a "cross country" trip—a once-in-a-lifetime adventure never to be repeated any other day. How do you wish to spend your time? By enjoying every minute and sometimes stopping to savor a unique opportunity? Or will you simply focus on your goal for the night and achieve that?

On any evening, you can reach any destination you set for yourself. But how you do that will determine how enjoyable and memorable the night will be. The runner who only looks down at the road will surely reach her destination, but won't have the same experience as the runner who looks at all the natural beauty and sights along the way.

From this night on, resolve to pay attention to what's happening in your world. Notice the people in it, the tastes of foods you prepare, the words you read, and the music you hear. *Appreciate* each night's journey.

☆

If I were on a cross country trip, I'd probably make a lot of stops along the way. I'll open my senses at night and let go of a time-table so I can experience everything and everyone around me.

Laziness is nothing more than resting before you get tired.

—*Jules Renard*

The last time you felt draggy or irritable during the day, you may have blamed how you felt on a lack of sleep. As your temper grew shorter and you were less pleasant with family members and coworkers, you may have vowed to get more sleep. To you, "how much" was the reason for your low energy. So you may have started taking naps, going to bed earlier, or sleeping in later. Yet you may still be as edgy, anxious, and irritable during the day.

Research has shown that you can actually sleep *too* much. Staying in bed excessively long or napping late in the day can make your sleep shallower and more fragmented. So your daytime grumpiness may instead be caused by your inability to face up to things you may be reluctant to deal with: emotional or physical stresses, problems in your intimate relationship, the illness of someone close to you, lack of interest or challenge in your job, or low self-esteem.

Using sleep as an excuse not to deal with the "real" problems in your life is like always choosing to hike the easiest trail up a mountain. From now on, use your evening time to exert greater effort into conquering a difficult path in your life. Instead of napping in front of the television, talk with a friend about something that's troubling you. Together, you may find a solution that can "wake" you up.

☆

I know that the longer it takes me to deal with something that's affecting me, the worse I'll feel. I'll remember that there's always a price to pay for procrastination.

I think the most important thing is caring about someone. It's being by themselves that does people in, makes them old and bitter. . . . I think real happiness only comes when we are joined to another human being. Otherwise we are lonely, and we suffer for it.
                                                        —Thomas Tryon

One day a member of a tribe living in a remote area in central Brazil left his village and journeyed to São Paulo. After spending a few years experiencing the bustling modern city of 13 million people, he went back to his small village of 300. When he got home, he told the members of the tribe why he had returned. "Here," he said, "we know each other and are with each other." He explained that he hadn't found security in the city; rather, the close personal and social connections that were typical of his way of life in the tribe were lacking in the more modern society.

What's an example of a connection of tribal life? Tribal society doesn't abandon old people the way many in society do, as they shuttle grandparents and aging parents to the homes of siblings or nursing homes. In tribes younger family members, as well as everyone else in the village, have a reponsibility to help support the aged.

Tonight, think about an older member of your "tribe"— your biological family, adoptive family, or family of friends— with whom you've lost touch. Resolve to write a letter, make a phone call, extend an invitation to your home, or visit this person in the near future.

☆

Society can be a very alienating place to live. That's why it's important that I take the initiative in connecting and reconnecting with those who are important to me.

The difficult things of this world must once have been easy; the great things of this world must once have been small. Set about difficult things while they are still easy; do great things while they are still small.
—*Taoism*

Very often you may not pay attention to things until they reach a crisis stage. For example, you may put off paying bills—even when you have the money—until you receive past-due notices in your mailbox. You may ignore the suspicious sound your car engine is making and instead drive to and from work every day with your fingers crossed. Or you may avoid working on communication issues in your relationship until your partner gives you an ultimatum of couples counseling or separation.

Handling events *before* they get out of hand is like practicing preventive medicine. Rather than be rushed to the hospital with a heart attack, it's less risky to eat right, exercise in moderation, and get a yearly check-up. Taking action *before* things escalate can avert future trouble or keep a bad situation from growing worse.

From this moment on, resolve to become a "troubleshooter." Consider one area of your life that runs the risk of reaching a crisis. Decide what you can do to avert a crisis— pay the phone bill before your service is shut off, work through a confrontation before your partner decides to leave, or call a mechanic to repair your car. Remember, what you do can eliminate a problem instead of make it more difficult.

☆

Am I tempted to put off things I know must be done? I'll remind myself that there are no excuses for delaying handling a condition that I know exists.

*He that always gives way to others will end in having
no principles of his own.*

—*Aesop*

One of the most difficult skills to learn is how to set appropriate boundaries for yourself. Yet *knowing* you need to set limits on your time and energy and actually *setting* them are two different things. Oftentimes you may be afraid to tell your boss that you have to cut back on your overtime because you fear jeopardizing a future promotion or greater responsibilities. You may be reluctant to delegate some of the tasks you've assumed for a long time because you feel others need you or are depending upon you. You may feel pressure to single-handedly assume the obligations of working a full-time job as well as being a single parent or the primary caretaker in your home. Or your overdeveloped sense of pride or the need for an ego-boost may entice you into accepting a position of leadership that necessitates a great deal of your time and energy.

Tonight you may discover that your fears, doubts, and insecurities have led you to a critical crossroads—a place where you need to make a decision. Can you continue to maintain a schedule crammed full with nighttime obligations, or do you need to set limits that respect your need for a "time out"? Resolve in future evenings to find out what limits are right for you so you can create boundaries that address your needs first.

☆

I can recognize how my old boundaries got me to where I am today. Am I too afraid to say no? Maybe now is the time for me to learn how to say it—and mean it.

Failure is an event, never a person.
—William D. Brown

There's a story from the early days of the automobile about a Model-T Ford that was once stalled in the middle of a road. The driver couldn't get it started no matter how hard he cranked or how much he tried to adjust the spark plug. Just then a chauffeured limousine pulled up behind the car. A man hopped out from the back seat and offered his assistance. After looking under the hood and tinkering with something for a few minutes, the man said, "Now try it!" The engine started right up. It was then that the man from the limousine identified himself as Henry Ford. "I designed and built this car," he told the driver, "so I know what to do when something goes wrong."

What do you do when something goes wrong? Maybe things didn't go right today at work. Perhaps you and your intimate partner haven't been able to see eye-to-eye. Maybe your child is having difficulty in school. Or perhaps you haven't been able to improve your workouts. Do you tend to blame yourself or focus on all the things you could've, should've, or ought to've done? Or are you able to see any setbacks, mistakes, and failures as events that simply need some adjustment?

Today, stop blaming yourself for all the people, places, and things that didn't go right today. Instead, be more like Henry Ford. Don't scrap the entire invention; instead, be satisfied that you will find an appropriate solution.

☆

When nothing seems to go right, I can think of ways they can be mended. I won't drift aimlessly at sea as I blame the wind for my torn sails. I'll make my repairs so I can once again sail on course.

Laughter is a tranquilizer with no side effects.
—*Arnold H. Glasow*

Sometimes you may not see the importance of laughter during dark times because you're blinded by your tears, immobilized by your grief, or incapable of feeling anything other than anger. But being able to laugh at life's ongoing daily hassles as well as in the face of incredible tragedies such as illness, death, and loss can provide you with the same much-needed physical and psychological benefits that laughter can give you at other times, including helping keep things in perspective as well as keeping you in balance when your life seems totally out of balance.

In addition, remaining open to levity in even the most solemn situations can help you, as a survivor, stay both mentally and physically healthy. Being overly serious in the grieving process can actually be unhealthy, as a study of the immune systems of grieving spouses showed: The spouses had lower activity levels of T cells—one of the body's most important defenses against illness.

From this moment on, how can you keep your perspective through your difficulties? Rabbi Harold Kushner, in his book *When Bad Things Happen to Good People*, recommends changing your focus from being on the past or on the pain. Instead of asking, "Why did this happen to me?" you should instead ask " . . . the question that opens doors to the future: 'Now that this has happened, what shall I do about it?' "

☆

Tonight I'll keep in mind an old Chinese proverb that states: "You cannot prevent the birds of sorrow from flying over your head, but you can prevent them from building nests in your hair."

It is never wise to seek or wish for another's misfortune. If malice or envy were tangible and had a shape, it would be the shape of a boomerang.
—*Charley Reese*

When Lee Iacocca brought Chrysler back from near bankruptcy in the early 1980s, he often publicly declared that one of his primary motives for succeeding at Chrysler was to get revenge on Henry Ford II for firing him years previously. Did Iacocca succeed in his revengeful desires? At first it seemed as if he had. Financially, Chrysler became profitable. The minivan idea that the Ford Motor Company had rejected became a profitable hit for Chrysler. Henry Ford II got to see Iacocca's success, but died in 1987. But now, years later, Chrysler is still the number three U.S. auto maker. So what did Iacocca prove by seeking Ford's misfortune so he could succeed?

It's important to realize that it will be inevitable, at some point in your career, in your parenting, in your intimate relationship, in your friendships, or in your interactions with your parents, you'll be taken for granted. You'll sometimes be mistreated. Your contributions may not be fully recognized or rewarded. You may not be fully loved or deeply appreciated. But that doesn't mean that you need to retaliate or seek revenge. Instead, focus on responses that are constructive, rather than destructive. Seek motives that will serve you, but not at the expense of others.

☆

Revenge isn't compatible with the character I'm building—someone who's compassionate, kind, positive, and forgiving. I'll do the best I can and remember that I'm not the one in charge of distributing justice in this world.

How do people go to sleep? I'm afraid I've lost the knack. I might try busting myself smartly over the temple with the night-light. I might repeat to myself, slowly and soothingly, a list of quotations beautiful from minds profound; if I can remember any of the damn things.
—Dorothy Parker

If you have trouble from time to time getting to sleep at night and staying asleep, here are some strategies you can use to counteract things that can spoil your sleep.

Skip a nightcap. People who have had several drinks before bedtime often sleep very deeply during the first part of the night but then, after the alcohol has been metabolized into their systems, sleep poorly for the rest of the time. So it's a good idea to limit evening alcohol consumption to one drink two hours before turning in.

Avoid stimulants. Coffee, tea, and chocolate aren't the only sources of caffeine. Many sodas and diet drinks contain caffeine, as do some diet pills, over-the-counter decongestants, and pain relievers.

Use sleeping pills sparingly. At first, most sleeping pills may help you to sleep, but after awhile they can lose their effectiveness or become addictive.

Be in touch with your stomach. Don't go to bed hungry or shortly after eating a heavy meal—both situations will interfere with your sleep. Also, if any food has a tendency to irritate your stomach, avoid it in the evening. You can add spice to your life—but not to your sleep!

☆

By identifying some of the ways I can sleep better, I can improve my pre-sleep activities and behaviors. After a more restful night, the next day can be easier to get through.

I think all of life is going out and going back. You get to your job, you want to get home, you get to your home, you want to go out. When you're out you say, "I gotta get back." Wherever you are in life, you gotta get the hell out of there.

—Jerry Seinfeld

Are you at peace with your body? Your career? Your relationships? Are you satisfied with your family? Your finances? Yourself? Oftentimes being upset with one or more aspects of your life can lead you to think that the only solution is to get out of the situation that's making you distressed. So if you're not at peace with your body, you may opt for surgery to resculpt it. If you're unhappy with your career, you may want to give it up completely. If an intimate relationship is upsetting to you, you may decide to end it. Whenever you experience conflict in any part of your life, you may only be able to think of resolution in terms of black and white, right and wrong, stay in a crummy situation or get the hell out.

Yet when there's disharmony in your life, the steps you can take towards reestablishing harmony rarely come from such dramatic tactics. Rather, the best things you can do are to shift your attitude and think about small changes you can make.

Tonight, think about one area of your life that's causing you disharmony. Then think of at least five small things you can do to create greater harmony in your life.

☆

Dualism can make me cling to the status quo or charge into a radical, 180-degree turn. Tonight I'll be a gentle problem solver so I can create peaceful change in my life.

Tears may linger at nightfall. . . . Carefree as I was, I had said, "I can never be shaken." But, Lord, it was Thy will to shake my mountain refuge . . .

—*Psalm 30*

Visitors to the Fiji Islands tell about a strange custom among its native people known as "Calling to the Dead." A mourner climbs to a high tree or cliff and, after calling out the name of the deceased, cries out, "Come back! Come back!" The cry is made even more heartrending by the echoes that reverberate in "reply."

Aren't there times when you wish you could climb to the highest point and release a despairing wail during a time of difficulty or stress? You might want to cry out, "Please let me get this job!" "Will someone please listen to me?" "Can't anybody help me in my time of need?" or, simply, "I hurt!"

Yet there's a great force in your life that can hear your cries during times of isolation, desolation, grief, and despair. Believing in a power greater than yourself—a Higher Power, God, a goddess, a deceased loved one who watches over you, or your spiritual guide—can help you feel safe and secure even though you may sometimes feel as if you stand alone and exposed to the elements of the world.

Tonight, offer a prayer to your Higher Power. Cry out your pain, beat your hands against your chest, let your tears fall, get on your knees, or simply close your eyes and silently ask for help. You *will* get an answer.

☆

What can prayer do for me in my time of need? Tonight I can pray in faith and confidence, or I can pray out of desperation and utter hopelessness. Either way, I know my prayers will be heard.

What is a kiss, anyway? A pucker, a smack, a smooch, a brushing of lips. There are passionate kisses and po- lite kisses, long heartfelt kisses you anticipate all even- ing long and those that take you by surprise.
—Susan Lewis

Once upon a time, when you were very young, you learned that kisses had magical powers. Fairy tales taught you that a frog could be turned into a prince and a beauti- ful princess could be awakened from eternal sleep by a kiss. Your parents may have told you that kisses could heal scraped elbows and knees, keep cruel words and unkind ac- tions from hurting you, and make everything better. As you got older, you may have discovered that kissing the right person could feel wonderful; it created an electrical charge that sparked and then energetically surged from your lips throughout your body, warming you inside and making your toes and fingertips tingle. Now, as you grow older, you may be learning that kisses aren't always sexual in nature; sometimes they can be physical reassurances of safety and security—a way of communicating to another, "I'm here for you."

When was the last time you kissed your parents? Your best friend? Your children? Your life partner? Someone who returned to your life after a separation?

Why not take someone by surprise and give a kiss? Let- ting those you care for know how safe and secure, loved and cared for they are can make you both feel better.

☆

If kisses can heal the wounds of childhood, can't they also do good things in adulthood? I'll be open to discover the emotional and phys- ical healing powers that come from the simple act of kissing.

We crucify ourselves between two thieves: regret for yesterday and fear of tomorrow.

—*Fulton Oursler*

Many women who have been victims of nighttime rape, domestic violence, or sexual harrassment have banded together in some cities in "Take Back the Night" public demonstrations and empowering discussion groups. Rather than hold onto the shame, humiliation, regrets, or fears about what happened to them in the past and what might happen to them in the future, they have chosen to live in the present moment without fear.

You can "take back the night" from your own fears. Maybe you fear an upcoming work presentation or job interview. Perhaps you have a doctor's appointment or have to enter the hospital for medical care. Maybe there's someone you need to get together with tomorrow who you really don't want to see. Or perhaps you fear taking a walk at night around the neighborhood in the dark.

Yet any night is yours. That means you need to pull your mind away from the stresses of the day and from your nervous anticipation of tomorrow; both take you away from the present moment. Let go of any fearful thoughts you have so you're at peace in your home and with yourself. Then block out any fearful thoughts you have by telling yourself, "It's my time now for enjoyment, gentle rest, pleasant dreams, and uninterrupted sleep. I'll take back *my* night and let nothing spoil my enjoyment of it."

☆

The past is gone; tomorrow is still waiting for me. That means tonight is here with me right now. I'll feel peace, trust, and serenity by living in the present moment.

Reach high, for stars lie hidden in your soul. Dream deep, for every dream precedes the goal.
—Pamela Vaull Starr

It has been said that if you tell yourself what you'd like to dream before you go to sleep, over time you can teach yourself to dream your own dreams. If you've been troubled by restless nights, confusing dreams, or nightmares that disturb your sleep, beginning tonight you can reprogram your mind. How can you do this? One way is to train your mind to think positive thoughts. Say, for example, "I don't want to dream about my day at work. Instead, I'd like to dream about this weekend" or "I don't want to have another confusing, stress-filled dream. Instead, I'd like to dream about an island paradise."

Another way to reprogram your dreams is to ask for the answers to questions that are troubling you to be revealed in your dreams. Before going to sleep, for example, you can ask, "I've been bothered lately by physical ailments. What can I do to improve my health?" or "What's the best way to handle my latest conflict with my boss?"

A final way is reprogram is to prepare yourself for a night of relaxing or revealing dreams by visualizing what you'd most like to dream about. Close your eyes and "see" yourself doing what you want to do or being who you want to be. Immediately after this visualization, go to sleep. A good night's sleep may actually help you finish the dream you already started.

☆

What will I dream tonight? I can imagine the most positive thing and let it become part of my sleeping thoughts. After a night of positive dreams, I'll wake up refreshed and ready to continue thinking positively.

I just wrote Chris Webber a letter. I told him some things he'll have to deal with, all kinds of people who'll be very critical of him, people who will come at him with support and sob stories.

—Fred Brown

When Michigan forward Chris Webber called for a time-out his team didn't have in the final seconds of the 1993 NCAA basketball championship against North Carolina, he received a technical foul. North Carolina's foul shot clinched the lead for them and ended Michigan's comeback bid for the championship.

Yet Webber isn't the only athlete who has had a momentary lapse during game play that resulted in a loss. When Fred Brown was playing for Georgetown in the 1982 NCAA championships and his team was one point behind, he tossed a game-ending pass directly into the hands of an opposing player. Red Sox first baseman Bill Buckner let an easy ground ball dribble between his legs in the 1986 World Series, setting the stage for the Sox's loss. Roy Riegels ran the wrong way in the 1929 Rose Bowl, costing his team the win and earning the nickname "Wrong Way" Riegels. And there have been many, many other examples of mistakes.

Tonight, keep in mind that while no one wants to make a "major league" blunder, you might from time to time. The best way to handle your mistakes are to talk about them, get them out of your system, and then get on with your life.

☆

Fred Brown turned his mistake to his advantage, using it as free advertising to help him become top salesman of the year for a major corporation. Tonight I'll remember that I can turn any mistake into an advantage.

Eleven o'clock in Grovers Corners. Tomorrow's another day. Everybody is resting in Grovers Corners. You get a good rest, too. Good night.
—*Thornton Wilder*

The last lines in Thornton Wilder's classic play, *Our Town*, are spoken by the narrator as he stands alone on an empty, darkened stage. Rereading the above lines can recreate Wilder's setting of a small, sleepy, silent town where all the windows in the modest homes are darkened and all the town's citizens are settled into their beds, without a sound to rouse them from their slumbers.

Nighttime noise in and around your home—from a television, from others who live with you, from planes flying overhead, or from automobile traffic—is a common source of sleep interruption. In fact, studies have shown that most people who live near airports or busy streets rarely fully adjust to the racket, leading to poor sleep.

Rather than let a noisy environment impact on your sleep, you can take steps to minimize the effect of the noise. If you live near an airport or busy street or room with others who are on a different sleep schedule than you are, deaden the noise by padding your floors in your bedroom with thick carpeting. Cover your windows with heavy drapes or invest in soundproof windows. Block out unwanted sounds by wearing earplugs to bed or by playing a tape of soothing music. Or drown out the noises with a fan, an air conditioner, or a white-noise machine.

☆

To improve the way I sleep, I'll improve my sleeping environment. I'll pay attention to noises that keep me up at night or wake me up from a sound sleep, then take measures to make the noises less annoying.

Worry often gives a small thing a big shadow.
—Swedish proverb

Worry does absolutely nothing for your emotional, physical, or spiritual health. It can take a small situation and enlarge it to the proportion of a giant who looms above you and casts a long, dark shadow over your life. Over time, you may become a constant worrier whose life is ruled by fear as you expect the worst to happen all the time.

That's why "How important is it?" is a good question to ask at night when you're worried. Your answer can help you put the worry into its proper perspective. Another question you can ask is: "What can I do about this right now?" By focusing on what you can actually *do* about a worry, you may discover that your worry involves something that has already happened or something that hasn't yet happened—both of which you can't change or control.

You have the power within you to shrink your worries into a more manageable size. To do so, resolve not to waste your present time worrying over things left undone or things that have yet to come. Choose instead to live for right now and to leave your worries where they belong.

Tonight, think of something that worries you. Then position a light in a way that allows you to create a "shadow puppet" on the wall. Give your puppet the name of a worry and let it dance around for a while. Then turn out the light so it goes away!

☆

Tonight I'll remember that there's nothing to be gained from worrying except more time spent worrying. So while I can spend time making "worry shadows" appear, I can also make them disappear—and have more time for myself.

If you have knowledge, let others light their candles at it.

—Margaret Fuller

Are there people in your life who need your reassurance at night to help them sleep better? Maybe your children need you to tell them a story or tuck them in at night. Perhaps a family member who lives alone needs your nightly telephone call to feel safe and secure. Maybe a friend who's bedridden or going through a difficult time could use some of your concern and attention at night. Or perhaps new members of a 12-step support group would benefit from your message of strength and hope in order to guide them through another night of sobriety.

If you've ever seen a candlelight ceremony, you know how powerful just one candle can be. Countless tapers can be lit from that one small flame until a room, a large meeting hall—even a darkened avenue—is brilliant with light,

Sometimes others may see you as a small flame from which they can light their candles of hope, health, and happiness. Each night, give the gift of your light to others. Offer encouragement to those who could use it, give support to those who are in need, provide strength to those who are weak, relate hope to those who are losing their faith, and share your experience and knowledge with those who will listen. Don't leave anyone in the dark. Let others light their candles from yours.

☆

We are all candlelighters to each other. This gift assures me that I'll never be in the dark; I'll always have the ability to gather light and to give it to others.

I still find each day too short for all the thoughts I want to think, all the walks I want to take, all the books I want to read, and all the friends I want to see.
—John Burroughs

Have you ever observed squirrels in your backyard or in a nearby park? With their boundless energy, they seem to be on a never-ending mission of joyous union with life. They scurry up and down tree trunks, hang from branches, leap gracefully from tree top to tree top, and then jump down to the ground. There they locate nuts and other edibles and either bury them as a dog would bury a bone for future snacking or furiously nibble at the food. Sometimes, in mid-meal, they dart off once again—this time, perhaps, to greet another squirrel, roll playfully around on the grass together, then chase each other around and around the base of a tree trunk.

Squirrels are like individualized packets of joy. Everything they do seems to give them pleasure: walking across telephone wires like circus acrobats, jumping from tree to tree, wiggling their noses, scampering about, and swishing their long, bushy tails.

What the squirrels seem to capture is a joy of life—a happiness in being alive and having many enjoyable things to do from the moment they wake up to the time they need to rest.

From this moment on, decide to be like a squirrel. Don't take yourself or your life too seriously. Instead, think about all the things you'd like to do, pick one—and then do it!

☆

Did I laugh today? Did I take time out to play? Did I enjoy my meals, the company I kept, and the things I did? Each night I'll strive to see my life as an adventure and enjoy every part of it.

Prayer should be the key of the day and the lock of the night.

—Old Proverb

Some people believe that prayer is something that needs to be scheduled—a once-in-the-morning or a once-at-night routine. Yet do you know that prayer isn't so much a ritual or a necessity as it is a *conversation* with a Higher Power—an open, honest communication with a trusted spiritual partner? That means you can pray anytime and as often as you'd like.

Prayer in the morning can be a wonderful way to open the day, but oftentimes your life can get so busy in the morning that your prayers are like your breakfasts—unsatisfying, incomplete, and grabbed on the run. So morning prayers may become just one more thing you try to fit into your life—something to do while shaving or showering or when you're driving to work on the freeway.

That's why it's important to keep in mind that tonight the door is still open to your prayers. Your Higher Power is still there to listen to you. You can share your feelings of the day as if you were talking to a close friend. All you have to do is start talking.

Then you can close the door to today with prayer, knowing that you now have with you the good, warm feelings that faith can bring. When you finally lay down to sleep tonight, you can say goodnight to your Higher Power and rest in peace.

☆

Let me begin my prayers tonight with "Now I lay me down to sleep, I pray to my Higher Power my soul to keep . . ." Then let me give my heartfelt thanks for the day.

*It fascinates me how differently we all speak in differ-
ent circumstances . . . there is the language with no
clothes on; the talk of couples—murmurs, sighs—open
and vulnerable language, at its least self-conscious.*
                                        —Robert MacNeil

Throughout the day, you speak in many different languages. There's the formal language you use for your clients
and professional contacts, business letters, job interviews,
and resumes. There's the less formal language you use with
those who work in stores where you shop or who provide you
with services in your home. There's the casual language you
use with your close friends. There's the assertive language you
use with providers of goods and services who ignore your
needs, overcharge you, or who exhibit unfriendly or abusive
attitudes. And there's the family language you use when
you're in your childhood home or with your own children.

Yet none of these languages are appropriate to use when
you're intimately communicating with your partner. Then
you need to "speak" in a way that comes not only from your
voice, but also from your eyes. You need to communicate not
only the feelings in your head, but also the feelings in your
heart. You need to touch, to taste, to listen, to caress, to care.
You need to use the language you've learned together.

Make up your mind to take time to communicate with
your lover from this moment on. Together, express in words
and actions the strength and meaning of your connection
with one another.

☆

*When was the last time I talked with—not to—my partner?
When was the last time we connected by touching each other's
heart? I'll look forward to opening up the channels of our special
communication with my partner.*

. . . the darkness was encumbering only because I relied upon my sight for everything I did, not knowing that another way was to let power be the guide.
—Carlos Castaneda

You don't need to be blind in order not to see. Haven't there been times when someone has pointed out a different way of looking at things or an easier way of doing something that you couldn't see? Weren't there times when you put on a blindfold of denial so you didn't have to see something that was too painful to acknowledge? Hasn't it sometimes been hard for you to focus on a difficult situation so you could see your way to a solution?

What have you done when you've felt blind? Sometimes your pride may have gotten in the way and haughtily informed you that you could do it alone. Other times you may have refused kind offers of guidance others gave you. And still other times you may have felt strong enough to "go it alone." But during those times, were you always able to safely and effectively find your way?

But even the blind person has a cane or an animal for guidance. Maybe you, too, can benefit from the help of a "sighted" friend—a trusted companion who can guide you on the path of life so you don't stumble or lose your way. Ask, "Have I been blind to the help offered by others? Can I take them up on their offers of support and use their help so I can 'see'?"

☆

I've already felt the effects of my blind gropings in the past. I've stumbled into too many walls and taken more than my share of wrong turns. From now on, I won't be blind to admitting that sometimes I need the help others can give me.

Change, like sunshine, can be a friend or a foe, a blessing or a curse, a dawn or a dusk.
—William Arthur Ward

When you enter into the second half of your life—your midlife years—you may be surprised at the inner struggles you face. Suddenly all the people, places, and things that once seemed comfortable to you may now be uncomfortable. All the answers to the questions you had may now seem wrong. All the dreams and goals you once strived to reach may seem meaningless and insignificant.

Some people call this time "midlife crisis." But Mark Gerzon, author of *Coming Into Our Own: Understanding the Adult Metamorphosis,* calls it " . . . 'midlife *quest'*—the time we begin questioning—from the Latin *quarerere,* 'to search'—the lives we have created so far . . ." Perhaps now you seek meaning in your aging. You may yearn to find wholeness and completion in your life. You may want to find your "calling." You may want to increase your spiritual awareness. Or you may crave a more intimate, romantic, passionate, or loving relationship.

Remember that your midlife quest will be different from everyone else's. But your goal will be the same as everyone's—to seek wholeness in your life. To find what you're looking for, you need to be "in touch" with how you feel as well as aware of *why* you're feeling the way you are. Then you need to recognize that sometimes making a change simply for the sake of change won't make you feel better in the end.

☆

It's one thing to say, "I'm dissatisfied with my life." But it's another to say why I am and what I want to do about it. Before I start to look for "greener pastures," I'll figure out why I want to change.

Enthusiasm is the yeast that makes your hopes rise to the stars. Enthusiasm is the sparkle in your eyes, the swing in your gait, the grip of your hand, the irresistible surge of will and energy to execute your ideas.
—Henry Ford

Do you know that Babe Ruth struck out 1,330 times in his baseball career? Yet if he had concentrated on his outs instead of his hits, he might not have been able to set nearly 50 baseball records—many which still stand today.

Did you know that it took Thomas Edison over a thousand tries to discover which filament to use for the incandescent light bulb? "You have failed a thousand times!" his critics told him. "No," answered Edison. "But what I have done is found a thousand materials that *won't* work!"

Enthusiasm can be a catalyst for improvement. If you think back tonight to those times in your life when you've felt enthusiasm for something, you'll realize now the benefits of that positive, energized feeling you had. Perhaps you secured a job promotion, scored the winning point for your team, got a date with the person who's now your life partner, or completed your first novel. From your persistence to achieve a dream came the drive you needed to accomplish it.

So don't let the minor setbacks that occur during the day dampen your enthusiasm at night. Don't be afraid to strike out or to continue to search for the "right" solution to a problem. Use your failures—as well as your successes—as ways to liberate your enthusiasm to keep trying.

☆

Failure can help me succeed because it can make me more courageous to try something new, something different, or to simply try again. I won't be afraid to step up to the plate and swing away.

This formulation—love thyself, and then thy neighbor
—is a license for unremitting self-indulgence, because
the quest for self-love is endless. By the time you have
finally learned to love yourself, you'll find yourself
playing golf at Leisure World.
                                        —Charles Krauthammer

There's a story told about a king who suddenly awakens in the middle of the night and summons the kingdom's wisest seer into his bedchambers. "Oh, Great Seer," the king says, "my sleep is troubled for I do not know the answer to this question: What is holding up the earth?"

"Your Majesty," replies the seer, "the earth rests on the back of a giant elephant."

The king sighs in relief, and then goes back to sleep. But it isn't long before he awakens in a cold sweat and once again summons the seer to his bedchambers. "Tell me, Great Seer," the king says, "what is holding up the elephant?"

The seer replies, "The elephant stands on the back of a giant turtle."

The king sighs again, reaches for his bed candle to blow out the flame, and then stops. "But Seer . . ." the king begins.

The seer holds up his hand. "You can stop right there, your Majesty. It's turtles all the way down."

Tonight, rather than put yourself through such intense self-exploration, focus instead on the best thing to do at the moment: sleep.

☆

Tonight I'll recognize that it's okay to examine myself from time to time. But to endlessly do so gives me an inward instead of an outward focus. I need to look at myself, but I also need to see my relationship with life around me.

No day is so bad it can't be fixed with a nap.
—*Carrie Snow*

In the heat of an intense sports competition, one of the best strategies a coach can use is to call a time-out. When the players step away from the action and take a breather, they have a chance to replenish their depleted energy, review their strategy, and renew their efforts to win.

After the "heat" of your stressful day, how often do you give yourself a time-out—a chance to unwind from the day's events, to shift your focus from work-related activities to leisure-time interests, and to readjust your energies? Just as a deep-sea diver needs time to "decompress" after a dive before being ready to reenter the world on the surface of the water, so too do you need time after your day-time activities have ended so you can be ready not only to enter the world of night-time activities, but also to enjoy them.

From now on, decide to set aside at least fifteen minutes between the time you walk through the door to your home and the time you start doing any evening activity—cooking or eating dinner, looking at your mail, returning telephone calls, cleaning or doing a yard project, or talking about the plans for the evening. Change into comfortable clothes, lie down for a few minutes, close your eyes, breathe deeply, and let go of the day. Make this a regular part of your work-day routine, and you may find that your nights are much more peaceful.

☆

I'll set aside a fixed time during the next few days to unwind from day-time activities. I'll use this time to take a "power nap"— a short time of light rest—to release the stress and tensions of the day.

Sorrow looks back, worry looks around, faith looks up.
—*Quoted in* Guideposts Magazine

Loss of any thing in your life—a job, a home, a means of transportation, financial independence, a goal or direction, your health—or of any person dear to you—through separation or divorce, because of relocation, or due to an illness or death—can be devastating. Expressing your sorrow may be about the only way you have of getting through your grief over the loss.

But then, when your sadness has eased, you may become fraught with worry. "What am I going to do now?" you may nervously question. "Where will I go? What shall I do? How am I going to get through this time? Is it always going to be this way? Oh, this is *terrible!*"

Some people, when faced with a loss, can only feel sorrow and worry. Back and forth their emotions go as they alternate between crying and trembling. But what they forget is that while their emotions can go down, they can also go up. John Steinbeck has said that "Somewhere in the world there is defeat for everyone. Some are destroyed by defeat, and some made small and mean by victory. Greatness lives in one who triumphs equally over defeat and victory."

Triumph over your defeats by looking up from time to time. Trust that you can get through your loss, no matter how hard that may seem right now. Tell yourself, "I *will* get through this tough time," rather than ask, "How will I get through this tough time?"

☆

It doesn't matter how *I'll weather the tragedy in my life right now. What matters is that I* will *weather it. I need to have faith and trust that somehow, I'll get through it. I will survive!*

Time is a dressmaker specializing in alterations.
—*Faith Baldwin*

A man who had moved from the east coast to California had so much unpacking and readjusting to do that he missed most of the summer planting season. He finally had time in September to go to the nursery to buy seeds so he could bring in a winter harvest.

When the nurseryworker looked at the man's seed packages she said, "It's much too late for you to be planting beans and squash. You might want to plant your winter vegetables now. I'd recommend broccoli and onions."

The man ignored her advice. He planted yellow squash and green beans and was later rewarded when the plants sprang up through the soil. But it wasn't long before the plants withered and died, for they needed long, hot summer days in order to flower and bear their fruit.

To conquer your impatience over not getting what you want when you want it, you need to learn that sometimes what you get instead is what you need. The man who wanted his summer vegetables really wanted them, but what he really needed was to learn to work with the seasons.

Your projects, goals, dreams, and desires will come to you when you're ready to receive them. So accept where you're at right now. Each step you take leads you closer to your goal, but you'll reach that goal when the time is right for you.

☆

John Milton once despaired about how little he had accomplished at the age of 23, but at 59 wrote Paradise Lost, *which some believe to be the greatest epic in the English language.* Have patience. *You may be progressing more slowly than you'd like, but you* are *making progress.*

Some degree of loneliness is absolutely part of the adult experience.
—*Dr. John T. Maltsberger*

When you're a child you often have adults who take care of you, tell you what to do, and provide you with a sense of direction in life. But when you reach adulthood, oftentimes you're the one who has to provide such things for yourself. At times this can feel exciting being in charge of your own life and your destiny; at other times it can feel isolating and lonely being the sole provider of your emotional, physical, and spiritual needs.

If you feel good about yourself, times of loneliness often leave as quickly as they came. But if you're troubled by low self-esteem, you may have difficulty weathering such times of alienation. Sometimes you may see so many things in yourself that need changing or immediate attention that you can easily become overwhelmed, depressed, or burned out. At such times you may wish that someone would come along who could take care of things for you so you felt less alone.

Yet everyone needs to "go within" from time to time. You need time for creative day dreaming, developing empowering thoughts, weighing options in order to make appropriate decisions, reading words of inspiration and wisdom, and attending to what you need to do. You need to see that taking care of yourself is not an isolating burden, but an exciting adventure that can provide you with meaningful challenge in your life.

☆

Tonight I'll close my eyes and see myself doing something wonderful for myself. I'll feel the joy, dedication, and adventure in this act. I'll keep this feeling with me whenever I do something good for myself.

Living well is the best revenge.
—*Anonymous*

When William White was editor of the *Emporia Gazette*, he received many articles from aspiring writers. As with most publications, many submissions were returned to their authors with rejection slips. Sometimes White saw the same names cross his desk again, with much improved articles.

But one bitter and disappointed writer responded to White's rejection of her article with these words: "Sir, you sent back a story of mine. I know that you did not read it because, as a test, I pasted together pages 19 and 20. The manuscript came back with the pages still stuck together. So I know that you are a fraud and that you turn down articles without reading them."

How did White respond? He sent the woman a brief reply: "Madam: At breakfast when I open an egg, I don't have to eat it all to determine if it's bad."

What do you do when someone treats you badly, something you've worked hard for is rejected, or the reward you felt you deserved is given to someone else? The woman who responded to White did so out of bitterness, anger, defeat, hatred, and negativity. But another response is to learn and grow from disappointment so when you try again, what you gain is what you had originally intended.

You can be disheartened from your setbacks or take heart from them. Which will you choose?

☆

My intention at all times needs to be this: to stay positive and not let anything interfere with that goal. If something happens to drag my spirits down, I'll remind myself that the best way to overcome any negative is with a positive.

*Panics, in some cases, have their uses. Their duration
is always short; the mind soon grows through them
and acquires a firmer habit than before.*
                                        —Thomas Paine

Anytime you experience an anxious feeling, that's a signal that needs your attention. Perhaps your palms are sweaty, you feel edgy and restless, your breathing is rapid and shallow, you can't seem to stop shaking, or you feel dizzy and lightheaded. Those are all physical signs that your body's trying to communicate with you, to tell you that there's something going on inside.

If you ask yourself what's going on, you might hear answers like, "I'm really scared to be alone," "I'm having a hard time letting go of this problem," "I'm afraid to say what I feel or ask for what I need," or "I don't know that I'm a good person." You may be feeling frustrated, ashamed, guilty, or fearful about things that are over and done with or things that have yet to come.

One of the best ways to get through a panic attack is to center yourself in the present. You can do this by remembering such things as the date, the time, and the temperature. Then you can identify objects around you as well as what you're wearing. This simple, two-part exercise can bring you back to the present and ground you in a way that removes you from the space you were in that contributed to your attack. Once you're grounded, it can be easier to work through your anxiety and ease your anxious feelings.

☆

*I need to keep myself in the present when I'm anxious. I'll identify
the things and people around me that exist so I can replace my
anxious feelings with ones that are more centered in the moment.*

Faith is the bird that feels the light and sings when the dawn is still dark.

—*Rabindranath Tagore*

In 1957 Lieutenant David Steeves hiked out of California's rugged Sierra Mountains 54 days after reports that he and his Air Force trainer jet had disappeared. To his superiors and the media, Steeves related an unbelievable tale of how he had lived in the wilderness after parachuting from his disabled plane. But when a military search conducted shortly after his return failed to turn up the wreckage of his airplane, the Air Force suspected a hoax and forced him to resign from the military. It wasn't until 20 years later that his story was finally confirmed, when a troop of hiking Boy Scouts discovered the wreckage of his plane.

Sometimes you may hold onto dreams, ideals, or goals that others think are unbelievable, unattainable, or unrealistic. Do you let their feelings influence you, or do you continue striving to reach the place where you've set your sights? Thinking dependently means basing the things you say and do on the input of others. But thinking independently means living with the courage of your convictions, no matter what skeptics may say.

Tonight, think for a moment about something you'd like to achieve or have come true in your life. Then close your eyes and visualize this happening. Belief in a dream, ideal, or goal can begin with such simple faith.

☆

Tonight I'll strive to understand the power of faith in the bird that sings while looking at a darkened sky. Can I have as much faith in myself?

You have learned something. That always feels at first as if you had lost something.
—George Bernard Shaw

Do you remember coming home from school as a child and having a parent ask you, "What did you learn today?" You were usually quick to report an historical fact, a geographical location, the answer to a math problem, or the synopsis of a book you had read.

But when you're an adult and someone asks you the same question, often what you respond is not as simple and straightforward as the name of the capital of a particular state, an important date in history, or the square root of a certain number. Rather, your learning in adulthood often impacts on your growth, maturation, and emotional development. Because of this, what you gain in knowledge and experience can often feel like it's taking something away from you in the process.

For example, coming in touch with an unhealthy pattern of drinking in your life may help you to learn that you have a drinking problem. But giving up drinking may at first make you feel as if you're losing part of your identity; attending Alcoholics Anonymous meetings may initially make you lose self-respect. But, over time, the losses you may feel as a result of a lesson you learned may help you grow.

From now on, strive to think about a situation in your life that you once viewed as a loss as a gain.

☆

Sometimes I wish my life as an adult was as simple as learning my ABCs. But I'll remember that what I know today is a result of all the hard lessons I've had to learn in the past.

*And remember, we all stumble, every one of us. That's
why it's a comfort to go hand in hand.*
            —Emily Kimbrough

Coping with stress depends not only on your inner resources, strengths, and abilities, but also on the quality, experiences, and connections you have with people who are
part of your life. Just as you need professional support from
coworkers, mentors, and information and service networks,
so too do you need personal relationships from which you
can receive emotional support.

The greater the number of people available to you who
can offer advice and help during times of crisis or difficulty,
the healthier you're likely to be. Those who have been laid
off from work and are now reemployed can attest to this fact.
If you ask these people how they were able to land another
job, most will probably respond that first they built a network
of support they relied upon not only for professional leads
but also for emotional support. In addition to attending meetings related to their careers, going on job interviews, and
regularly keeping in touch with recruiters, they may have
also joined a support group for the unemployed and sought
help from a therapist or nurturing friends.

Resolve to start building a support network *before* you
need it. A good beginning is to create your own "Help
Line"—a listing of telephone numbers you can use during
your next time of difficulty.

☆

*I'll think about making a list of supportive people I can call on
in my times of need. I'll include family members, close friends,
a partner, a college buddy, and those I know professionally.*

*Making the simple complicated is commonplace;
making the complicated simple, awesomely simple,
that's creativity.*

—*Charles Mingus*

At the end of the day, are you still often overwhelmed with responsibilities, concerns, or an impossible work load during your evening hours? If so, you may have so many pressing demands that it may be difficult to rank all of your tasks in order of importance and attend to them in a logical, orderly, and effective fashion.

When you're under this kind of pressure, the first thing you can do is list every one of your priorities that faces you in the evening. From work to family responsibilities to social obligations to personal needs, compile all the things you feel you need to do. Next, separate your list into those things that are most essential and need to be accomplished right away—"top drawer priorities," such as making and eating dinner. Then decide which things can be put off for a short time, but are still important—"middle drawer priorities," such as doing a load of laundry. Finally, determine which tasks can easily be put off for a longer time with no harm done—"bottom drawer priorities," such as answering a letter you just received from a friend.

Once your list is prioritized, rank the top drawer items in the order in which they should be accomplished, from most critical to least critical. Then focus your attention on doing only one or two of the top drawer items in an evening.

☆

Sometimes I try to accomplish too much in too little time. From now on, prioritizing and then setting limits as to what I'll do at night can simplify my evenings and ease my stress.

*You go on a diet. Then you eat some chocolate cake,
and you punish yourself by feeling guilty. Half an hour
of punishment for the chocolate cake. It's absurd.*
—Peter McWilliams

Guilt over anything is really anger at yourself—anger at
something you didn't think you should have done, but did,
or at something you should have done, but didn't. Either
way, you lose because you not only didn't do what you feel
you ought to have done, but you're also mad at yourself.

Guilt is an absolutely useless emotion. The only purpose
it serves is to inflict self-punishment. If you enjoy feeling
guilty, then you probably enjoy punishing yourself. But if
you're like most people and are angry at the anger you have
at yourself for being guilty in the first place, then it could be
time to change your guilt into something positive.

The next time you're feeling guilty, backtrack a bit. In your
head, return to the beginning of a guilt-producing situation.
What you'll probably find is that you were faced with a
choice. For example, you could eat the chocolate cake or you
could refuse to eat the cake. By eating the cake, you made
a decision. While making a decision is positive, what isn't
positive is the *attitude* you then had about your decision.

From this moment on, resolve that when you're not feeling good about a decision you made in the past, you will
respond differently. Change your attitude so you can let go
of your guilt and stop punishing yourself.

☆

*I can fret and fume at myself over something from the past, or
I can say, "Well, I guess I learned something from what I did.
Next time, I'll respond a bit differently." The choice is mine.*

Don't blame stress on your environment. Stress has less to do with your immediate surroundings than with your psychological makeup.

—Dr. Kenneth L. Lichstein

Do you think that if you had a better job, a more attentive spouse, a different childhood, fewer money problems, or more time in a day that you could eliminate the stress in your life? While it's true that some situations are inherently stressful—the job of an air traffic controller, being laid off, an emergency that drains your bank account, or living with an active alcoholic—many people who go through such things remain stress-free. Yet you may not only experience a great deal of stress in those situations, but also in even the calmest circumstances.

Stress is not something outside you, but a product of your mind—something that you create and which you, therefore, can control. Rather than react stressfully to every little frustration that occurs, you can calm yourself by changing your way of thinking and speaking. To do this, avoid exaggerated descriptions. A person who cuts you off in traffic and almost causes an accident didn't "nearly kill" you. A day where a lot of minor frustrations occurred wasn't "terrible." And the mess in your home isn't going to take "months and months" to straighten up.

Calm yourself by calming your way of thinking. Don't use extremes in your descriptions of unpleasant events that overstate the reality—and needlessly cause stress.

☆

From now on, I'll think about choosing words to describe my day that accurately tell what it was like. I'll save the "most awful" words for major life crises that deserve them.

Life is, for most of us, a continuous process of getting used to things we hadn't expected.

—Anonymous

The barbeque preparations for the evening were moving along as planned. The hostess had dashed frantically about the house and kitchen all morning preparing enormous quantities of food for the large crowd that could only be handled outdoors. By early afternoon she proudly beamed at the numerous dishes she had prepared and surveyed the immaculately groomed backyard, the spotless patio furniture, and the festive decorations.

But as the afternoon wore on, it began to drizzle and then break into a torrential downpour. Weather forecasters warned of high winds, thunderstorms, hail—even tornadoes. One by one, the dinner guests called to cancel.

Like the hostess, you may face times when even your best-laid plans go awry—the copying machine breaks down before an important business meeting, a highway accident snarls traffic and you have no way of telephoning your date to say you'll be late, you lose a sales slip for an expensive item you need to return, or the fish market is out of the seafood you needed for a planned dinner menu.

How you react to such unexpected events can determine how well you cope with change. When something out of the ordinary occurs, you can ask: "Is there anything I could have done to have prevented this from happening?" If there is, do it next time. But if there isn't, *accept* the change.

☆

When something suddenly comes up, do I immediately get down? I'll learn to recognize that when things happen that are out of my control, I'll simply relax and let go.

Soon it will be dusk, then dark again. Always the lone-liest part of the day to me, that painful, slowly descending interval before the night ultimately comes down.

—*Thomas Tryon*

When you're caught up in the hustle-and-bustle of the day, you're often surrounded by people—coworkers, family members, other consumers, fellow public transportation riders, other students in your class or on campus, and people who provide you with services. But when it's time to return home for the evening, you may dread the feelings of isolation and loneliness you have.

The first thing you may want to do is push yourself to be with another person simply to escape your loneliness. Yet there are positive qualities to being alone at night. You can view your time of loneliness as a healing period that can allow you to experience yourself in a whole new way. Rather than escape this beneficial time, you can use it for introspection, reflection, growth, meditation, and inner development.

Or you can take yourself "out on a date." Plan something special one night of the week when you'll be alone. Then prepare your favorite dinner or make reservations for one at a restaurant you've wanted to try, treat yourself to a double feature at the movies or a play, or take a walk through the woods and eat a picnic dinner at a scenic spot. Learning to value your own company can increase your sense of self-worth and make you mentally healthy.

☆

I know that the sign of a healthy person is someone who can treasure time alone as well as time spent with other people. At night I won't seek to escape from my loneliness but to enjoy it.

When you dream, you dialogue with aspects of yourself that normally are not with you in the daytime and you discover that you know a great deal more than you thought you did.

—Toni Cade Bambara

Listening carefully to yourself can help you recognize your own attitudes and emotions. But while it may be hard to "hear" yourself think above the clamor of the people and activities that need your attention during the day, the time when you're asleep can present the perfect environment for such inner communication.

With silence as your background and your subconscious mind "on alert," what you dream at night can put you in touch with yourself. That's the time when some of the thoughts and feelings you may have suppressed or put "on hold" during the day have the chance to be "heard." That's also the time when you rehash the problems of the day before going to sleep—"Should I fire that employee?" "Is it time to hire a financial manager?" "How can my partner and I fight less?"—can resurface in your dreams with suggested solutions.

Before going to bed tonight, place a pad of paper and a pen on your bedside table. Then, when you wake up in the morning, write down your dreams. Review what you've written from time to time. Ask, "What do my dreams say about me? What am I learning about myself?"

☆

After recording my dreams for awhile, I'll review them to discover recurrent patterns, possible solutions to the problems in my life, and more about myself.

Death, when it approaches, ought not to take one by surprise. It should be part of the full expectancy of life.
—Muriel Spark

At the end of Dostoevsky's *The Brothers Karamozov*, a young man dies. After the funeral, his friend Alyosha reminds those gathered of the custom of eating pancakes. The purpose is to mix sweetness with the bitterness of death.

When you can only see death as a terrible loss or a devastating upset, it will continually cause you pain. When death only leaves you with sorrow, you'll never be able to experience a little sweetness with the bitterness. In either case, it will be hard for you to accept how much death is part of life.

The process of living includes many dimensions. Some are joyful. Some are not. Yet if you can allow some lighter moments in ceremonies such as funerals or remembrances of anniversaries of losses, such events can become a celebration of a life lived rather than just a mourning of a life lost.

To do so, focus on the wonderful memories you have of someone dear, the accomplishments made during that person's life, or a favorite story or anecdote you shared together. Just as you accept life, it's also possible to have an attitude of acceptance about death.

☆

Death can be a homecoming for anyone I've known in my life. Tonight I'll keep the love and memory of a lost loved one in the "home" of my heart.

Thy will be done this day! Today is a day of completion; I give thanks for this perfect day, miracle shall follow miracle and wonders shall never cease.
—Florence Scovel Shinn

Many people believe that the quality of each day depends on how it begins. So if their day is initially set with a late start, rushing around, squabbling, and then spending the rest of the day trying to catch up, that'll be the direction for the rest of their day—one of tension and frustration—and until it mercifully draws to a close.

Yet no matter how your day begins, you always have the power to change its direction and how you respond to it. At any moment today you could've said, "Wait! This is not the type of day I want to have. Starting now, things are going to be different. I'm going to wipe the slate clean and start over again."

You can do the same thing at night. While you may find it difficult to shake off the tensions of the day; to stop the negative tapes that play, rewind, and then replay in your mind; to not rehearse the conflicts of tomorrow; and to not live in yesterday's hurts or tomorrow's fear, *you can do it.*

Before you turn out the lights tonight say, "I had a great day! I'm proud of myself and my accomplishments. I'm happy about all the things I was able to enjoy." Ending the day with such powerful affirmations can point you in the right direction for a pleasurable evening—and the promise of a wonderful new tomorrow.

☆

I'll give thanks for this day. I'll praise the miracles that are already on their way for tomorrow. And I'll express my gratitude for the precious gift of tonight.

You are the best friend you will ever have. In the presence of your true self you will become the most peaceful, the most relaxed, the most natural person possible.

—*Bartholomew*

In your endless striving to find "The Right Person"—the one who will treat you right, give you good feelings about yourself, always be there for you, and make you feel healthy and whole—did you ever consider that *you* may be the perfect "right person" for you? Yet for as long as you expect that the right relationship will come along that'll make you feel better about you, you're keeping yourself from exploring and strengthening a relationship with yourself.

Looking to others to help you live more comfortably or feel better about you is like grocery shopping when you're hungry. To fulfill the need you have inside, you pack your shopping cart high as you travel up and down the food-laden aisles. Yet when you arrive home, what you discover is that you had your favorite leftovers in your refrigerator.

Wholeness, happiness, good health, and a high level of self-esteem aren't given to you by other people. They're gifts you give yourself that others can nurture, respect, and support.

Tonight, recognize that your best friend and life partner is you. Stop expecting others to give you the time and attention you deserve. *Give it to yourself.*

☆

Tonight I won't neglect myself. I'll enjoy my company, attend to my needs, and be a kind, loving friend to myself.

The best things you can give children, next to good habits, are good memories.

—Sydney J. Harris

Every parent wants to raise the best kids. But too often you may assess your parenting skills on how well or how badly your children behave. While it may be easy to feel like a "good parent" when your children are behaving like little angels, that self-assessment may be replaced with the belief that you're a "bad parent" when your children act up or act out. Then—when you're yelling at your kids, delivering a stern lecture, or doling out punishment—you may question whether you're acting like your own far-from-perfect parents: the ones you said you never wanted to be like because of the bad memories they gave you.

How can you raise your children well and still give them good memories? One way is to stop overidentifying with your them. Seeing your children as reflections of yourself may make you overly identified with their concerns. Your children are not yourself, nor can they ever be the child you always wish you could've been when you were growing up. That means your children need to have room to make mistakes, to work through some of their difficulties with some level of independence, to feel pride in accomplishments they've achieved for themselves—and to be less than perfect.

You don't always have to step in to fix your children's problems. From time to time you can let them find their own solutions.

☆

When I'm older I hope my children will say to me, "The best memory I have of my childhood is that you let me be me." I can let my children grow into who they need to be—not who I want them to be.

When it gets dark enough, you can see the stars.
—Lee Salk

The tiny points of light in the darkened sky have long been used to plot navigational courses. In fact, sailors have learned to trust the stars as more reliable than even their most sophisticated instruments. You, too, can look at the sky tonight no matter where you are and find reassurance in its light.

Perhaps you're on a business trip that has taken you away from your family or loved ones. Maybe you're on the first vacation you've taken in a long time and are feeling uncomfortable being away from work obligations and your daily routine. Perhaps you're in the military, stationed overseas, and feeling like a stranger in a strange land. Or maybe you're feeling alienated from others around you because of your gay lifestyle, the color of your skin, your cultural background, your level of education, or your religious beliefs.

As you take a moment to look at the sky tonight, consider that each star has meaning. Whether it's part of a major constellation or merely a pulsating, burning mass in the sky, there's a reason for that star to be there. It belongs in the sky, just as you belong in the world.

Tonight, know that you're never alone and never far from home. You're a star in the night who shares the expansive heavens with all the stars around you.

☆

Whether I'm miles away from home or simply feeling miles away from others because of my differences with them, I can still feel that there's purpose and meaning in my life.

*Every year I live I am more convinced that the waste of
life lies in the love we have not given, the powers we
have not used, the selfish prudence that will miss nothing, and which, shirking pain, misses happiness as well.*
— Mary Cholomondeley

When you were a child, your teachers or parents may have
said, "You're a bright child and do wonderful things," they
may have said, "but you're not working up to your full potential." Now, as an adult, you may wonder, "Am I living up to
my full potential?" What exactly is your full potential? And
how do you work up to it?

You've been blessed with certain talents and abilities.
When you express these talents and abilities, often the world
opens up before you. Then you can learn, play, create, love,
mature, take risks, make decisions, speak your mind, experiment, set records, and achieve goals.

When you avoid developing a talent or an ability—when
your employer offers you a promotion you won't take, when
those at a party ask you to play your favorite musical instru-
ment and you don't, when a coach urges you to compete and
you refuse, or when a partner praises your commitment to
the relationship but you shy away from further intimacy—
those are times when you're not realizing your full potential.

From now on, realize your full potential by giving one
talent or ability the freedom to be recognized. By experiencing its full potential, you're making a contribution towards
becoming a *whole* person.

☆

*I can identify one of my long-ignored talents or abilities and "dust
it off" so I can use it again. It may be rusty at first, but I'll be patient so I can see its full potential.*

. . . a father who cares enough to wait and worry, who cares enough to counsel and be concerned, is among the greatest blessings God has given.

—*Richard L. Evans*

The memories you have of your childhood may be filled with joy, sorrow, happiness, or misery. The child within you may still be crying out for a father with whom you can share your gains as well as your upsets, your pain as well as growth, your failures as well as your successes. As an adult, you may feel cheated out of a wonderful relationship with him because of your past history or saddened because your relationship with him ended when he died.

A loving, healthy father is a great blessing; you may not have had such a blessing. But instead of thinking back to your childhood with feelings of anger or bitterness, sadness or regret, dejection or depression, tonight believe that your father did the best he could to raise you. He had to deal with his own childhood as well as his adulthood—at the same time he was also trying to be your father.

Tonight, look back and remember three good things about your father. Maybe he always baited the fishhook for you, never missed one of the games you played in, or paid for your college education. By looking at some of the good in your father rather than noticing all of the bad, you may be able to see him as human instead of imperfect.

☆

Tonight I need to see my father as another human being who has shared my path in life. Can I see the good in him, as I hope he sees the good in me?

As long as we're taught to believe we are victims to whatever health hazards come our way we won't have the necessary strength to change the conditions that gave us the trouble in the first place.
—Margo Adair

No disease in modern history has captured as much attention as AIDS has. Whether you're gay or straight, black or white, male or female, American or foreign, young or old, or single or married, as long as you're sexually active you're vulnerable to the disease. While abstinence is the best prevention of transmitting the HIV virus, practicing safer sex is also a responsible choice two consenting adults can make.

Yet safer sex can't help those who are already infected with the disease. AIDS, like cancer, is proving to be more powerful than medical science as it eludes attempts to eradicate or suppress it. But while a cure may still be years away, that doesn't mean the situation is hopeless or permanent.

As with any sickness or injury, only *you* can heal yourself. Your health is like a full-time job; day and night, you need to create the best conditions for optimal healing to take place.

Tonight, use your head and not your heart—practice safer sex with your partner. Build up your immune system through proper nutrition, adequate rest, and positive thinking. And even if you're HIV-positive or have full-blown AIDS, *don't give up hope for a cure.*

☆

I can heal my body by living in the healthiest ways I can. Tonight I'll be my own doctor, caretaker, healer, and nurturer so I can help my body heal and mend.

Day after day the sun rises in the east;
Day after day the sun sets in the west.
—*The Gospel According to Zen*

Time and how you experience it can be perplexing. When you have a sense of expectation and familiarity that comes from a daily routine or a usual way of doing things, time can seem to drag. Yet time seems to fly by when you're doing the unexpected or something pleasurable. That's why two weeks composed of ten days at the office and four days doing household chores can seem like a month, while a two-week vacation is over before you know it.

When your days and nights begin to blend together in a mundane, unappealing, boring mixture, then perhaps you can find ways to interrupt the usual progression of your time and do something out of the ordinary. Ronald Graham, an internationally renowned mathematician at AT&T Bell Laboratories, has always enjoyed the passage of time. In a forty-year time span he has " . . . mastered Chinese, learned to play the piano and kept up his juggling and acrobatics, all while writing dozens of papers and traveling tens of thousands of miles a year."

Make time soon to go for a drive or a bike ride to a place you've never been before. Take note of the unfamiliar scenery and the novelty of your journey. Then, when you return home, write in a journal about the most interesting thing you noticed on your trip.

☆

Taking a different route to or from work on occasion, spending my evenings learning something new, or doing something out of the ordinary are just a few ways I can make the passage of time much more interesting.

To love oneself is the beginning of a life-long romance.
—Oscar Wilde

If you were in the midst of the most perfect, wonderful, satisfying love affair, what do you imagine your lover would be doing for you? Listening to the kind of day you had at work? Cooking a delicious dinner for you? Surprising you with a bouquet of flowers or a special gift? Paying attention to your needs? Giving you nightly massages?

You deserve to have such time, attention, and energy lavished on you. But it's unhealthy to expect or believe that such things ought to come from someone else. You need to live each day as though you're in a wild, glorious, satisfying, and never-ending love affair—with yourself!

How can you demonstrate such self-love? Start by doing at least one thing you might think is a little outrageous or a little corny. Give yourself a little gift—a take-out order from your favorite restaurant or a bunch of freshly picked flowers. Compliment yourself about the things you did today, your appearance, or the type of person you are. Set aside enough time in your day for play, for exercise, for rest, and for meditation. Say affirming statements to yourself such as "I deserve to be treated well; such treatment will begin with me." Then, each night before you go to bed, tell yourself, "I love you." After awhile, your self-love may change from a casual affair into a life-long love interest.

☆

When I look in the mirror, can I smile at myself? Can I think warm thoughts when I meet my eyes? Tonight I'll treat myself as if I were a perfect lover by viewing myself in warm, loving ways.

Do not take life's experiences too seriously. For in reality they are nothing but dream experiences. Play your part in life, but never forget that it is only a role.
—*Paramahansa Yogananda*

How very easy it is to be extremely serious about life! Because there are so many things to be serious about—your employment (or unemployment), financial problems, relationship issues, family matters, and personal difficulties—you may not view life as an enjoyable experience. Instead of proclaiming, "Life is an adventure," you may grumble, "Life is hard."

But have you ever noticed how much better you feel after a good laugh? That's because laughter stimulates the production of endorphins, the body's natural painkillers. Laughter also improves respiration, activates your immune system, relaxes your muscles, and relieves stress. With laughter and a lighter attitude towards life can come the realization that all things will come to pass; that *everything* evolves through the cycle of change.

Tonight, you have a choice. You can either look forward to the cycles of life and enjoy them when they occur, or you can resist. Enjoying the cycles can bring joy; resistance can bring pain. Can you find something to enjoy? Laugh at life's ironies, chuckle at a comedian's sense of humor or a funny television sitcom, or laugh at yourself. Don't take life too seriously. As it has been said, "You'll never get out of it alive!"

☆

When I lose my sense of humor, I forget how to enjoy life. Tonight, rather than take myself or my circumstances too seriously, I'll put on a happy face and rediscover my sense of humor.

When we play the role of a saint with one-word answers, we don't help people. We help when we listen and share our pain. We must live the sermon, not just deliver it.

—*Bernie S. Siegel, M.D.*

When Dr. Bernie Siegel's son Keith was four years old, he was scheduled to undergo a hernia repair in the hospital. The doctor reassured his son about the surgery by slowly and carefully explaining in great detail all of the medical details of the procedure. But when Keith awoke after surgery and saw his father standing by his bedside he mumbled, "Daddy, you forgot to tell me something."

"What's that?" his father asked.

"You forgot to tell me it was going to hurt."

Sometimes when your children, an employee, a coworker, a friend, or your partner come to you with problems, you may be quick to provide them with solutions. But what those in need may want from you aren't simple answers, rational advice, or logical thinking. Rather, what they may need is someone to simply hear them. They need you to listen, to pay attention to their emotional outpouring, and to give them a space in which they can vent their feelings without having to think beyond how they feel at the moment.

From this moment on, strive to be a good listener and not a good preacher. The best communicators are not the most eloquent orators; rather, they're often the most patient and most caring listeners.

☆

I won't expect my words of advice to be like a magic wand I can wave over someone's problems to make them go away. A listening ear, however, can often magically lighten almost any burden.

My experience has been that in the end when you fight for a desperate cause and have good reasons to fight, you usually win.

—*Edward Teller*

On the job, your future may seem uncertain. You may see mounting problems at your company or sense an impending crisis that could put your job in jeopardy. You can spend restless nights worried about being laid off, or you can start tonight to lay the groundwork for changing jobs if you need to.

The most important step you can take is to build or rebuild your professional network. By reestablishing contact with former employers, clients, or friends in the same line of work, you can discreetly begin to put out "feelers" so you discern what's going on in the job market.

Another step you can take is to begin post-layoff planning *before* you receive a pink slip. Update your resume. Start preparing for interviews. Consider temporary work as an option so you can get to know another company or another line of work before you make a permanent decision. Think about becoming a salesperson in your own industry—if you've worked for a computer manufacturer, for instance, you could possibly be in demand as a computer salesperson. Finally, consider going into business for yourself. If you can be optimistic about a potential layoff rather than pessimistic, you *can* do something so you'll end up a winner rather than a loser.

☆

I can think about turning a hobby into an occupation or a new business I could start up on an after-work basis. Why take a layoff lying down when I can fight for something I might really want?

*Worry is most apt to ride you ragged not when you are
in action, but when the day's work is done. Your imagination can run riot then . . . your mind is like a
motor operating without its load.*

—James L. Mursell

During the day your mind may operate like a train engine.
For as long as you stay on the tracks to reach a certain destination, you stoke your engines and burn a ton of coal to
give you the power to charge "full steam ahead" down the
tracks. Going to and from your job, attending classes, being
a full-time parent, or operating your own business are the
"stations" your engine steams to throughout the day.

But when the day's activities are done and you're left with
an evening of free time, your mind may be like an engine
that can't be slowed down as it heads into a curve. You may
have built up such a hot "head" during the day that you
don't know how to cool down at night. You may become so
frantically worried about what you're going to do in the unstructured hours that lie ahead that you steam into the turn
at too high a speed—and derail.

Your mind doesn't have to be on full speed all the time.
When the day's work is done on a railroad, the engines are
guided onto sidetracks to cool until morning. Tonight, cool
your engine. Guide the engine of your mind onto the relaxing sidetracks of sleep.

☆

*I don't need to continue to fuel my mind with agitated worries.
I'll bring peace to my inner "engine" by focusing my attention
on peace and serenity.*

But, realistically speaking, it's when someone gets sick that it really creates what I call 'the teachable moment,' the prime opportunity to share feelings and attitudes about death.

—Joan McGiver Gibson

How do you talk about death? If you're like most people, you probably avoid talking about it as much as possible. But with the AIDS epidemic, the proliferation of cancer-related illnesses, the rising costs of nursing homes for aged and ailing parents, and the growing availability of living wills, the opportunity to talk about death has never been greater.

If you're exploring the scenario of your own death or the death of someone close to you, then there's no better time than the present to have an initial conversation about what alternatives you'd like to consider for health care. It's highly important that you make your medical wishes known or that you learn the wishes of those close to you—a parent, a partner, a close friend, or a sibling.

Tonight, make a promise to yourself to investigate the option of creating a living will—a document that tells what kind of life-sustaining procedures are desired when a person is unable to make or express such decisions—or a durable power of attorney for health care so someone can make medical decisions if a patient can't. Whether you're young or old, well or ill, or single or married, acknowledging your mortality and doing something about it is a sign of wisdom and maturity.

☆

"Let me tell you about some things that matter to me," might be one way to open up a discussion on the topic of dying. I'll consider the positive aspects of my decisions so I can encourage open, honest communication.

*The first three times you came with the same story
[they] would listen and try to help. But if you showed
up a fourth time and it was the same old tired things,
the others in the circle would just get up and
move . . . it was time you did something about it.*
—Anne Cameron

Often you may hold fast to something so tightly—a fear,
a way of doing things, a past relationship, or your youth—
that you hold yourself back, preventing forward motion as
well as your growth. Instead of taking a risk, trying something new, getting on with your life, or accepting your limitations, you may remain mired in some internal conflict. Like
an old tree that has to remain rooted in one spot, you become unbending, rigid, and inflexible.

For centuries Chinese calligraphers have painted bamboo
as a symbol that shows how to harmonize with change and
growth. Bamboo is thick on the outside, but hollow inside,
so it's open to new possibilities; it's strong on the outside, but
bends with the wind and doesn't break, so it's capable of being yielding.

You, too, can be more like bamboo—strong even while being flexible, firm yet able to yield to the winds of change. To
resolve an internal conflict that keeps you stuck in one place,
remember to ask, "What would I really like to do about this?"
Think of all the possible ways you can get there. Then accept a possibility and make an action plan.

☆

*Whenever I'm faced with a dilemma in my life, I'll throw off the
blinders of custom and look beyond it. I'll come up with at least
three alternatives that can take me out of the conflict so I can
get on with my life.*

To wake in the night: be wide awake in an instant, with all your faculties on edge: to wake, and be under compulsion to set in, night for night, at the same point, knowing from grim experience, that the demons awaiting you have each to be grappled with in turn, no single one of them left unthrown, before you can win through the peace that is utter exhaustion.
—Henry Handel Richardson

Everyone has to endure an occasional nightmare. What do you do when you awaken in the darkness of your bedroom and the stillness of the night feeling frightened? How you handle nightmares when they occur can often spell the difference between once-in-a-while terrifying dreams and recurring or more frequent nighttime terrors.

While it may sometimes take you awhile to reorient yourself to your surroundings and to settle down after you awaken from a bad dream, once you're conscious it's a good idea to turn on the light and then get out of bed. You may wish to drink a glass of water or prepare a cup of warm milk or decaffeinated tea. Take slow, deep breaths, then relate your dream to someone or say it aloud to yourself so you can hear how unreal it really was.

Then return to your bedroom. Straighten up the bed covers and fluff up your pillow. After you turn out the lights, reassure yourself with the thought that a bad dream is like a television channel—and you can always change it!

☆

Tonight I won't let a nightmare influence me for more than a few minutes after I awaken from it. I'll control what I "see" at night by saying, "I don't like this dream, so I'm going to switch to another dream channel."

There is a divine plan of good at work in my life. I will let go and let it unfold.

—*Ruth P. Freedman*

Have you ever marveled at how fate has drawn you to someone? Maybe you met the person of your dreams through a very interesting turn of events. Perhaps you stopped at a store you've never been in before and discovered a childhood friend working there. Or maybe you were laid off from work and, for some reason, attended a meeting in a different state and met an employer looking for someone with your qualifications.

There's a lesson to be learned from each person you meet. Your contact, however brief or long, happens for a reason. Sometimes when you meet someone at a particularly meaningful time you may feel as if you're part of a play, sharing a stage with characters you know will have an important influence upon your character. Although not all the lessons you'll learn will be easy or all the contacts you make feel wonderful—some people may treat you badly; others may leave you with pain and heartache—all will have given you a valuable lesson.

Tonight, trust that your life is being guided not only by the decisions you make, but also from the input of a divine resource. Rather than marvel at chance meetings and interactions that have a positive impact and question those that have a negative influence, accept *all* as fulfilling a useful purpose. *Every* lesson you learn is meaningful.

☆

Because I'll always be meeting new people, I'll always be learning. Tonight I'll trust that there's a divine plan at work in my life that's helping me to learn and grow from each lesson I'm given.

Love where you are, love who you're with, and love what you do.
                            —*The Findhorn Community*

Throughout history individuals have chosen to live in communities so they could structure their lives according to their beliefs with other like-minded individuals. From St. Francis of Assisi and religious communities of the Middle Ages to the Puritan and Quaker settlements; from communes of the 1960s to gay-sensitive communities in San Francisco, Fire Island, Provincetown, and Key West; to recent New Age ventures and group collectives that follow a particular religious or political leader, such separatism encourages people to believe that they're better off living with others who share their same philosophies or lifestyles.

Yet harmony with humanity means being able to be a separate individual as well as someone who can connect with the diversity of many individuals. It's easy to cooperate, to resolve conflicts, and to interact in peaceful harmony when you're linked with others who think, feel, and act in similar ways. It becomes much harder when you're divided by who each of you are individually and by each set of wants and needs.

Would you like to create a community spirit within your family of origin or your extended family? Resolve to make a conscious effort to cooperate within the safety of your home or with those with whom you share a common bond. Then it can be easier to harmonize with others who are different from you.

☆

Instead of complaining or finding fault, I can praise, compliment, and provide support. I'll build a peaceful community close to me so I can reach out to others in the larger community.

My dog Treader loved being on tour. I got him when I got sober, and he's helped me to keep my perspective, see life through a dog's eyes. You're doing all right if you've got food, a place to sleep and someone to pet you.

—*Izzy Stradlin*

When you felt bad in the past, you may have numbed your feelings with drugs, alcohol, food, or sex. As your addiction negatively impacted on your life, you may have attempted to give it up. But each time you did, you may have been abruptly confronted by such emotional pain, amplified by pangs of withdrawal, that you soon returned to the protective cocoon provided by your numbing addiction.

Now, or at some time in the near future, you may finally reach "the point of no return" when you finally concede to yourself that your addiction is neither a helpful nor a positive alternative to dealing with your feelings. When you do, you're sure to be confronted by a wide array of feelings that will attempt to push you back to drinking, drugging, food binging, or using sex as an escape.

To work through such times, remember that the feelings of fear, anxiety, loneliness, and depression just *seem* unbearable. They truly *are* bearable; you *can* get through them.

Tonight, if you're going through a rough time, repeat over and over again, "This too shall pass." Then rework the familiar slogan of recovery to be: "One *night* at a time."

☆

Tonight, when I'm faced with painful feelings that create an emotional chain linked so tightly I can't break through it, I'll remember that there are ways I can get through it. I can always go under it, jump over it, or go around it!

No one can make you feel inferior without your consent.
                                    —*Eleanor Roosevelt*

Self-talk can be very powerful. On the one hand it can develop a healthy ego, build self-esteem, create confidence, and help you strengthen problem-solving skills. On the other hand it can trigger ego deterioration, destroy self-esteem, lower confidence, and create more problems in your life. How can you communicate to yourself in ways that are positive rather than negative so you can build a strong, secure individual?

First, avoid asking yourself questions. Self-questioning can erode self-confidence and instill self-doubt. Rather than ask, "Can I handle this situation?" say, "I *can* handle this situation." A wavering query will rarely push you into action the way a firm statement can.

Second, replace negative words in your vocabulary with positive words. Rather than say, "I can't make a change" or "I won't be able to do this right," say, "I *can* make a change" and "I *will* be able to do this right." Negative words encourage negative responses; positive words beget positive changes.

Finally, eliminate the words "should" and "ought to" from your self-talk. Such words are based on the expectations of others or what you *believe* is appropriate—not what you really want or what you truly think is right for you.

Success is as close as the words you use to talk to yourself. *So choose your words carefully.*

☆

From now on I'll be conscious of my self-talk. I'll use positive, affirming statements that emphasize all the power and potential I have within myself.

What must I do is all that concerns me—not what people think. It is easy in the world to live after the world's opinion; it is easy in solitude to live after our own;—but the great man is he who in the midst of the crowd keeps with perfect sweetness the independence of solitude.

—Ralph Waldo Emerson

At times are you like a chameleon, changing colors to please others? Chameleons survive because they're adept at hiding from predators. So you may hide your sad feelings and pretend to be happy and content. You may avoid sharing your truthful thoughts so you don't hurt someone close to you. You may go along with the decisions or choices of others even though what they choose aren't your preferences.

By doing such things, you may feel that you're being a nice person, are living well, or are showing that you're someone who's easy to get along with. But who's getting to see your "real" colors? Aren't you ignoring your own needs while making someone else's more important?

Today, you may have changed colors constantly to please others—a boss, coworkers, teachers, friends, family, or a partner. But you don't have to be a chameleon any more. There are no predators to hide from—only people, just like you. Their thoughts and feelings may be different from yours, but that's okay. Dare to be different. Don't be afraid to disagree or to show your own brilliant colors!

☆

When I go along with the crowd, I lose my individuality and identity. I won't become just a face in the crowd. I'll distinguish myself in some way that calls attention to my different thoughts, feelings, or beliefs.

*Nothing was handed to us, so it made me realize that
if I wanted something, I had to work for it.*
　　　　　　　　　　　　　　　　　—Kim Jones

A slip on melting snow five weeks before the 1992 Olympic trials ended Kim Jones's dreams of running the marathon for her country. She had to slowly work her way back after pulling a ligament and cracking a bone in her ankle. In August, she found herself in the lead of the Hokkaido Marathon. But at the ten-mile mark, as she bent down for a water bottle, she pulled a hamstring. In October the asthma-prone runner had to battle flu symptoms in the Tufts 10K in Boston; in November, after the New York marathon, she headed to bed for a month with pleurisy. But those were just Kim's injuries. Before the Olympic trials, she lost four loved ones, including a grandmother and mother-in-law. Yet in the spring of 1993 she was ready to run her usual 5:30 mile pace in the 97th Boston Marathon.

How did Kim keep up her spirits through the frustrating injuries and unfortunate tragedies in her life? Her determined nature may have come from growing up in a household with ten other children. "I think it's made me very aggressive," she comments. "It was a struggle just to get what you wanted."

Tonight, think about something you really want. Then reflect on Kim Jones's tortuous path to fulfill her commitment to running. Can you be as committed?

☆

*I can't expect that something I want is going to be handed to me.
Tonight I'll strengthen my determination to work hard for something that's important to me.*

Walk on a rainbow trail; walk on a trail of song, and about you will be beauty. There is a way out of every dark mist, over a rainbow trail.
— *Navajo song*

Each day you pay attention to your physical needs—you eat, you exercise, you sleep. But do you also pay attention to your spiritual needs? Everyone needs some time each day for spiritual renewal. If you neglect taking care of your body, it will eventually break down in some way. So, too, can you become emotionally imbalanced and find your world filled with continual conflict if you avoid addressing your spiritual needs.

Setting aside time for moments of reflection is the best way to pay attention to your spiritual needs. Taking time for reflection may seem like self-indulgence when you feel there are so many other things you need to do or that there are "better" uses of your time. Yet it's one of the most *responsible* things you can do for yourself.

When you're confused and uncentered, restore your inner harmony and vital energy by making contact with nature. Take a walk on a nature trail near your home. Watch the setting sun. Lie down on your balcony or in your backyard and seek out familiar constellations in the night sky. Listen to the sounds of bullfrogs and crickets. Crush a handful of fresh herbs in the palm of your hand and inhale the aroma. Your quest for harmony can be as close as the nature that surrounds you.

☆

When I'm spiritually centered, I can see things more clearly, act more effectively, and feel healthier. Tonight I'll accept the responsibility of balancing my physical needs with my spiritual ones so I can achieve peace and harmony in my life.

America wasn't founded so that we could all be better. America was founded so we could all be anything we damn well pleased.

—P. J. O'Rourke

When you were growing up, you may have been told that you were never good enough. Today you may still carry unfair judgments about yourself that your parents gave you. Or you may have a hard time accepting who you are because you're gay, black, Hispanic, disadvantaged, physically challenged, or different in some other way. You may negatively judge yourself because of these differences. But to what useful purpose do such judgments serve?

In nature everything is valuable. Everything has its place and purpose. Only human beings suffer from low opinions of themselves. A rose, a robin, or a rabbit never feel badly about themselves; each flower has its fragrance, each bird has its song, and each animal has a purpose. So, too, do you.

Tonight, declare your independence from past criticisms, society's judgments, or your own chastizing. Recognize a talent or ability that makes you unique. Then resolve from this moment on to nurture that special part of yourself by painting, drawing, taking pictures, playing music, or doing whatever makes you feel independent of others. *Be yourself*—not who others think you should or shouldn't be.

☆

Too often I feel inferior because I don't feel that I fit into some stereotype. But I can learn to honor my uniqueness by being myself, not by imitating others so I can be just like them.

The person who fears to try is thus enslaved.
—Leonard E. Read

Immobilization is the result of fear. In its grip, you fail to move forward. You fail to think new thoughts, live new experiences, meet new people, and change in new ways. All that life offers you may refuse; all that you're capable of achieving may go unrealized.

If you're not careful you can allow fear to overtake you until it becomes a trap that catches you whenever you try to go anywhere or do anything different. Although you can't see, hear, or touch fear, you can give it so much power that it almost has a life of its own.

Tonight, believe that you've been given the gift of life. With this gift comes an obligation to test your wings and spring forth. You can get rid of the traps of fear that have been set by having faith that you're safe wherever you are and whatever you choose to do. Even when a fear trap crouches close to your heels, ready to catch you in its grasp, you can elude it by repeating the message, "All is well. No matter what happens, all is well."

Remember that because life is a series of opportunities presented to you for your emotional, spiritual, and intellectual growth, no opportunity for action or experience is beyond your capabilities. Look to every moment as a time to participate in all experiences. And trust that "All is well."

☆

Tonight I'll cut the ties of fear that bind me. Rather than cower in fear, I'll greet life with open arms. Without fear, all will be well.

"Okay, Marlowe," I said to myself. "You're a tough guy. You've been sapped twice, choked, beaten silly with a gun, shot in the arm until you're as crazy as a couple of waltzing mice. Now, let's see you do something really tough—like putting your pants on."

—*Raymond Chandler,* Farewell My Lovely

Is "I can handle it" one of the phrases you use most often? Yet take a look at the most difficult times you handled at the office, at home, with a life partner, with your close friends, for an organization you belong to, or for a course you're taking. What happened *after* what you chose to handle was completed? Did you come down with a stomach bug or a summer cold? Were you so exhausted you had no energy left to do anything else? Were you so wound up that you couldn't calm down? Did you become so intently focused that afterwards it was hard to concentrate on anything else?

Like detective Phillip Marlowe in Raymond Chandler's classic novel *Farewell, My Lovely*, you may become so wrapped up in trying to "solve" the "tough cases" that you forget to handle one of the most basic and important "cases" in your life—yourself.

Rather than get caught up in a succession of activities you feel you can handle, take time to catch your breath. "Solve" one case, then don't take on another until you've had time to restore your inner peace.

☆

Whenever I contemplate handling something new, I'll ask: "Is it necessary? Is it healthy? Will it bring greater peace to my life?" If what I want to take on doesn't fit any of these criteria, I won't do it.

*One often learns more from ten days of agony than
from ten years of contentment.*
                                        —*Merle Shain*

Imagine driving in your car. Suddenly the alternator light
goes on. You pull off the road, reach under the dashboard,
and pull the wire out to the alternator light so the light goes
off. You dust off your hands, start the car, and go merrily on
your way.

While this may sound like a ridiculous way to solve a
major problem in your car, it may symbolize the way you
handle pain in your life. Do you try to avoid pain at all costs?
Do you often fend off painful memories from the past or painful feelings in the present with the philosophy, "Not now—I
haven't got time for pain"?

You can either face the pain or you can deny it. But no
matter which you choose, *the pain exists*. Denying it may delay dealing with it, but at some point you'll once again be
confronted by it. Denial of pain is like not seeing a doctor
when you've broken your arm. Your body's natural powers
of healing will eventually mend the break, but your chances
of breaking it again are greater than if you had effectively
dealt with it when it first happened.

Resolve to face your pain. Let it gently push you—or even
forcefully shove you—into making or accepting changes in
your life so you can mend the injury or make the necessary
repairs. Then you can safely continue on in your life travels
free of pain.

☆

*While I don't welcome pain, I know I won't attain peaceful times
without dealing with some times of pain. I'll accept all experiences that come my way as necessary to my development.*

But he himself went a day's journey into the wilderness, and came and sat down under a broom tree. And he prayed that he might die, and said, "It is enough!"
—*1 Kings 19:4*

The prophet Elijah—a man of great faith—was once reduced to despair by a battle with fatigue. He had overexerted himself by running nearly 120 miles from Carmel to Berrsheba—*and* then ran an extra day's worth through the Sinai desert! Elijah's mistake may be similar to ones you make all the time. You think you can put in an extra few hours of work, do the carpooling for the neighborhood a few more days, pull an all-nighter, run an extra mile, or stay up another hour to watch the end of a baseball game.

When you do such things, you deprive yourself of much needed rest and relaxation. But does that stop you? While you may drag yourself through the next day speaking the same words as Elijah—"It is enough!"—you may push yourself once again that night!

When you find yourself revved up to "go an extra mile" at night, soothe your restless mind and body by preparing an aromatic bed for yourself. Before crawling under the covers take a warm bath in a scented bath oil, lightly dab your favorite cologne on your pulse points or pillowcase, or burn incense or a scented candle in your bedroom. "Often simply inhaling a pleasant aroma," says Susan Knaski, an environmental psychologist, "can trigger a change in mood and have a soothing effect."

☆

I'll lure myself away from an exhausting day or the desire to do more by creating a luxurious and inviting bedroom filled with scents conducive to evening relaxation. Then I'll breathe deeply and fall fast asleep.

When health is absent, wisdom cannot reveal itself,
art cannot manifest, strength cannot fight, wealth be-
comes useless, and intelligence cannot be applied.
                                      —Herophilus

Just because you break a habit that's detrimental to your health—smoking, drinking, overeating, or sugar binging—doesn't mean your health is automatically restored. You still need to pay attention to your need for sleep, good food, and exercise. You need to address your intellectual needs to bring about a sense of newness, vitality, and challenge to your life. And you need to take care of your spiritual needs by meditating and taking time off to unwind.

Breaking an addictive or negative behavior doesn't mean you're "cured." Your work may just be beginning. When you stop smoking or eating poorly, you often need proper exercise and nutrition to restore health to your body or to expand your lung capacity. When you stop drinking or drugging, you often need to rediscover your faith in yourself and a Higher Power so you can address the problems in your life rather than anesthetize them.

Take time to identify an area of your life that needs rebuilding. What is one thing you can do to work on your outer appearance as well as on your inner healthiness? Good nutrition, plenty of rest, exercise and play, meditating, and a balance between work hours and home hours may be some of the things you can focus on for your best health.

☆

Tonight I'll reward the first step I've taken towards better
health—by ceasing an addictive or unhealthy behavior—by get-
ting ready to take the second step towards building a better self.

Let your tears come. Let them water your soul.
—Eileen Mayhew

When you were growing up, you may have tried hard not to cry when you were sick, hurt, angry, or frustrated. You might have thought that being in control of your emotions was admirable or something expected of you because you were a "big boy" or a "big girl."

But boys, as well as girls, *do* cry. And so do adults. Being human means being in touch with all of your emotions—especially grief. If you try to stop your tears when grief surfaces, you'll only be damming up valuable emotions that can help you heal your grief so you can move on. Emotions are meant to be expressed, not repressed.

Tonight, let your tears come. It doesn't matter if your grief is related to past actions, missed opportunities, or things you never mourned, or to present-day losses. The source of the grief isn't important. What *is* important is expressing it. Remember, your tears are a necessary part of working through your feelings so that when you're finished crying—like the calm after a storm—you can feel more peaceful, clearheaded, and unburdened. So tonight let yourself cry, scream, and storm about. As Bartholomew says, "Your misery comes when you tighten up, when you do not allow your agony to move. . . ." Find the tight places in your body where you're holding onto your grief, then release it.

☆

Real freedom comes when I can openly and honestly express myself, alone or with the support of others. Tonight I won't try to protect myself or others from how I feel. I'll let my grief flow so I can let it go.

Jealousy is not a barometer by which the depth of love can be read. It merely records the degree of the lover's insecurity.

—Margaret Mead

When you become jealous you become a participant in a strange kind of competition. Your goal is to defeat your opponent, yet oftentimes you don't know who or what your opponent is. You may be jealous of the amount of time your partner spends at the office, working at home, or on business trips. You may be jealous of the friends with whom your partner wants to spend time or the activities your partner shares with them. You may be jealous of a person you think your partner may be interested in or who is interested in your partner. But what is the *real* source of your jealousy?

Oftentimes jealousy has little to do with outside events and influences. The problem often lies within you. Jealousy reflects a certain level of immaturity, a distorted sense of pride, and—especially—insecurity. When you're jealous you tend to compare yourself to others, seeing how you measure up. You engage in a one-sided battle in which the adversary you fight is yourself.

You can become less jealous by developing a more accurate perception of who you are, not who you are in relation to others. Tonight, build inner security by identifying at least two qualities you have that are appealing.

☆

Jealousy is a repellent that distances me from the one I love. Tonight I'll draw my lover close to me by proudly displaying the qualities I have that are attractive.

*I believe this: When people do things that are mean,
or, even unintentionally, that aren't good towards life
and people—they're the ones that suffer more than
anybody else.*

—*Tom Cruise*

The rival company softball teams were engaged in a tense competition. With two outs at the bottom of the last inning and their team behind by one run, a fiercely competitive baserunner waited on second base for the pitcher to deliver the pitch. As the pitcher started the wind-up, the baserunner tore to third for a steal. The catcher bulleted the ball to the third baseman just as the runner was starting to slide. The third baseman caught the ball, then bent low for the tag. Realizing the call would be close, the baserunner slid hard into the third baseman, sharply upending the player in the hopes the ball would be jarred loose. But the baseman held onto the ball, the umpire yelled "Out!"

The third baseman slowly got up, dusted off, then said to the baserunner, "I know you don't care that you hurt me, I'll heal. But I'd be feeling a whole lot worse if I had let my teammates down the way you did. You hurt your team more than you hurt me."

Did you do anything today that hurt someone? Rather than feel badly about what you did or said to a coworker, friend, family member, or partner, tonight think about what you can do to make amends. Take responsibility for your words or actions so you—and others—don't have to suffer.

☆

*I'll say "I'm sorry" for a personal offense I committed against
someone because of my insensitivity, thoughtlessness, or inability
to handle stress. I'll offer no excuses—only a heartfelt apology.*

Visualize yourself standing before a gateway on a hilltop. Your entire life lies out behind you and below. Before you step through, pause and review the past: the learning and the joys, the victories and the sorrows—everything it took to bring you here.
—The Book of Runes

Sometimes in order to move forward, you need to look back at where you've been. When you feel frustrated in the present, filled with anger, blocked or paralyzed, afraid, or overcome with sorrow, it may be because you need to deal with some unfinished business from the past. While you may not want to look back at old hurts, painful memories, or shameful experiences you've kept hidden, letting the secrets out may be the only way you can defuse the power they have over your life today.

How can you make peace with the past? You can write about an influential event from your personal history in a journal. Take your time as you allow the memory to slowly unfold. Be sure to include how you felt at the time and why things turned out the way they did.

Then, at some later time, share your story—with all of its untold secrets—with someone you trust. Once you do, you may find that such honest and open communication about the event can make it lose some of the power it has over you today. Then you can step through the gateway of the present into your future.

From now on I'll free myself of past hurts, wounds, and injustices by talking about them. Being willing to bring them to light will lighten the burden they've created in my life.

I am larger, better than I thought. I did not know I held so much goodness.

—Walt Whitman

Do you believe your critics? Your critics are the people whose opinion you value, but who often have done very little to deserve such attention. Perhaps one of your critics is a parent who brought you up to believe that you weren't a very worthwhile person. Another critic may be a sibling who has always tried to better you in senseless competitions. One of your critics could be a friend who rarely has a kind word to say. Or maybe your partner is a constant critic who finds fault with nearly everything you say or do.

Ralph Waldo Emerson said, "Whatever course you decide upon, there is always someone to tell you you are wrong." When you give your critics the authority to dictate how you *should* be, you allow them to fulfill the role of a powerful movie critic who has the power to destroy the hard work of a movie studio, director, screenwriter, or actor. Your critics can destroy your self-image—if you let them.

Tonight, "draw" a picture of yourself in your mind. Around your picture visualize phrases that praise who you are in ways that make you feel good about you. You might see, "A great cook!" "A must-see friend!" "A blockbuster parent!" "A four-star lover!" "Funny!" "Talented!" In so doing, you'll be creating a self-image that grows with praise.

☆

Tonight I won't be belittled by my critics. I'm much bigger and better than any critic.

How could we form an idea of beauty without a rose in the garden? Bending low before it, we take in its glowing color, its velvety petals, its fragrant scent, and feel blessed to have come across it on a warm summer afternoon, despite its glorious indifference to us.
—Linda Weltner

Who's your favorite hero or heroine? Everyone has their own definition of what qualities create an enviable role model. You may be swayed by those who project outer beauty: a sexy magazine model, a beautiful or handsome Hollywood star, an elegantly attired fashion designer, or a body builder. You may admire athletic prowess: an Olympic gold medalist, a professional athlete, a dedicated runner, or a skilled dancer. You may be enthralled by the fame and fortune someone has achieved. You may be awed by artistic ability or creative talents. Or you may respect someone's intelligence, the risks they've taken, or the work they've produced.

The qualities you most admire in a person you'd identify as your hero or heroine are usually the qualities you would most like to have. That's not to say that you want to be the next Amelia Earhart or Abraham Lincoln. But perhaps you admire the risks Earhart took or Lincoln's sensitivity to everyone, regardless of their skin color.

Tonight, think of at least one quality you most admire in one of your heroes or heroines. Then make up your mind to set a goal that can help you develop that quality in yourself.

☆

Tonight I'll use a hero or heroine as a role model from whom I can learn more about myself. I'll strive to be a rose in the garden instead of just someone who admires the garden from afar.

The moral is, no matter what you do, someone is always watching.
　　　　　　　　　　　　　　—General Colin L. Powell

Someone once told General Powell a story about three ditch diggers. One ditch digger leaned on his shovel when he should have been working and talked about owning the company he worked for some day. Another constantly complained about the hours and the pay. The third ditch digger neither complained nor took a break; he just kept digging.

The years went by. The first ditch digger was still leaning on his shovel, dreaming the same dream. The second ditch digger had faked an injury and retired on disability. And the third ditch digger? He *owned* the company.

One of the first jobs General Powell had was mopping floors at a local soft-drink bottling plant. One day 50 cases of soda crashed to the floor, spraying the sugary beverage everywhere. Powell mopped and mopped. The next summer, he was promoted to filling bottles. His third summer on the job, he was given the job of deputy foreman. "As I have learned," Powell says, "someone is always watching."

Tonight, don't belittle the contributions you make at home or on the job. Keep doing all the good things you're doing. While you might not always get the recognition you feel you deserve or sometimes think that what you do is taken for granted, someone *is* watching.

☆

"I'm worth it" is an affirmative statement I can tell myself whenever I feel my efforts are being ignored. Tonight I'll believe that the things I do do matter—if not to anyone else—to me.

One of the most tragic things I know about human nature is that all of us tend to put off living. We are all dreaming of some magical rose garden over the horizon—instead of enjoying the roses that are blooming outside our windows today.

—Dale Carnegie

There's a difference between dreaming of castles in the sky and dreaming creatively. One is symbolized by the question, "What if . . . ?" while the other is manifested by the response "Here's how . . .". To dream creatively means to think of all the "what ifs" and then transform the possibilities into probabilities. To simply dream is to stay stuck in one spot, mired like a car in mud, spinning the wheels of fantasy without ever knowing how to enjoy the reality.

One of the best ways to dream creatively is to set aside twenty minutes to an hour in the evening to simply let your mind go where it wants to. Encourage this dream state by doing something to stimulate the nonrational part of your mind. You could choose an introspective activity such as meditation, a creative activity such as painting, or a physical activity such as running.

Winston Churchill painted every day to open up the channels of creative dreaming. By avoiding rational thinking, when he was finished painting he often felt refreshed, renewed, and resolved to meet the troubling issues he faced.

☆

I can be a creative dreamer. What would I really like to do in my life? What problem would I like to solve? I'll use the nonrational part of my mind to come up with ways to accomplish something I'd like to do.

Either you reach a higher point today, or you exercise your strength in order to be able to climb higher tomorrow.

—Nietzsche

It has been said that the truth will set you free. But what is truth? Truth is not simply being honest with yourself and others. Truth also involves the ideals you'd like to live by. Some people spend their lifetimes never knowing truth, while others search for it in vain. To find your truth, you need to set off on an individual journey.

In many Eastern countries, people believe that truth is found after scaling a high mountain peak and consulting with a wise sage. That's almost what you need to do to find your truth. You need to set off on a challenging journey that will bring you into closer consultation with your Higher Power. Yet you don't have to reach the top of some majestic peak, walk the Appalachian trail, or run a marathon in order to find your spiritual resource. Rather, you can realize the truth along the way. As you use the knowledge about truth that you discover, your journey through life can become easier and less painful.

No matter how good or bad today was, you've gained ground on your search for truth. You may now have some insights into your life. Even if you didn't progress as far in your journey as you would have liked, you still have tomorrow. Your search for truth is an on-going quest.

☆

Higher Power, help me find the strength to press onward and upward in my quest for the truth. Let my find my ideals and learn to live by them. Then I'll experience great rewards.

"I am troubled by insomnia."
"Well, I know a good cure for it."
"Yeah?"
"Get plenty of sleep."
    —*Otis Criblecoblis, a.k.a. W.C. Fields,*
     in Never Give a Sucker an Even Break

There's nothing better than having a positive attitude when you're going through a trying situation to help you get through it. But when you're in the midst of a difficult time such as another night of insomnia and you're stuck counting sheep, drinking warm milk, or listening to a meditation tape, you may find it hard to see anything positive.

No matter how troubled you may feel, you can choose which pair of "attitude glasses" you'll wear. If you wear dark glasses, everything around you will appear dismal. But if you put on a pair of rose-tinted glasses, things can appear brighter. So you can either wallow in your suffering of having to go through yet another sleepless night, or you can alter your attitude and change your outlook.

Tonight you can moan, "Not another sleepless night," as you toss and turn in your darkened bedroom or watch the numbers change on your digital clock. Or you can proclaim, "Another sleepless night! What fun and exciting thing can I do to pass the time?" You may find that by taking your mind off of your inability to sleep, you can begin to relax so you *can* get to sleep!

☆

Tonight I'll create a list of the positive things I can do to help me relax when I'm restless. I'll keep the list by my bed so I'll have it on hand during the times I'm troubled by insomnia.

It's really a lot less complicated than we usually think.
Life is playfulness. Children know this. That's why they
spend so much of their time playing. They are aware
of wonder. Adults often need help remembering how
to play. We need to play so that we can rediscover the
magic all around us.

—*Flora Colao*

No one has to teach a child to play. They come into this
world prepared to experience everything as if it were new.
Can you imagine a child thinking, "I haven't taken time off
from my busy schedule this week to go to the playground.
So maybe I should set aside some time to have some fun."

As an adult, you may be too busy to play. Or you may be
so caught up in your ambitious career endeavors, in taking
care of your family, in working on your intimate relationship,
in attending to the priorities in your life—in short, in doing
serious, responsible, adult-like things—that you've forgotten
what it's like to be a child.

When was the last time you felt like a kid? Building a sand
castle on the beach, flying a kite, or playing on the equipment on a playground are a few of the ways kids have fun.
What can you do?

From now on, decide that you'll do something playful,
different, and spontaneous at night. Read a children's book
like *Winnie-the-Pooh* or *The Secret Garden*. Play a board
game or card game. Have a charades party. Or sing a silly
song to yourself. Rediscover the fun in life by *being* a child.

☆

I'll strive to look at my world through a child's eyes. What things
are wonderful, marvelous, and exciting? What can I do to help
me feel as happy and carefree as a kid?

*Have you learned lessons only of those who have ad-
mired you, and were tender with you, and stood aside
for you? Have you not learned great lessons from
those who braced themselves against you, and dis-
puted the passage with you?*

—*Walt Whitman*

Wouldn't it be grand if you could have everything go *your*
way and have everybody do what *you* want them to do?
You'd have people at your beck and call—a boss who
wouldn't criticize you, a parent who wouldn't find fault, or
a partner who wouldn't push you into doing things he or she
wanted. You'd be able to do what you *wanted* to do—not
what you *needed* to do. You'd never have to take responsibility for yourself, never have to struggle for anything, and
never have any wish or desire refused.

But how would you learn and grow? Learning involves
gains you make based on efforts you expend; in addition,
learning comes from experiences you go through that often
run contrary to what you expect. Growth comes from the
process of maturing; you mature when you put your time
and energy into making personal changes, taking risks, making gains, and suffering setbacks.

Recognize that some things in life will come easily, while
others won't. Don't be afraid to put your energy into someone or something that's important to you. You'll find that,
in the end, the things that often require the most motivation
and determination are the ones that *really* matter.

☆

*I can't listen to a music box unless I wind it. Tonight I'll wind
the music boxes in my life so I can learn and grow as a
person—and enjoy the rewards of my efforts.*

Perhaps someday it will be pleasant to remember even this.

—*Virgil*

There's nothing like a little time and distance from a trying situation to find something positive in it. But sometimes it may take hours, days, weeks, months, or even years before you can look back and find something good in a misfortune. Now may not be the time to see what's right about a minor car accident, lost airline tickets, a burned dinner, or an argument with a friend. It takes a strong faith in yourself and trust in time being able to heal all wounds to get through an unfortunate situation without having it totally disrupt your life.

But when you feel overwhelmed, upset, baffled, or alone, you may see a circumstance as awful or overwhelming. How can you develop the skill to be able to say, "Things will ultimately work out for the best" in the midst of a challenge?

Art Linkletter says, "Things turn out best for people who make the best of the way things turn out." Accept that life is full of all kinds of hassles and upsets—that's what life is all about. Recognize that you're not the only one who goes through them. Then strive to look for a positive aspect in a setback. Focus on what you can *gain* from a circumstance—a new opportunity, a change in your routine, or a different way of looking at something or someone. Find the silver lining in any dark cloud that comes your way.

☆

Finding something positive in a misfortune doesn't make it go away. But it helps me from getting caught up in the negativity of a setback and allows me to see some good that can come out of it.

You have to live on this twenty-four hours of daily time. Out of it you have to spin health, pleasure, money, content, respect, and the evolution of your mortal soul. Its right use, its most effective use, is a matter of highest urgency.

—Arnold Bennett

Like everyone else, you have twenty-four hours every day to accomplish what you need for your emotional, physical, and spiritual growth. But just because you read your morning meditation, you completed your work or school day, or your evening is over doesn't mean the time for growth is over, too. There's still much time left—*if* you want to use it.

The first twelve hours of a day are usually spent housecleaning, raising children, commuting and working, running errands, or attending classes. By the time the daily whirlwind of your activities has ended, you may feel as if there's no time left to the day. But you still have another twelve hours left in which to accomplish things you weren't able to do during the day: to relax and unwind, communicate with friends and family members, socialize, prepare and eat dinner, and get a good night's sleep.

Use the time you have left in the evening to your best benefit. Focus on an emotional, physical, or spiritual need you may have ignored during the day. Often there's still time left for you to attend to it—if you make the time.

☆

My most effective use of the day involves accomplishing the most I can for myself. At night I can continue to build a relationship with myself by helping to grow in some way.

I have to laugh at the times I've knocked myself out over a tough spot only to find out afterwards there was an easier way through.

—Robert Franklin Leslie

One day a robin flew into an apartment through open sliding glass doors. Confused and frightened by its confining new environment, the distressed bird frantically fluttered about the living room, banging into walls and hitting the ceiling. In a panic, it repeatedly hurled itself against the windows and screens in its efforts to get out.

Finally, exhausted and dazed, it perched on the back of a chair. As the small creature panted through its wide-open beak, it suddenly cocked its head to the side. It listened to the sounds of other birds coming from outside the open glass doors. It hopped down from the chair, fluttered across the floor to the doors, then quickly flew outside to a nearby tree branch, where it soon began to sing.

When you're distressed by a troubling circumstance, sometimes the best thing to do is what the robin did—take a breather. But often what you do is continue to struggle, which exhausts your physical, intellectual, and spiritual resources.

Tonight, don't knock yourself out over a tough spot. Take a break. Stop struggling and rest. Tomorrow, when your mind and spirit are refreshed, you may find the open doors that can help you find "the easier way through."

☆

I remember a time when I pushed and pushed against a door that was clearly marked PULL. Tonight I won't spend a lot of time and energy pushing against closed doors. I'll relax and read the signs that can help me to open doors.

If all difficulties were known at the outset of a long journey, most of us would never start out at all.
—Dan Rather

"Hard times" is a label you may often hear during times of social and economic change. But even "bad" or "troubled" times offer opportunities. While the Great Depression was, economically, a miserable time, it was also a great time in the entertainment industry. In fact the 1930s are known as the "Golden Age of Entertainment," for wonderful music, great radio programs, and two outstanding movies—*Gone With the Wind* and *The Wizard of Oz*—were created then.

What if those things you perceive today as barriers, road-blocks, or hard times are really times of great opportunity? What you may now view as an obstacle on your road to success—a job layoff rather than a promotion, a loss of financial security rather than the ability to pay your debts, an ending of a marriage rather than the celebration of your anniversary—could actually be the paving stones you need for building a *new* road to success. It depends on how you look at your roadblocks: as obstacles or opportunities.

Tonight, believe in what Peter McWilliams, co-author of *Do It! Let's Get Off Our Buts!* says: "An obstacle is like the hurdle in a steeplechase—ride up to it . . . throw your heart over it . . . and the horse will go along, too."

☆

Tonight I'll strive to distinguish between what's new and harmful to me and what's new and exciting for me. The only roadblocks on my road to success are the ones I erect.

*It's easy to lose our focus, to get lost in other people,
external goals, and desires . . . we lose our connection
to the universe inside ourselves. As long as we focus
on the outside there will always be an empty, hungry,
lost place inside that needs to be filled.*

—*Shakti Gawain*

Codependency is the act of becoming so absorbed in other
people, places, and things that you don't have any time left
for yourself. Caring so deeply about others or focusing so obsessively on externals can lead you so far away from yourself that you may forget how to take care of yourself or that
you have your own needs.

Losing yourself in a love affair or relationship, in work or
school obligations, or in caring for an aged or ailing loved
one can make you go days, weeks, months, or even years
without conscious contact with yourself. When this happens
you may forget that you even exist apart from whatever it
is you're lost in.

From now on you need to tell yourself, "I'm still here." To
bring some of the focus back on yourself, spend time during the day writing in a journal about how someone or something has impacted on your life. Then consider what it would
be like to *detach*. Ask, "If I didn't have this person or thing
in my life, what would I be doing with myself and for myself that's different from what I'm doing now?" Make a list
of what you'd be doing. Then choose one thing—and do it!

☆

*Detach is the opposite of attach. Has staying attached helped
me? How do I feel about detaching? Each day I'll make a choice
about remaining firmly attached to someone or something, or
gently detaching myself.*

. . . to have a crisis, and act upon it, is one thing. To dwell in perpetual crisis is another.
—*Barbara Grizzuti Harrison*

Every crisis has a negative side and a positive side. The negative side is that sometimes a crisis can seem so big or serious that it can be difficult to ride it out or to effectively handle it. New situations, a new job, a new challenge at work, asking for a raise, starting a family, buying a house, or making an appointment with a therapist or doctor can be positively frightening. So rather than work through whatever it is that frightens you, you may despair and stay mired in it.

But the positive side of any crisis is that it can push you out of your fear-based paralysis and motivate you to take *action*. Sometimes fear can actually work to your advantage, for it can provide you with the energy you need to do your best in a new situation. Then, when you see that you *can* make it through a rough time under your own direction or power, you learn to trust that even the most difficult things *can* be faced.

The best approach to any crisis is one of sanity, not insanity. Tell yourself, "No matter how bad this situation seems to be or how afraid I feel, I know I can get through it." Then think of at least three responses to the question, "What can I do about this?" and try it.

A crisis can present me with unknown opportunities and a chance for change and growth. From now on I'll resolve to do the thing I'm afraid of doing so I can learn and grow from the experience.

Nobody grows old merely by a number of years. We grow old by deserting our ideals. Years may wrinkle the skin, but to give up enthusiasm wrinkles the soul.
　　　　　　　　　　　　　　　—Samuel Ullman

Most people would agree that the worst thing about aging is the physical erosion that occurs in the body—the general physical slowing down of the body that puts you in touch with the fact that you're not a youngster anymore. While you may have heard it said that "You're as young as you feel," sometimes you may not feel very young.

That's why the attitude you take towards how your body slows down is extremely important. Denying an ache or pain or ignoring muscular stiffness won't make it go away. You need to respect such physical limitations by not pushing yourself. Similarly, you need to deal with your physical needs when they come up by taking care of yourself.

But then you can move past the physical limitations and focus on the many satisfactions that are still possible. While your body is subject to deterioration because of age, you still have the capacity for intellectual and spiritual growth. You still have time to enjoy the simple things in life. You still can appreciate the value of life. And you still have the ability to laugh. As actor Hume Cronyn once said about the lines on his face: "Let them get deeper—particularly the laugh lines!"

☆

Tonight I'll forget my chronological age and think instead about how young I feel inside. I'm still young in many ways, with lots of time to grow.

Constant togetherness is fine—but only for Siamese twins.

—*Victoria Billings*

When you were growing up, you may have spent hours fantasizing about how wonderful an intimate relationship or marriage would be. You may have placed so much hope in dreaming about the "perfect" relationship that once you met someone you may have unconsciously smothered the other person in togetherness. You may have feared time apart, believing that being separate meant abandonment, rejection, or that your partner didn't love you anymore.

Fusion in relationships can be self-destroying. Bonding so tightly with one person, with little time spent apart, is a perfect setup to addiction. When you become addicted to a person, you can become as desperate and suffering as an addict without a fix.

Tonight, think about all the flowers in a garden. Each flower has a separate set of roots, separate stems, leaves, and buds. Although the flowers may be the same variety, each is different from the other in subtle ways. Similarly, you and your partner are different from the other. You both need to grow separately—as well as together. So don't hesitate to take advantage of opportunities to spend time alone. Let your partner spend time apart from you without being jealous, threatened, or angry. You can still grow and flourish together, but on your own.

☆

Tonight I'll spend time by myself, relaxing for a peaceful night's sleep. In that way I'll create a garden of intimacy that has plenty of room in which to grow—and is not choked by clinging weeds.

Analysis is not the only way to resolve inner conflicts.
Life itself still remains a very effective therapist.
—Karen Horney

One day during her lunch hour, a receptionist in a busy medical office building smelled smoke. She searched for the source and eventually discovered that carpenters who were remodeling an examining room had left a soldering iron on. The unattended iron had burned into the flooring. She unplugged the equipment, then returned to her desk.

But when the office reopened after lunch, a commotion ensued. Doctors smelled smoke and began screaming at the nurses, who in turn began shouting at the office assistants. It took the receptionist several minutes to restore calm, having to explain and reexplain what the problem was and how she had solved it.

In far too many conflicts people often become so agitated that they forget what the problem is and how simple it is to solve. They'd rather assess blame, become defensive, ponder the root of the conflict, or overanalyze what's really going on. Sometimes a solution is as easy as pulling a plug.

When fear, confusion, insecurity, or defensiveness are the tools you use for resolution, you rarely have an easy time reaching a solution. So from now on, take time to examine a conflict. Ask, "What can I do to create greater harmony to resolve this conflict?" See yourself as that person, doing what you need to do. Then apply your vision and take action.

☆

Life always offers me a multitude of simple solutions to its conflicts. But I need to be willing to relax and find them. From now on I'll stop focusing on a conflict and instead seek its resolution.

. . . the healthy, the strong individual, is the one who asks for help when he needs it whether he's got an abscess on his knee or in his soul.

—Rona Barrett

It's not meant that anyone should shoulder all the trials and triumphs in their life alone; you're tied into the company of others by design. You have a voice so you can express your needs, hands so you can reach out to others, ears so you can listen to advice and encouragement, and a heart so you can trust and feel the love and caring around you. But it's not always easy to use those inner resources with others—or for others to use them with you.

Part of the experience of being with others involves not only relating the need for support during times of sorrow and suffering, but also communicating the need to share times of joy and celebration. But how can these needs be related?

You need to make a clear request, as well as a clear invitation, for help or sharing you're willing to extend or to receive. Communicate as openly and clearly as you can what it is you want or need when speaking with someone else. Or, when extending an invitation to help, be sure to be clear about what you're capable of giving.

Ask, "What do I need or want to communicate to someone?" or "What am I willing to give to someone in need?" Then you'll be prepared, no matter who makes a call for help or support tonight, to be willing to give or receive.

☆

One of the greatest gifts I can offer others, or which they can offer me, is comfort. I'll accept that others need me just as much as I need them.

May August moon bring gentle sleep. Sayonara.
—Marlon Brando addressing the audience
in the last lines of Daniel Mann's
The Teahouse of the August Moon

The moon rules the oceans; as tides ebb and flow under its influence, the moon shows its presence and power. The moon is a symbol for the intuitive self; it's purported to hold court over emotions. The moon signifies abundance; the Harvest moon signals a time for relaxation after the summer's labor and a time for giving thanksgiving for a bountiful harvest. The moon represents new frontiers and great challenges; the lunar landing was a great scientific achievement. The moon is a cyclical, evolving presence; every month it moves from full and bright to black and dark.

The moon is your constant nighttime companion. Even when it isn't visible to the naked eye, its presence can still be felt. It can sway your emotions and affect your mental health, your moods, your relationships, and your energy. Because of this, the moon can serve as a reminder of your connection to all things as well as your relationship to yourself.

Zen Buddhists have said that " . . . a finger is needed to point to the moon, but that we should not trouble ourselves with the finger once the moon is recognized." Tonight, take time to look at the moon. Notice its color, size, and position in the night sky. *Feel* the moon—allow its energy to fill your heart. Then sleep peacefully tonight, knowing that the moon is watching over you.

☆

The moon can remind me that my emotions are part of me, too. Tonight, when I express or feel my feelings, I'll remember that I'm nourishing the soul of my inner moon.

Prayer is one of life's most puzzling mysteries. I have sometimes feared it is presumptuous to take up God's time with my problems.

—Celestine Sibley

How do you learn to pray? What do you ask for? What do you say? Do you get down on your knees, bow your head, or lift your face to the heavens?

Sometimes, in trying to answer such questions, you may forget the purpose of prayer. You may feel inhibited to pray to an unseen presence. You may feel self-conscious. You may feel your prayers don't measure up to the eloquence of the sentiments expressed by a moving preacher or inspirational literature. These may be just a few reasons you may feel unworthy of communicating with a Higher Power.

Tonight, when you begin to think like this, remind yourself why you pray and what it has done for you. Although you may never describe your prayers as articulate or perfect, it's the act of praying that matters. You pray as an expression of your gratitude as well as your suffering, of your helplessness as well as your purposefulness, of your fears and doubts as well as your trust and faith, of your powerlessness as well as your strength. As Hannah More says, "Prayer is not eloquence, but earnestness; not definition of hopelessness, but the feeling of it; not figures of speech, but earnestness of soul." What's most important is *making* the effort to pray.

☆

Tonight I'll remember that my Higher Power hears me, no matter how I choose to pray. Whether I spend several minutes talking aloud about my day or a few moments in silence, my Higher Power listens.

Language has created the word "loneliness" to express the pain of being alone and the word "solitude" to express the glory of being alone.

—Paul Tillich

Why do you sometimes feel lonely? Sometimes it may be because you feel no contact with anyone or anything else. So you ride crowded subways or buses each workday or live in a home filled with the voices of others, but feel lonely. Sometimes you may feel that you're not valued or important to someone or something. So while you have a life partner, close family, or an enviable position of responsibility in a company, when others don't respond to you in ways that show your worth, you feel isolated.

Yet there are people who may have few friends, no surviving family members or family that lives far away, or a job where they work alone, and they never feel lonely. That's because they combat loneliness by being self-sufficient. Self-sufficiency doesn't mean that you need to learn how to live outside of your community or without loved ones around you. What it means is that whether or not you have loved ones, you don't suffer from loneliness because you have a sense of connection to yourself and the world around you.

Strive not to depend upon others for your sole source of union or feelings of self-worth. *Look to yourself.* Rather than despair in your loneliness, see it as an opportunity to enjoy your own company for a change.

☆

Although I'm a very social person, I can balance my need for interaction with the need to be by myself from time to time. With true self-sufficiency, I can connect with others as well as with myself.

Human beings are born with just two basic fears. One is the fear of loud noises. The other is the fear of falling. All other fears must be learned.

—Ronald Rood

One of your greatest fears may be the loss of your financial security. Maybe you've lost your job or are having a tough time making a profit in your business. Perhaps you're having difficulty paying off a student loan, house mortgage, or credit card balance. Maybe you've had to assume the burden of paying for a medical emergency or long-term medical care. Perhaps an unexpected car or home repair has drained your bank account. So you may think, "If only I were rich, I wouldn't feel so scared whenever I think about my financial future."

Financial independence has nothing to do with being rich. It's simply knowing when you have *enough.* Enough for you may be different from enough for someone else. But your "enough" needs to be a real figure that's within your current financial means.

Although you may not have much money right now, you can feel like you have more by using a few simple saving techniques. For example, if you're one of the seventy percent of adults who visit a shopping mall on a weekly basis, you may be tempted into making spur-of-the-moment purchases. So don't go shopping unless you *really* need something; also, wait until you have the money *before* you buy something.

☆

I'll save the money I have, rather than spend it. For the next week I'll resolve to keep track of every cent that comes in and goes out so I can be more conscious of how to better handle my money.

My children often disagreed with me, thank God! I'd no objection at all to their being disobedient. Parents should remember that beside being parents, they are also the bone on which the puppy can shape its teeth.
—Peter Ustinov

Are you a parent who lets your kids be themselves, or do you try to mold and shape them in the way you want them to be? One father insisted his daughter continue much-hated piano lessons. "We're a musical family," the father told her. "And we're also not quitters! So you need to learn how to be a great piano player like your Aunt Elizabeth." Another mother had a son who signed up for an expensive kids' cooking class. He went a few times, then stopped going. "We paid a lot of money for that class," the mother informed the son. "So you're going back, and that's that."

Children who are forced into doing things so they can continue a family tradition or avoid disappointing their parents rarely enjoy what they do. Rather, they often end up resenting the very things you think will bring them—and you —pleasure.

From now on, give your children the opportunity to say how they honestly feel about the things they do in their lives. Instead of focusing on your children's failures or the ways they let you down, encourage them to do things they're good at or enjoy. In so doing, your kids can feel better about themselves now—and in the future.

☆

I'll make it a point to sit down soon with my kids and help them create a "Wish I Could List." Together we'll write down all the things they might like to do. Then I'll let them do at least one of those things on a regular basis.

Finish every day and be done with it. You have done
what you could. Some blunders and absurdities no
doubt crept in; forget them as soon as you can.
                              —Ralph Waldo Emerson

Are you living in the present moment right now, or are
you still reliving the events of the day? If you're still looking
backward, you're viewing a tedious television rerun—one
where you already know the plot, the characters, the dialogue, and how it turns out in the end.

Today is done. Whatever mistakes, confusions, disappointments, or problems that occurred in it are also done. But if
you can't seem to let go of the day, then perhaps you need
to "watch" the "rerun" one more time before you let it go.

Right now, set aside ten minutes in which you can worry,
process, rehash, and review all the occurrences of the day.
If you'd like, you can even create a list of all the leftover
things that are still bothering you. When you complete your
list, look at each item and ask, "Is there anything I can do
to change the situation?" Think about or jot down a solution
next to each item. At the end of ten minutes, stop writing and
put the list away. Tell yourself, "There's nothing I can do to
alter the happenings of the day. So I'll pay attention to the
present."

Then turn off the "rerun." Rather than continue to watch
the past, be excited for the new "shows" to come. You can
start new programming—*right now.*

☆

When I look backward at the day, there are no surprises and
no new wonders for tonight. I don't need to experience what I've
already experienced; I'll participate in something fresh and new.

Opportunity is often difficult to recognize; we usually expect it to beckon us with beepers and billboards.
—*William Arthur Ward*

Have you ever tried to follow the flight of a hummingbird? It's not only the smallest bird in the world, but its wing motion is so rapid that the wings appear blurred—even when it's hovering as it feeds on a flower's sweet nectar.

A hummingbird can be seen as a symbol of the times of opportunities that may be presented to you. In the midst of great difficulties or changes in your life, a tiny opportunity may open up to you—if only by chance. As in spotting a hummingbird, you must be sharp enough to discern this time of opportunity, quick enough to catch it, and then determined enough to do something with it. If you let it pass, you may be filled with regrets.

The *Tao* says, "A green bird darting in the night. Will you be able to see it? Will you be able to catch it?" This book of Chinese wisdom recommends that you cling to all the events in your life like a shadow. Wherever life takes you, you go, so as soon as life throws you an opportunity, you'll be in the best position to catch it.

Tonight, trust that times of oppression and adversity won't last forever. Be prepared for quick movement in a new and positive direction—and be ready to capture it. Move like the hummingbird: keep up with life and move at its speed. Then you'll be able to seize opportunities that come your way.

☆

If I wait for an opportunity to be formally announced like a guest at my grand ball, then I'm just sitting back and waiting for things to come to me. Tonight I'll open the doors of my life so I can be ready to let in any unannounced guest.

Make it a rule of life never to regret and never to look back. Regret is an apalling waste of energy; you can't build on it; it's only good for wallowing in.
                                        —*Katherine Mansfield*

Life is dynamic. Like a river it constantly flows, its currents forming new patterns based on change. If you live your life as a dynamic person, then you aren't afraid to travel on that river. You go where it takes you. You remain becalmed when its waters run calm; you race along when its waters rush; you make twists and turns as the water forges its path. As the river of your life changes, so does the way you move through it.

But when you live your life holding onto the past—by remembering the pains of childhood or by reminiscing over "glory days" gone by—then you're not able to flow with the river. Instead, you watch the river go by or fight wherever the river wants to take you. Your regrets keep you from enjoying your travels down the river.

Many people resist enjoying their river journey or looking forward to where the waters of life take them. But there's an old Chinese adage that says, "Flowing water does not decay." When you go with the flow, you move. When you don't, you stagnate. From now on, get into motion. Move your mind, body, and spirit. Do something new, different, exciting, and challenging. Be like Huck Finn. Build your raft and journey to wherever the river of life takes you.

☆

Life is a flow of energy. Each day I'll let the energy flow carry me with its strong, determined current.

I want to hit a routine grounder to second and run all out to first base, then get thrown out by a half step. I want to leave an example to the young guys that that's how you play the game: all out.

—George Brett

Kansas City Royals star George Brett is one of the most dedicated players in professional baseball. Once, when a reporter asked the three-time batting champion and future baseball Hall of Fame nominee what he wanted to do at his last at-bat, he gave the above answer. Rather than retire after a grand slam home run, he wants to be remembered as a player who played all out up to the end—even when he knew he would be called out.

Are you willing to work as hard for something you want, or do you often wish things came to you much easier? A team of researchers at the University of Chicago analyzed the careers of concert pianists, sculptors, research mathematicians, neurologists, Olympic swimmers, and tennis champions to determine what led them to high levels of achievement. What they discovered is that ultimate excellence is a product of total commitment and hard work over the long-term.

So talent alone won't make you great at something. You need daily practice to develop the strengths necessary to be successful. Each day, set aside time in which to practice a skill you want to strengthen. Doing something "all out" will help you get the most out of it.

☆

No matter what my talent or interest, I can always improve it. Every day I'll believe in the adage, "Practice makes perfect."

While science may help explain how a virus multiplies,
it leaves unanswered why a tear is shed.
—Bernard Lown, M.D.

Have you ever noticed how children react when they fall while playing? Some children will stay on the ground, clutching their bleeding knee or elbow while crying at the top of their lungs. Yet there are others who slowly pick themselves up with faces grimaced with pain, obviously wanting to cry, but who choke back their tears. Rather than admit they're hurt, they quickly dust themselves off and jump back into play. While the scrapes and cuts they sustained in their fall will later receive healing treatment when they get home, the pain they felt won't get healed.

When you have a cold, a stomach virus, an injury, or a medical emergency, you often know how to treat such things. So you drink plenty of fluids, prepare bland foods, take it easy for awhile, or seek medical treatment so you can physically heal. But when you're unhappy, grief-stricken, upset, or depressed, do you know how to treat your pain so you can emotionally heal?

While society values stoicism, repressing emotions such as sadness over a period of time is like shaking a bottle that contains a carbonated beverage—and then expecting to be able to open it without the liquid cascading everywhere. Tonight, show your pain. Rant. Rave. Cry. *Let it out.* For that is how you emotionally heal.

☆

Tonight, when I stumble on the playground of my life, I won't repress my tears. I'll let them come so I can heal my emotional pain.

I live on earth, where I am surrounded by people who bless me for "sneezing," and not for living, singing, or breathing.

—Tom Hopkinson

Years ago a group of California teachers were told that some of their students would have an intellectual growth spurt. The students' names were revealed in confidence to the teachers. By the end of the year, the academic performance of those particular students *had* dramatically improved. Then it was announced that the students had been selected not because of their intellectual abilities, but merely at random. But because their teachers had expected more of them, the students had expected more of themselves; therefore, they had tried to perform up to the expectations. The moral of the story is: When others expect wonderful things from you, then oftentimes you can meet those expectations. *Expectations affect your experience.*

When you're surrounded by supportive, positive, and encouraging people who believe in you, then you're more apt to create such beliefs in yourself. Your self-esteem, self-worth, and self-confidence will grow. But when you're surrounded by self-centered, negative, and critical people, then you're more likely to take on such attitudes about yourself. You might not feel good about yourself, lack confidence in your abilities, and be self-critical.

From now on, surround yourself with people who will expect the very best you can do—not the very least.

☆

Why am I waiting for some people in my life to notice that I'm a good person? From now on I'll pay attention to those people who pay attention to me. They are my true blessings.

Nothing happens that God doesn't have a reason for. . . . He tries to reach down and shake us out of our ignorance. I know He made me crippled for a reason. He wants me to learn something. It may be patience or it may be forbearance or it may be how to dress without standing up. He doesn't tell you what it is, you just have to learn it.
—*Ruth, in* Marvin's Room, *by Scott McPherson*

Social worker Margaret Sangster once told a story to a group of colleagues about a young boy in an urban ghetto who was little more than twisted human flesh. He had been struck by a car and had healed over a period of several months without receiving proper medical attention. Sangster took the boy to an orthopedist, who performed surgery on his legs. Two years later the boy was walking without crutches, his recovery complete. Sangster proudly thought, "If I accomplish nothing else in my life, I have made a real difference with at least this one."

Several years passed. "Where do you think that boy is today?" Sangster asked her audience. Suggestions were called out to her: school teacher, physician, or a social worker. "No," she said, sadly shaking her head. "He's in the penitentiary. You see, I was instrumental in teaching him how to walk again, but there was no one to teach him *where* to walk."

Tonight you need to accept that your broken body, broken dream, broken home, or broken heart can't be fixed if that's all you're focused on. Such things are not your *whole* life—they're just part of it.

☆

In order to understand my life, I need to see how all the pieces of it fit together to make up a whole. There are reasons for everything I've been given. It's up to me to learn from these reasons.

You don't just luck into things as much as you'd like to think you do. You build step by step, whether it's friendships or opportunities.

—Barbara Bush

Clint Black, Country Music Association Male Vocalist of the Year in 1990, never attributed any of his success to luck. Rather, while holding down a job as an iron worker he took advantage of every opportunity to sing. He performed in clubs, on porches, and at church gatherings. His hard work led to his distinctive singing style and earned him a large following.

Similarly, a study of musicians who competed in six major piano competitions, including the prestigious International Tchaikovsky Competition, revealed that the musicians worked an average of 17.1 years from the day they began taking piano lessons to the day they won a major competition.

While luck may make some opportunities come your way—a winning lottery ticket that pays off a debt, a chance meeting under a canopy on a rainy day that introduces you to your future life partner, or being in the right place at right time that lands you a dream job—luck doesn't help you to attain or even sustain such things. That's where hard work comes in. Luck just showed you the door, but you had to open it.

Tonight, reflect not only on the good things that have come your way because of luck, but also on the wonderful things you've attained because you've worked hard for them.

☆

Dumb luck is just that. It doesn't require much effort or ability on my part. But smart success is a result of my efforts and abilities. Tonight I won't pray to be lucky; I'll pray to be a successful person.

I could tell where the lamplighter was by the trail he left behind him.

—Harry Lauder

Before electricity was installed, city dwellers were dependent upon lamplighters to light the gas lamps before dark so they could walk at night in safety. Without light the streets were dark and ominous—almost impassable.

Do you sometimes feel as though you're floundering about in the dark, wishing you had a lamplighter to light your way? Maybe you were dependent upon someone who lit your way for awhile, but then left. Perhaps you're blindly groping your way from job interview to job interview or scanning the Help Wanted section every day in the hopes of finding a dim prospect. Maybe you feel in the dark after moving to a new neighborhood or relocating to a different part of the country, far away from friends, loved ones, and familiar surroundings. Or perhaps you feel like you're in a black hole as you fall deeper into an unhealthy addiction.

Your lamplighter doesn't have to be a new lover, a new job, new friends, or recovery. Your lamplighter can simply be someone who has traveled the same darkened road you're traveling now. Reach out to a lamplighter who can help light your way by sharing some of his or her strength, hope, and experience. Until you can carry your own light, it's okay to walk under the protective safety provided by this lamplighter.

☆

Everyone is a lamplighter from time to time, both for themselves and for others. I'll seek out a lamplighter to guide me through my darkness or reach out to help light the path of a fellow traveler.

The secret of a happy life is to accept change gracefully.

—*Jimmy Stewart*

Isn't it easy to make changes when the world around you changes in ways that can be dangerous? When street crime increases, you may have no problem changing what time and where you walk at night or taking precautions you wouldn't normally take. If there's the threat of stormy weather, you may easily change your plans from an outdoor barbeque or boating on the ocean to an indoor pot luck dinner or shopping.

When your life is in danger or going through with a planned event will result in discomfort, you may have no problem making changes. But can you make other changes with such grace and ease? You may have a hard time making changes in yourself or in your life. You may be afraid to change a familiar pattern, to let go of a particular behavior, or to try something new. No matter how bad a situation may be in your life—a dead-end job or an unhappy relationship—unless the situation is killing you you may not want to do anything about it.

Yet the only constant in life is change. Everything in the world is evolving and changing. Tonight, don't be afraid or hesitant to change. The next time you face a new challenge tell yourself, "I can handle this." Then readily accept the change.

☆

As my life changes, I'm going to gain some things and lose others. That's all part of change. Tonight I'll keep in mind that if I make a change and don't like it, I can even change the change!

AUGUST 18

Scientific research has proven that color and light play a
significant role in influencing your mood. But even if you
don't totally believe in the effects color and light can have
on your emotional, physical, and spiritual state, you can
recall how you feel when you see a brilliant sunrise or
breathtaking sunset. You can remember how you feel after
three or four days of gray, overcast skies. The bright and
vibrant colors may evoke a positive stimulus to your senses,
while the gray, dark colors can negatively impact on or
depress your senses.

The colors you wear and the way you decorate your living space can also be seen as pretty accurate reflections of
the positive or negative feelings you have about yourself and
your life. Sometimes dressing in a more brilliant or softer
color can subtly change your mood from sadness to happiness. Sometimes imagining that you're surrounded by a healing color or a brilliant white light can help lift your spirits.

Tonight, just as you would give a coloring book and
crayons to a child, you can give yourself a palette of beautiful colors with which to "paint" yourself and your world.
Close your eyes and imagine colors that glow within and
around you. Select the color of the energy that your living
space emits. Picture the color that surrounds your bed at
night. Then take these colors with you as you sleep so you
can have colorful rainbow dreams!

☆

*Can I color me peaceful and happy tonight? I'll "paint" not from
the depths of despair, but from the heights of happiness.*

Everyone has talent. What is rare is the courage to fol-low the talent to the dark place where it leads.
—Erica Jong

A writer knows that a first draft is just a first step towards creating a manuscript. There's often much polishing and revising that needs to be done before the writer can send the manuscript to a publisher. And even when the writer is will-ing to share the book with the world, what's then involved is the process of waiting to hear from a publisher, possible rejection letters, or disappointment in needing to do more research or further rewriting.

Every day in your life is like a first draft. It's just a first step you take in working towards the kind of person you'd like to become and the kind of life you'd like to have. Sometimes this can feel bright and exciting, like finishing your first draft of a novel. So you may end the day on a satisfied, relaxed note. Other times it can feel dark and depressing, like the hard work and dedication that's involved in believing in your book when others don't. Then you may end your day feel-ing restless and unfulfilled.

The writer uses a belief in his or her talents to get through the "dark times" of self-doubt and waiting for a publisher. Tonight, so too can you make it through your dark times by focusing on the skills you have. Before you go to sleep, iden-tify at least three of your strengths. By seeing what you do best, you'll be sharpening talents that can lead to your success.

☆

When do I feel most confident—when I'm recalling a moment of success or a dark time of defeat? Tonight I'll visualize my strengths clearly so I can remain positive.

You will forget your misery; you will remember it as waters that have passed away.

—*Job 11:16*

Do you have a painful memory you carry around with you like a picture in a wallet? Maybe your memory revolves around a difficult childhood. Perhaps it's a friend who treated you badly. Maybe it was a time you lost something or someone you really wanted. Or perhaps it was a missed opportunity. Why are you so attached to such unpleasant memories?

It may be difficult to let go of memories—no matter how unpleasant they are—because the pain they evoke is familiar. They remind you of a past time which, in a perverse way, provides you with a certain level of comfort today. Why do you need such unhealthy comfort? You may have fewer painful times now. You may have worked through much of your childhood issues in therapy, have wonderful and supportive friends, win more than you lose, and are successful in ways you never imagined. Because you have little to feel badly about but feeling badly has been so ingrained, you may continue to dredge up the pain of the past. *You don't know how to feel good.*

Tonight, let go of a painful memory of the past. Say, "This is how *it was* for me before. But now, this is how *it is*." Then hold onto the feeling of the present rather than clutch the pain of the past.

☆

Tonight I'll empty my "wallet" of one bad time from the past. In its place I'll insert the picture of a good time from the present. I'll keep this good time as a reminder that can become familiar and comforting over time.

Simply to live is a wonderful privilege in itself. . . . But to what are you alive? Is it merely to a daily routine. . . . How much do you really live outside of your chosen profession or occupation?

—Henry Wood

From a tiny acorn to a majestic tree, the oak focuses all its energy into growing as strong and tall as it can. Moisture, sunlight, and nutrition are gathered through its roots for the growth of its leaves, branches, and trunk. Yet if the oak tree monopolizes all the moisture, sunshine, and nutrition around it, other nearby trees will be weaker and smaller.

You are just one "tree" in a "forest" of trees that demands attention for their growth. There's also a career tree, a family tree, a relationship tree, a parent tree, and a friendship tree. But if you spend more time and attention on one tree, the neglected ones will not grow strong.

Every "tree" in your life should be treated equally—your family tree as well as your career tree, your relationship tree as well as your friendship tree, your parent tree as well as your tree of individuality. For example, while it may strengthen your career tree to receive a promotion after long hours, nights, and weekends spent "nourishing" it, the nearby relationship tree, family tree, parent tree, and tree of individuality may have suffered. Every part of your life needs attention in order to flourish. Tonight, seek balance in your time. Make sure that each tree in your "forest" receives some attention *every day.*

☆

To devote my life to one person, one cause, or one routine means I'll be neglecting other important areas. Every day, I'll seek ways to balance my time so all areas in my life get the time and attention they deserve.

I guess we are now small enough to go to bed.
— *Theodore Roosevelt*

Have you ever bragged to another person about your achievements only to discover that this person has surpassed your achievements, but chooses to remain quiet about it?

At a friend's barbeque one night a woman thought she would impress a man she had just met. She boasted to him, "I just started running. I'm up to three miles a day."

"That's great," the man replied.

"And I've lost a ton of weight," she bragged. "I've dropped almost twenty pounds!"

"You look wonderful," the man smiled. "Stick with it."

A little while later, the woman went up to her friend. "So tell me about the man I was talking to."

"Well," her friend began, "he runs every day after work. I think he's even competed in some local marathons. And recently I learned he lost 50 pounds."

It's easy to get off on an ego trip—feeling that what you've done is the best—when you've reached a personal goal, resolved a difficult problem in your life, or have successfully kicked a bad habit. But feeling cocky or even seeing yourself as larger than life doesn't prove anything to anyone.

Tonight, be grateful for the positive, constructive energy you have from your achievements and the great strides you've made. Feel good about yourself—but don't forget that you're human!

☆

Tonight I'll remember that everything is where it belongs. The stars are up in the sky and I'm just another human being on earth who's looking up at them.

*Is there any stab as deep as wondering where and
how much you failed those you loved?*
—*Florida Scott Maxwell*

To be kind and loving to others every day and as you go
through every situation can sometimes be difficult. When
you're tired or your body is wracked by pain, when you've
just learned that you have a medical problem for which
there's no cure, when you've lost your job or are having a
hard time making ends meet, when you see the health of a
family member deteriorating, when you're unhappy, or
when a cherished relationship has been broken, the last
thing in the world you may want to do is be nice to someone close to you. In your anger, frustration, pain, or misery,
you may lash out at this loved one.

Treating your loved ones as you would hope to be treated
by them—no matter what the circumstances—is your best
assurance against failing them. When you can look beyond
your infirmities and distresses to the love you feel inside,
then you can exhibit the right behavior, provide thoughtful
and calm responses, and assume a respectful posture.

Scottish author and preacher George Matheson, who was
blind, often expressed this prayer: "I have thanked Thee a
thousand times for my roses [and] . . . for my 'thorn'. . . .
Show me that my tears have made my rainbow."

From this moment on, teach others how to treat you in
their times of difficulty by treating them in loving ways.

☆

*How I treat someone I love invites like treatment. Let me be
mindful that I'm sharing my experiences in this life with others
I care about—and who care about me.*

*I am not a gold coin—not everyone is going to love
me.*

—Anonymous

Have you ever felt animosity directed at you from a boss,
coworker, member of a committee or group you belong to,
or a friend of a friend? You may feel confused about this person's negative reaction. You may question, "What did I ever
do to be disliked?" You may wrack your brain about the
things you've done for the person or the way you've com-
municated in an effort to seek the cause of the hatred. You
may become obsessed with thinking about changing that
person's feelings. In fact, you may even bend over backwards, change your plans, or go out of your way to be
friendly and courteous in an effort to show that person that
you can be liked.

Yet just because someone doesn't like you doesn't mean
you've done something wrong or that you're wrong as a person. After all, are you comfortable with everyone you work
with or with whom you have contact? Letting the opinions
of others determine how you react to them or influence how
you feel about yourself only gives them control over your
self-esteem.

Tonight, remind yourself that just as you don't necessarily like everyone you know, so too may some people not like
you. A goal to be universally liked simply isn't realistic. Instead, make your goal to love yourself enough so that the
outside approval of others isn't necessary.

☆

*I like myself, but that doesn't mean everyone's going to like me,
too. Tonight I'll accept how others feel about me, but I won't let
that change how I feel about me.*

What did I do today?
I exercised. I said good-bye
To a departing friend.
I went to market, ate my meals.
Took a walk. Took out the garbage.
Read a little. Meditated. Slept.
This was my mandela.

                                        —Tao

A mandela is a painting that's often used during meditation. The brightly colored and extremely complicated picture
is used to increase concentration during meditation so the
meditator can become completely absorbed in it. By beginning mind-focusing at the outer perimeter of the picture and
then slowly working inwards, the meditator gradually stops
paying attention to the outside world and becomes inwardly
focused. When the meditator has reached the center of the
mandela, that's when the meditative mind is supposedly its
most open and focused.

Each day can be viewed as a mandela that can prepare
you for an evening of inner peace and relaxation. By performing simple rituals each day—taking a walk or going for
a run, eating meals around the same time, performing routine tasks at work or at home, or reading a little—you can
still your mind.

Tonight, change the way you look at the mundane routines you perform in your life. Rather than resent them, revel
in them. Let them keep your concentration absorbed in
soothing, positive ways.

☆

My daily activities can be my mandela. Tonight I'll stop look-
ing for relaxation in spectacular events and instead concentrate
on the peace that comes from the usual and the mundane.

When I hear somebody sigh, "Life is hard," I am always tempted to ask, "Compared to what?"
—*Sydney J. Harris*

Do you see life as difficult, cruel, or brutal? If you do, you don't have far to look in order to find support for your viewpoint. Simply turning on the evening news or reading the newspaper will confirm that there are many things in life that are harsh and cruel.

It's not always easy to see life as wonderful, exciting, and filled with adventure. That's because there's often not much confirmation you receive on a daily basis that assures that life can be such things. Negativity makes the news; positivity rarely does. So you may be conditioned to believe in the horrors of life instead of the wonders.

But as Malcolm Muggeridge says, "There is no such thing as darkness; only a failure to see." So isn't there something you can see in today that was good? Maybe a stranger smiled at you on the morning commute. Perhaps your favorite baseball team won a game. Maybe a missing child was found. Or perhaps you were able to share a laugh with a friend.

There *is* much good in life. But you have to look for it. Tonight, rather than expect to find good news about life in the newspaper or on television, search for it in your own life. Ask, "What event happened today that I can feel good about? Who did I see today who made me feel good?"

☆

Life may be difficult at times, but it can also be quite fulfilling. Tonight I'll step down off my "Life is hard" soapbox. Instead of getting down about the day, I'll remember the humor, the smiles, the caring, and the good things that happened.

What, after all, is a halo? It's only one more thing to keep clean.

—*Christopher Fry*

Do you continually strive for perfection? If you do, you may find that from the moment you wake up until the time you go to sleep at night, you place incredible demands upon yourself. Instead of doing what you *want* to do, you do what you think you *ought* to do. One minute you may decide that you need to take a night off and pamper yourself; the next minute you're busy every night of the week so you can be the "perfect" employee, "perfect" teammate, "perfect" committe member, or "perfect" son/daughter. One minute you may say you're going to sit down and read; the next minute you're up cleaning the house, rushing from room to room in nervous energy in order to make everything look "just right."

Perfectionism places an incredible demand upon you to do everything right. But what is right? What is wrong? Who determines what they are? And is there a right way to do something and a wrong way?

The perfectionist in you may always be looking for "right"—and wearing yourself out in the process. That's because there is no right or wrong. There's only *whatever you choose*. So tonight remember: If you choose to wear a halo of perfection, keep in mind that even your halo may never be right. Halos can be tarnished, tipped to the side, or misplaced every once in a while!

☆

It has often been said that the key to life is progress, not perfection. To live well means that I'll sometimes take the wrong turn, choose a difficult path, or lose my way. Tonight I'll earn my angel wings and halo by living well—not by trying to live right.

I find it hard to accept anyone's death. I watched my mother die from cancer. I was overcome with grief and rage. I was told by someone trying to comfort me that we must all face death some day. "Some day, not now," I thought.

—David Keating

In death, as in life, your attitudes are the emotional paints you use to color your world. So if you see death as unfair, painful, and difficult, then most likely when you're confronted by it you'll feel angry, grief-stricken, and may have difficulty getting on with your life.

But you can change your negative attitudes about death to more positive ones. Instead of seeing terminal illness as a hopeless time, you can see it as a chance to slow down and take stock of life. Instead of feeling that death is unfair, you can accept it as a necessary part of life. Instead of seeing grief as overwhelming and insurmountable, you can view times of sorrow as opportunities of growth and renewal. By changing your outlook about death, you may even see a funeral as a time for loved ones to renew connections with one another and celebrate their lives together.

Tonight, it's okay to see the pain and suffering in death. But it's also okay to see the inevitability and purpose in it, too. Although no one wants to experience the death of a loved one or their own death, remember that you can do nothing about it—except enjoy the time you have.

☆

Samuel Butler once said, "The one serious conviction that a man should have is that nothing is to be taken too seriously." Tonight, whether I'm facing the death of a loved one or my own mortality, I'll strive to look around me and find something to enjoy.

Whatever with the past has gone, the best is always yet to come.

—Lucy Larcom

As the summer gradually draws to a close, you may feel regret that you weren't able to do all the things you'd said you'd do in the spring. Perhaps you wanted to have more time to work in your garden, but became sidetracked with too many other chores. Maybe you wanted to go somewhere exotic on your vacation, but finances limited you to taking day trips. Perhaps you wanted to learn to play tennis or exercise more, but other priorities took precedence. Or maybe you wanted to spend more time with your children, but never found the time.

Whatever you did or didn't do this summer is over and done with. You can never bring back the days of June or July. Yet rather than continue tonight to look back in regret, you can look ahead with anticipation to the beginning of autumn. What goals can you set for time that's to come?

What you have to look forward to now are times when you can harvest the vegetables in your garden or prepare the beds for the winter. You can look forward to cool, crisp nights lit by the Harvest moon. You can look forward to the annual leaf colorfest. You can look forward to times of cutting wood for romantic nights in front of the fireplace.

Tonight, what you can look forward to could be your best autumn yet—but only if you can let go of the summer days that are gone.

☆

Looking back prevents me from moving forward. Rather than bemoan the summer goals I didn't attain, I'll be excited about the new goals I can make in the fall.

Life is risky; we are all acrobats
Tiptoeing over one bridge or another.
—Chinese scrolls

After coming home from a hard day at work, a woman went out to her garden to cut fresh herbs for dinner. While she was there, she noticed that the pumpkin vines had meandered over much of the garden. Feeling pressured to begin dinner but anxious to keep up with her gardening, she quickly began pruning. As she rushed through the task, she hurriedly made a cut in the vine and then realized too late that she had made an error. In her haste to complete the project, she had cut into a massive vine—the lifeline to several maturing pumpkins. Sadly, she realized that the pumpkins would never fully ripen.

Have you ever ruined something before you completed it because you were impatient to reach the end? Oftentimes all it takes is one false move and, like the acrobat on a highwire who loses balance, you tumble to the ground.

Everyone likes to bring a project to completion. Whether the task is large or small, reaching the end can bring about feelings of exhilaration and a sense of accomplishment. Yet being too obsessed with closure can result in carelessness or the need to stop to make repairs.

Before you blindly set off on a task or feel the urge to rush to the end of a project, tell yourself to "Slow down!" Sometimes even a few seconds hesitation can spell the difference between success or self-sabotage.

☆

Patience is a necessary ingredient I need to add to all the tasks I'm trying to complete. From now on, whenever I feel the urge to pick up my pace or seek out a shortcut, I'll tell myself, "Slow down."

When they are alone they want to be with others, and when they are with others they want to be alone. After all, human beings are like that.

—Gertrude Stein

Do you ever say that you want something but then, when the time draws near, say you really don't want it after all? Perhaps you and your intimate partner have made plans for separate time, but then cancel those plans at the last minute in order to be with each other. Maybe your desire to switch jobs changes when you receive a job offer from another company. Perhaps the things you tell others you'd like to do never materialize. Or maybe, after the first few months of graduate school, you drop out.

At such times you may ask yourself, "What's going on?" You may feel confused, angry, frustrated, or impatient with moods, goals, and dreams that seem to change from one minute to the next. But just because you *think* you'll be happy doing or having something doesn't mean you *will* be, just as talking about your dreams doesn't mean that those *are* your dreams. You're a changing, evolving person, and what may seem right for you one minute may be totally wrong the next.

Tonight, accept that it's okay to change your feelings or opinions about something, to revise a dream or a goal, or even to "to switch horses midstream." Be patient with yourself. Let yourself grow. Learn to accept where you are when you're there.

☆

It's only natural that changes in myself or my life can make how I feel inside change, too. Tonight I'll realize that just because I'm happy, content, and filled with purpose one minute doesn't mean I'm going to feel the same later. And that's okay.

Your profession is not who you are, it is only a costume.
—Anonymous

Sometimes those who retire from their profession become depressed or even die. Because they define who they are by what they did, once the "costume" of their profession was taken away they felt naked and vulnerable. Without it, they lacked direction and purposefulness in seeking out and enjoying other interests.

Yet a career "costume" is just one of many you may wear. There's the costume of a full-time parent, a college or graduate school student, a member of a self-help group, or a leader in the community. You "wear" a costume when you devote all your time and energy to a special cause or group, when you plaster your car with stickers that proclaim your interest or affiliation in a belief or organization, or when you actually wear clothing that identifies your connection to a company or special interest.

When you *need* to wear a costume—to proclaim to the world your job, your school insignia, your self-help group slogan, or another "costume"—then you're showing you aren't comfortable with being yourself. You need something outside you to create your identity.

Think about the externals in your life that help identify who you are. How would you feel if these externals were taken away from you without warning? From this moment on, resolve to nurture what's beneath the costume so being without one won't matter.

☆

What kind of person am I? What are my hobbies or interests? What are my talents and abilities? Each day I'll devote time to getting to know and appreciate my naked, vulnerable self.

Learn to know yourself to the end that you may improve your powers, your conduct, your character. This is the true aim of education and the best of all educations is self-education.

—*Rutherford B. Hayes*

Every day, modern life assaults your senses with full-scale attacks. Lights and colors are flashing, brilliant, sparkling, and glowing neon. Advertisements scream at you, loud music pounds your eardrums, and heavy machinery reverberates through your head. Unhealthy appeals lead you to believe that alcohol makes you a good athlete or romantic lover, drugs free your inhibitions, sex makes you a total woman or man, and fast food, sugar products, coffee, and empty calories get you through the day. After a day spent being assailed by such sensory overloads, how can you unwind at the end of the day?

The best way is to create an evening or nightly ritual that reduces sensory overload, instills relaxation rather than exhaustion, and restores your center. Set aside a period of silence when you arrive home—a time when you can turn off the radio and television, unplug the telephone, or close the door to your room and appreciate the absence of noise. Spend some time alone each evening—take a walk, read a good book, or listen to your own thoughts. Or connect with the natural world by working in your garden or sitting in a nearby park. Such things can create just the right sensory balance to restore inner peace.

☆

Each night I'll do something to create stability in my life after an unstable day. I'll make this into an important ritual I can perform at night so I can get into the habit of shutting off the day—and tuning in the night.

The main difference between optimism and pessimism resides in the notion of memory. The pessimist aptly recalls the hurts and failures of yesterday, but simply cannot remember the plentiful possibilities of a new tomorrow. The optimist has a hopeful future already memorized.

—Charles E. Jinks

Do you have a propensity for remembering old hurts and past mistakes? You probably can't practice forgiveness when old grudges stand in your way; you certainly can't look forward to the future when you get a kind of perverse pleasure out of hanging onto past failures.

According to American Indian tradition, enemies such as failure and hurt are sacred because they can make you strong. The unfortunate things that have happened in your past can teach you how to become stronger in the present and how to succeed in the future. But if you can only see hurt and failure and can't look ahead, then you're going to remain a perpetual pessimist.

How can you change this? Take a moment to recall a hurt or failure from the past. Ask, "Has it opened new doors for me? Has it made me stronger or wiser? Has it provided me with lessons that have helped me to grow? Has it brought new opportunities in my life?" Focus on the positive aspects of yesterday's hurts and failures to create a positive foundation on which to build your optimistic future.

☆

I'll start to live by Helen Keller's optimistic philosophy: "When one door of happiness closes, another opens, but often we look so long at the closed door that we do not see the one that has been opened for us."

Chasing desire can drive us mad.
—*Lao Tzu*

In the 1950s a woman renamed herself Peace Pilgrim and began a walk across America to raise awareness about living a simple, peaceful life. Before she left on her pilgrimage, she pared down her possessions to a "need-level," keeping a few items in her pockets and limiting her clothes to the ones she was wearing.

Do you operate on a "need-level" or a "want-level"? You may live in a space that's crammed with furniture, knick-knacks, and numerous electronic gadgets. You may have run out of closet space because your closets are filled with clothes you haven't worn in years. Your kitchen cupboards may be stacked full of canned goods and impulse items you're probably never going to eat. Your garage may even be so full of clutter that your car is parked outside!

Living with clutter can be chaotic; living simply can be liberating and empowering. As Peace Pilgrim explains, "A persistent simplification will create an inner and outer well-being that places harmony in one's life."

From this moment on, bring greater order to your life. Discard what you don't want, give away what you don't need, and recycle what's left over. Work towards your need-level as you simplify your living space; it can have a profound effect on creating lasting inner peace.

☆

When I release old possessions, I'm freeing myself from the desire to have them. When I share these possessions with others, I'm fulfilling their needs. When I recycle discarded items, I'm producing more to go around.

The nice thing about football is that you have a score-board to show how you've done. In other things in life, you don't. At least, not that you can see.

—Chuck Noll

Competition may have been drummed into you from the time you were a kid and wanted the most marbles, the most ice cream, the best paper route, the most prize ribbons, or the most important position on a team. If you grew up in a dysfunctional home, then your competitive drive may be much stronger than that of other people. It may even go so far as to include an unwillingness to give to others because it may seem unfair to you. You may think, "Nobody ever gave me anything. I've had to fight for what little I've got. So there's no way I'm giving to anyone."

Such an intensely unhealthy drive to have more or to be better may be a hard lesson to unlearn in adulthood. There aren't many character traits that are so unsuitable—and so personally frustrating—as unhealthy competition. An unwillingness to let go of who has the most points, who has the biggest office, who has the most money, who has the nicest home, who takes the greatest vacations, or who has the best kids can doom you to a life of unhappiness, a sense of inadequacy, and a lack of true intimacy.

Tonight remember that not always being the winner, having the most, or owning the best takes nothing away from who you are as a person. In fact, you'll be a much better person when you can let go of the need to compare, to measure, or to score.

☆

There's no scoreboard that shows my "position" in life. So tonight I'll let go of the need to feel as if life's a game and everyone in it are my opponents.

Chop your own wood and it will warm you twice.
—American proverb

A young reporter who had worked hard in her profession was given the assignment of covering a formal gathering of the wealthiest people in her community. When a coworker asked about the gathering, the reporter replied: "I met two kinds of people there. The ones who had started out with little and achieved the most were wonderful people, filled with incredible pride and satisfaction. But the ones who were born with silver spoons in their mouths turned out to be some of the emptiest, most helpless people I've ever met."

To get the most out of life, you need to put effort into it. *You don't get something for nothing.* When you're willing to try, to do, to dare, and to risk, then you're living life deliberately—and are often rewarded by getting something out of your doing. But in order to get, you have to give; you need to expend energy.

Is there something you'd like to do? Don't hold yourself back from doing it. Give it your full effort. As Henry David Thoreau explains: "I went to the woods because I wished to live deliberately, to front only the essential facts of life, and see if I could not learn what it had to teach, and not, when I came to die, discover I had not lived."

Live life effortfully. Like chopping wood, when you expend energy you'll be rewarded.

I've made up my mind that I don't have time for half-hearted attempts or fantasies that good things will just be handed to me. If I want to stay warm, I'll have to chop my own wood.

Solitude is enjoying the richness of self. Loneliness is facing the poverty of self.

—*May Sarton*

It's a rare person indeed who never feels lonely at night. Even when you're surrounded by friends, family, roommates, or are in the company of an intimate partner, you can still feel lonely. You may question, "What's wrong with me? I'm not alone. I have others with me." What you may not realize is that having people around sometimes puts you in touch with how out of touch you are with yourself. Until you're happy being with yourself, it may be hard to be happy with others.

How do you create happiness in your solitude? Accept that no matter how close you are to another person or other people, you are essentially alone. You have to live within your own skin and be your own separate person. To do so takes practice. For example, instead of reaching for the telephone when you're lonely, you can listen to your favorite music. Or you can use your alone time to give yourself a manicure, massage your feet with an aromatic oil, or create different outfits from the clothes in your closet. Connecting with yourself, rather than relying on connecting to others, is the best way to create enriching experiences in your solitude.

Tonight, pay attention to your feelings of loneliness. Then be there for yourself. Learn that loneliness doesn't have to be bitter and solitude doesn't have to be frightening.

Tonight I'll savor the pleasure of my own company. I'll think my own thoughts, curl up with a good book, or relax in a hot tub.

The secret to not being hurt like this once again, I decided, was never depending on anyone, never needing, never loving. It is the last dream of children, to be forever untouched.

—*Audre Lorde*

How wonderful it would be if you could never be hurt again—for the rest of your life! You'd never have to reexperience divorce, separation, or termination of a relationship. You'd never have to endure another job loss. You'd never have to lose another friend. You'd never have to go through another difficult change. You'd never have to suffer through the death of someone close to you.

Yet hurt is part of the cycle of growth and learning. You had to skin your knees in order to finally learn how to ride a bike. You had to miss a longed-for event in order to learn how much it meant to you. You had to grieve over the loss of someone dear to you in order to learn how much love you felt.

Tonight, there are no assurances that you'll never be hurt again. No matter how hard you try to protect yourself or seal yourself off from emotional pain, you're going to have to go through it again. The best way to deal with hurt is to accept it, have faith that you can endure it—as you have before—and trust that you can grow from it. Shutting pain away in your head won't banish it from your heart.

☆

Have I been living in a childish never-never land, believing that if I shut myself off from people or deny that some things matter to me, I'll never be hurt again? Tonight I'll grow up and accept that pain is an inevitable part of life.

There is always danger for those who are afraid of it.
—Bernard Shaw

A woman who worked at a rape crisis center began to fear the possibility of a sexual assault she imagined could happen to her. After all, she had seen it happen to so many other women. But even though the woman took intelligent precautions in the way she lived her life, she couldn't shake her fear. Soon she grew so frightened she was afraid to leave her home.

While some amount of fear is good because it can make you cautious and conscious of your safety and welfare, too much fear can undermine your physical, emotional, and spiritual health. Living *in* fear—rather than living *with* fear—puts your physical senses on constant alert, encourages suspicion and mistrust, and leads you away from faith and belief in the existence of good in the universe.

Tonight your life can be filled with safety, security, and harmony, but only if you can see and face the real dangers in your life and not the imaginary ones. As Erica Jong has said, "I have accepted fear as a part of life—specifically the fear of change . . . I have gone ahead despite the pounding in the heart that says: turn back . . . ." Recognize that the only fears you really need to have are those that spring forth from the shadows of the unknown.

☆

To live a more peaceful life involves facing my fears, learning to distinguish whether each fear is real or imaginary, and then taking appropriate action.

Funding a will through action, yet unattached to outcomes, remaining mindful that all you can really do is stay out of your own way and let the Will of Heaven flow through you—these are among the hallmarks of the Spiritual Warrior.

—*Ralph Blum*

There's a story of a religious teacher whose daily sermons were wonderful and inspiring, and he often spent hours preparing them. He thought that someday he might collect them into a book and seek a publisher or even appear on his own television show. With these outcomes in the back of his mind, he was about to begin his sermon when a little bird came and sat on the window sill. It began to sing, and sang away with a full heart. Then it stopped and flew away. The teacher thought for a moment, folded the pages to his prepared sermon, and announced, "The sermon for this morning is over."

When you're attached to results or when you try to force things to go your way, then your sights may be set on satisfying your financial, intellectual, or emotional needs. But while many things can be sought after, worked hard for, or struggled over, some things simply exist—and exist well.

Tonight, accept that a more spiritual outcome to your efforts can be equally rewarding. Release your expectations, keep an open mind to new possibilities, and enjoy connecting with the energies of a Higher Power.

☆

Tonight I'll be a Spiritual Warrior. I can take action in my life but yet remain flexible and open to the will of the universe and my Higher Power.

I'm looking out a large window and I see about forty dogwood and maple and oak and locust trees and the light is on some of the leaves and it's so beautiful. Sometimes I'm overcome with gratitude at such sights and feel that each of us has a responsibility for being alive . . .

—Maya Angelou

How often do you take time to notice the wonders of the natural world—the rainbow after a rainstorm, the birds frolicking around your bird feeder, or the silvery brilliance of a full moon? How often do you go out of your way to discover a new path through the woods or a less traveled route to work? How often do you allow time in your schedule to quietly connect with nature in some small way—by getting up early to sit in a city park and watch the sunrise slowly awaken the city or by peering up at a star-filled night sky?

The mad rush of living—the crush of places to go, people to see, and things to do—can make you forget there's a natural world around you that's teeming with wonders. But these wonders won't come to you; you have to take time to notice them.

Decide tonight that no matter how busy you are tomorrow, you're going to slow down your pace and notice nature. Pack a bag lunch for work so you can eat outside and feel the sun on your face. Or schedule a walk in the early evening that will take you to a place you've never been before. By becoming more aware of the world around you, you can become more alive!

☆

Tonight I'll pay attention to the natural wonders of the world. By taking time and opening my senses, I can notice a whole new world around me.

How vastly different a troubled question looks to us at noonday and at midnight. We flinch in the hours of darkness from a problem we can meet bravely when we are on our feet, and under the momentum of the noonday vigor.

—*Charles B. Newcomb*

You may have often heard the phrase, "Things will look better in the morning." In the light of day, when you're caught up in the hustle and bustle of the daily routine, the problems that troubled you the night before may recede from the shores of your mind. Upon reflection about your sleepless, restless night you may think, "I don't know what I was so bothered about last night."

But then, as the hours slowly move from day into evening and then night—and the shadows lengthen and the stream of life gradually stills—your problems may once again arise in your mind. Like specters ready to materialize at your bedroom door, your problems may return to haunt you.

Perhaps you trust the day more because of its light and natural rhythm. At night the darkness obscures your vision, nature decelerates its movement, and people seem to be locked into their own rhythms. Yet you can trust tonight—and every night—by depending upon the light provided by inspirational tools. Read a favorite psalm, repeat aloud a self-help program slogan, listen to the soothing advice of a friend, or reread a familiar story. Tonight can feel secure and trouble-free when you make yourself more secure.

☆

I can work out the solution to any problem tonight by reaching out to others or using calming tools to help channel my objectivity. Tonight I'll trust that I'm capable of soothing my troubled mind.

*Here is the test to find whether your mission on earth
is finished: If you're alive it isn't.*

—Richard Bach

One experience that's particularly difficult to go through
is loss: the loss of a job, an expected raise, or promotion; the
loss of a close friend or neighbor who moves away; the loss
of personal possessions through fire or theft; the loss of a
loved one through separation, divorce, or death. Any loss
can leave a vacuum in your life—a space and time that was
once pleasantly filled but now feels empty and meaningless.
You may feel that it's nearly impossible to perform even the
simplest routines, to concentrate on anything, or to accept
that life must go on. You may feel as if your life is over and
you have nothing left to live for.

Everyone faces loss; some more than others. But as Elbert
Hubbard says, "The cure for grief is motion." You need to
grieve your loss, let go of the past, and then take action by
recommitting to life and being alive. You must go on and
raise your children, find a new relationship or friends, build
a new house, or look for a new job. You must *make* the commitment to being alive.

From this moment on, resolve to force yourself back into
the swing of living. Be prepared to do something that makes
you feel vital and alive again. Motivate yourself by saying,
"I *can* get through my loss." And then believe that, over
time, you *will* eventually feel good again.

☆

*How I respond to any loss in my life spells the difference between
having a hopeless "I-give-up" attitude and a hopeful "I-can-go-
on" one. Tonight I'll believe that I can go on living, despite the
loss I've suffered.*

Children have a magical ability not to place limits on their thinking and dreaming. Anything and everything is possible for those who believe, and children understand this better than anyone.

—Susan Smith Jones, Ph.D.

Do you place limits on your thinking and dreaming? You do when you use limiting words in your vocabulary such as *can't*—"I can't draw"—*shouldn't*—"I shouldn't change my career"—*don't*—"I don't have the right to ask for anything"—or *won't*—"I won't be able to fall asleep if I go to bed early." You do when you erect verbal boundaries that prevent you from even making an effort. Through statements such as, "It'll never work," "It's impossible!" or "I don't want to waste my time," you're telling yourself—and others—that you're not going to bother trying. Such communications signal that not only have you given up on a dream, but you've also given up on any dream—*period!*

When did your ability to be a child end? When did you stop creative thinking, planning, scheming, and dreaming? When did you cease having faith that anything was possible and change it to the belief that nothing was possible?

If you sit with these questions for a while tonight, you may discover that a past hurt, a recent failure, or a fear of change may be silencing your hopeful child within. Make a decision now to let that child be heard. Recover one lost dream or create a new one. Then be a child who believes in the dream.

☆

Now is the time to reclaim my ability to dream as a child would dream. Tonight I'll journey in my mind to a world where all things are possible. I'll believe in fairy tales with happy endings, lands filled with peace, and love everlasting.

If you feel as if your life is a seesaw, perhaps you are depending on another person for your ups and downs.
—*Anonymous*

When difficulties arise in your intimate relationship, are you able to communicate with caring, compromise, and concern? Or are you quick to try to take care of the other person's feelings, afraid to say what it is you want or need, or prefer to wait for your partner to take the initiative to make everything better?

True harmony in relationships doesn't just happen. Like two people who sit opposite one another on a seesaw, the actions of one person can't help but affect the other. In order to bring the seesaw into balance, you each need to adjust to one another and work together until you can still the board.

Each person in a relationship needs to be committed to discussing and resolving conflict. It's not enough to say, "Let's just get along" or "Why don't we just do what you want." Positive emotional health in a relationship can only be attained when neither partner allows the other to dictate his or her position or control the outcome. Each person needs to be willing to listen to what the other wants or needs and to communicate with similar openness and honesty.

From now on, strive to restore harmony in your relationship. Be ready to discuss and then work towards a resolution that gives each person some of what he or she desires. Then both you and your partner can enjoy a healthy emotional balance.

☆

I won't depend upon my partner to restore balance in our relationship. Tonight I'll remember that conflicts between us are best resolved through positive actions we both make.

There is an Indian belief that everyone is a house of four rooms: a physical, a mental, an emotional and a spiritual room. Most of us tend to live in one room most of the time, but unless we go into every room every day, even if only to keep it aired, we are not complete.

—*Rumer Godden*

For most people, serious prayer doesn't usually begin until after they reach the age of thirty. Then, the illusion of immortality and control one has over one's destiny fades and there's a need to rely on a guiding force who can provide "answers." But how do you make space in your "house" for such spiritual contact?

There are many ways you can begin communicating tonight with your Higher Power. You may wish to break the ice by using a familiar prayer, perhaps one learned by rote in childhood: "Our Father, who art in heaven . . ." "Now I lay me down to sleep . . ." or "The Lord is my Shepherd, I shall not want . . ." You may like to rely upon spiritual teachings from other religions or cultures. You may prefer to write your own prayer—one that addresses the particular areas of your life in which you feel you need spiritual guidance and wisdom. Or you may like to repeat an affirmation, a short proverb, or a helpful slogan.

What's most important about taking care of your "spiritual room" is that you do it every night. By making such communication part of your evening routine, you may discover a more profound—and much more rewarding—relationship with God.

☆

Tonight I'll find time to pray. It doesn't matter if I pray while I'm making dinner, when I brush my teeth, or right before I go to bed—just so long as I do it.

How hard it is to escape from places. However carefully one goes they hold you—you leave little bits of yourself fluttering on the fences—little rags and shreds of your very life.

—Katherine Mansfield

You may often think how wonderful life would be if things were easier. But think back to a particularly rough time you went through in the past. Maybe it was a difficult childhood, a hurtful relationship, an injury or illness, or the loss of a job. Would you be as strong today if it hadn't been for that experience? Hasn't that experience "marked" you in some way today—left a little piece of itself on your way of thinking, feeling, acting, or believing?

National Book Award winner Dorothy Allison, whose book *Bastard Out of Carolina* was based on her incestuous and painful childhood, talked about how the past has influenced her. "I'm past forty now," she says, "and it's taken me my entire life to figure out what happened to me as a kid. Because the things you do to survive with some kind of sense of yourself, the emotional maneuverings, really obstruct accurate memory."

From now on, when you're faced with a difficulty, don't try to find an easy way out or escape from it. Instead ask, "What will getting through this experience teach me? How will this make me a stronger person now and in the future?"

☆

Tonight I'll remember that I've had to climb a lot of fences in my life. Some were hard to get over; others not so hard. But each hard lesson I've faced has helped me to learn and grow in some way. Each fence mattered.

. . . life . . . is divided between waking, dreaming, and dreamless sleep. But transcending these three states is superconscious vision—called the Fourth.
                                        —from the Upanishads

Have you ever had a mystical, spiritual, or psychic experience? Maybe you dreamed of an event that actually came true. Perhaps you "saw" the right number to play in a lottery that resulted in financial gain. Maybe you heard the voice of a deceased loved one give you encouragement, guidance, or warning. Or perhaps you were able to make it through a particularly trying time because you "knew" your Higher Power was watching over you.

Such experiences may frighten or excite you. To be able to commune in some small way with another dimension or a supernatural world can be unearthly. To be able to use your "sixth sense" can challenge your belief in the three-fold connection between mind, body, and spirit. To be able to foresee events or to feel a protective presence may expand the boundaries of your existence. To feel like you can be more in touch with your destiny may make you feel empowered to make changes in your life.

But what do you do when you have such feelings? How do you handle the powerful impact they can have on you and your life? Tonight, don't be afraid to encourage and feel such mystical experiences. Use them to help you grow in ways other experiences don't.

☆

Tonight I won't shut off my ability to experience a mystical, magical, or psychic moment. I won't allow myself to be bound by traditional beliefs or the accepted "realities" of the world.

*I am not afraid of tomorrow, for I have seen yester-
day and I love today.*

—William Allen White

There's a parable about a group of congregants who were asked by their pastor to share what they often prayed for. One who had just lost her job said secure work. Another who had medical problems said health. And another who had been raised in poverty said financial security.

But one congregant shook his head at the responses. When it came his turn he said, "I don't pray to escape the things that frighten me. Instead, I pray for the ability to trust that no matter what happens to me each day, it is the *right* thing."

It has been said that there are two voices you can listen to. One is the voice of fear and the other is the voice of confidence. The voice of fear is high-pitched and frantic; it whines and warns and whispers messages designed to scare you. But the voice of confidence sounds soft and soothing; it tells you not to worry, assures you that all is well, and sometimes grows silent so you can listen to your Higher Power.

Tonight, still your voice of fear and let your voice of confidence grow louder. Pray for the wisdom to be able to live each moment to the fullest. A reassuring prayer is: "No matter what happens in the time between sunset and sunrise, I will never be surrounded by darkness."

☆

Tonight I'll view my past as a valuable asset, my future as a glorious new beginning, and the moment as a time of peace and relaxation. I'll rest assured tonight, knowing I have nothing to fear.

All of life is maintenance. Taking care of things. That's the pleasant part.

—Armistead Maupin

What do you want from life? Where are you going? How do you want to get there? Questions such as these can make you feel uncomfortable, especially when you don't have all the answers or don't know where to go to find them.

Sometimes you may find it disconcerting to go from day to day without a set plan in mind or a strong idea of who you are—especially when those around you seem capable of clearly defining themselves and what they want from their lives. So you may view them and what they do as exciting, and you and what you do as dull and boring.

Yet being flexible, spontaneous, and open to the circumstances each day brings can be highly rewarding. Being committed to taking care of yourself in healthy ways can be thrilling. Going through the rituals of the day can be reassuring and grounding. And simply enjoying the company of a dear friend or a loved one can be quite pleasant.

Each day holds the promise of new growth and new beginnings. Some days may seem full of purpose and meaning; some are pieced together by routine. But whether your day has been one of housecleaning or house building, car pooling or car purchasing, reheating leftovers for dinner or dining out at an elegant restaurant, or a date on a calendar or a date with destiny, you can view this day as pleasant.

☆

Tonight I'll give thanks for the day I was given and cease my search for more, better, or different. Today turned out to be a perfectly pleasant day—and just what I needed.

The thoughts that come unsought, and, as it were, drop into the mind, are commonly the most valuable of any we have.

—John Locke

Are you willing to take risks—to try something new to satisfy your inner desires, or are you afraid of doing anything that's out of the realm of what you think you "should" or "ought" to be doing? Are you able to give and take, or do you insist on going in only one direction? Do you take joy from your achievements, or do you just look at life as a series of tasks to accomplish? Do you exercise your creativity? Are you afraid to lose the security provided by always repeating the same ways of thinking, feeling, and behaving, or are you able to react in new ways by tuning into different thoughts, experiencing new feelings, and changing your behaviors?

As long as you act calmly and respond fluidly to all life has to offer—the smooth passages as well as the bumps and grinds—then you can learn and grow. That's because you're keeping yourself open to new experiences and reacting in new ways. But how can you do this on a consistent basis?

Tonight, reflect on how you go about your daily activities. Are you listening to everyone else *but* yourself? Ask, "What is it *I* want from life—not what others need, want, or expect from me?" Listen to your inner voice. By finding out what *you* want from life, you take the first step towards achieving it.

☆

Tonight I'll tune out the noise of opinions and ideas that come from every direction and tune in to just my own voice. By listening to myself, I'll be able to acknowledge my true feelings.

People want to give you easy consolation. Sure, it would be wonderful to be off the hook for things that easily—just blame it on God. I can't do that. It just isn't in me.

—Sally Jessy Raphael

When you're going through a difficult time or have experienced a profound loss, others may tell you, "It's God's will," "God never gives you more than you can handle," or "There's a reason for this; in time, you'll discover it." But such words, although intended to soothe your troubles, ease your pain, or make you feel less alone, rarely provide you with the comfort you truly need—that of validation, identification, and understanding that you're not the only person who has ever gone through what you're going through.

During one tough year, third highest rated talk show host Sally Jessy Raphael nearly lost her adopted son to a car accident and did lose her daughter within three weeks of each other. Prior to that, for twenty-six years she couldn't pay her credit-card bills, moved twenty-five times, was fired eighteen times. Sometimes her family lived on food stamps and slept in their car. "Yet," Sally says, "I consider myself a very, very lucky person." How did she make it not only through a tough year, but also a tough career? "I have a wonderful family," she answers, "and I hold on to the good vibrations of friends."

Tonight, think about who it is you can hold onto—a family member, your partner, or a close friend. Be ready to reach out to this person and hold on during your tough times.

☆

I live in a random universe, where tragedies sometimes occur without rhyme or reason. But tonight I'll have faith that no matter what happens to me, I'll pull through any difficulty with the help of my friends and loved ones.

The majority of us lead quiet, unheralded lives as we pass through this world. There will most likely be no ticker-tape parades for us, no monuments created in our honor. But that does not lessen our possible impact, for there are scores of people waiting for someone just like us to come along . . .

—Leo Buscaglia

Every day hungry and homeless men, women, and children wander America's streets searching garbage cans for scraps, lining up outside crowded shelters and soup kitchens, or panhandling. Every night these same hungry and homeless fight in the cold for the privilege of attaining the "luxury" of being able to catch a few hours of precious sleep on a park bench, over a subway grating, or wrapped in a blanket while huddled inside a cardboard box.

Do you take time to share your abundance with the homeless? You can donate a bag of groceries to a local food pantry, prepare or serve food at a soup kitchen or shelter, or offer to clean up after meals are served. Tonight, you can curl up with a full stomach beneath your soft, warm blankets in your comfortable bed and close your eyes to sisters and brothers in need. Or you can make a decision to become a more compassionate, giving person. There's much good that can come from donating an old sweater or coat to a charity or volunteering just a few hours at a shelter. Giving a little bit of your time or material possessions can make just one person in this world more comfortable.

☆

The next time a hungry and homeless person approaches me on the street, I won't turn away in disgust. Even the smallest act of caring—a smile, a kind word, or a hot cup of coffee and a sandwich—has the potential to turn a life around.

Choose your rut carefully. You'll be in it for a long time.

—Unknown

In his book *The Healing Power of Humor*, Allen Klein relates a story about two monks who were walking down the road when they noticed a young woman waiting to cross a stream. To the horror of one of the monks, the other picked the woman up in his arms and carried her across the water. The monks resumed their walking. "About a mile down the road, the monk who was aghast at his friend's action remarked, 'We are celibate, we are not supposed to even look at a woman, let alone pick one up and carry her across a stream. How could you possibly do that?' The other monk replied, 'I put that woman down a mile back. Are you still carrying her around with you?'"

When you can't let go of things that upset you, perplex you, or disappoint you, you remain mired in a rut. Like the monk who couldn't let go of what the other monk had done, you are—in reality—stuck back at the bank of the stream, unable to move on from that point in time. The only way out of your rut is to do as the monk who had carried the woman did—when he released the woman, he also released his attachment to that point in time. To move out of your rut, you need to accept and let go.

Tonight, move out of any rut you're stuck in by thinking about one thing you'd like to forget. Visualize writing this thought on a piece of paper, then rip it into tiny pieces and throw it away.

☆

The trick to maneuvering my way out of any rut is to give myself a kick from behind. Tonight I'll stop struggling, accept what I've been given, let go—and then move on.

Kindness in words creates confidence. Kindness in thinking creates profoundness. Kindness in giving creates love.

—Lao-Tze

Do you believe in the Buddhist law of karma, that what energy you give out will inevitably come back to you in kind? Karma teaches that every action produces a corresponding reaction. If you react violently to a violent person, you create more violence; aggressive reactions keep you in bondage so you experience further aggression.

But just as violence begets violence and negativity begets negativity, so too does patience beget patience and kindness beget kindness. It all depends on what you want to give out.

You can practice positive nonresistance to negativity every night. The next time someone is hostile, unkind, manipulative, or critical towards you, don't immediately react emotionally or in a way that will escalate the situation. Instead, take a deep breath. From a centered, calm space, listen and observe. Ask yourself, "What's *really* going on with this person? Can I figure out what it is that he or she *really* wants? Am I willing to use patience and kindness to help?"

Then, when you're ready, respond in ways that help you shift the negative energy to more positive energy. By not overreacting, you can defuse the situation and create a new, more peaceful pattern.

☆

When was the last time I did something kind for someone who wasn't kind to me? Tonight I'll recognize that the only way to change the way we interact with one another is for one of us to use positive energy to break the hostile cycle. I can be that person.

There are trees that seem to die at the end of autumn.
There are also the evergreens.

—Gilbert Maxwell

If you were a tree, what kind of tree would you be? Perhaps you'd like to be a maple that would blossom for three seasons and then provide sweet maple syrup for the winter months. Maybe you'd like to be a majestic oak that would someday be cut down and used to create a beautiful piece of furniture. Perhaps you'd like to be an apple tree that would provide food and fragrance for all to enjoy year-round. Or maybe you'd like to be an evergreen that would remain forever green, wearing a nest of robins in the spring, a garland of dead leaves from surrounding trees in the fall, and a blanket of snow in the winter.

Trees may remind you of some of the people in your life whom you admire. There may be those who stand tall, never letting the difficulties of life bend them over. There may be those who radiate power and majesty as they take incredible risks or make wonderful changes in their lives. Or there may be others who remain green year-round, radiating a positive outlook and bountiful energy that keeps them growing strong day after day.

Tonight, consider that while you're part of a forest of "trees" that surround you, you're also your own unique individual tree. Which tree will you be?

☆

Sometimes I may feel like a sapling—weak, young, and unformed; other times I may feel like old wood—tired, achy, and finished with my growth. Tonight I'll picture the tree I'd like to be and imagine what I'd feel like as this tree.

I dreamt I went to heaven and that heaven didn't seem to be my home and I broke my heart with weeping to come back to earth and the angels were so angry they flung me out in the middle of the heath . . . and I woke up sobbing with joy.

—Merle Oberon in the film version of
Wuthering Heights

Have you ever woken up from a nightmare and wept with joy over the realization that what you had just experienced was only a dream? Like Dorothy in *The Wizard of Oz*, upon waking you may have felt relief to find that you were safe in your bed.

Nighttime can be the scariest, hardest part of the day. As you prepare for sleep, you often review the day. In doing so you may discover leftover resentments, unprocessed anger, unresolved conflicts, twinges of jealousy or guilt, or imagined scenarios of things that could or might happen. Such things can keep you tossing and turning all night.

To rid yourself of the possibility of a sleepless night, before you go to sleep imagine that you're a guest on a talk show. The topic of the show is "Guilty Consciences." As the show begins, talk about the things that happened during the day that you wish could've turned out differently. Slowly, clear your conscience of the unwanted past and present events that may infiltrate your sleep tonight. Then enter into a restful, restorative sleep that's free from the nightmares of the day.

☆

I'm not going to sleep well if I can't begin my sleep with a mind that's free from unwanted clutter. Tonight I'll release those things from my mind that are negative or a waste of time and hold onto positive achievements and the things that make me feel good.

. . . And if you but listen in the stillness of the night you shall hear. . . . It is Thy urge in us that would turn our nights, which are Thine, into days, which are Thine also.
—*Kahlil Gibran*

When a child doesn't want to hear what a parent is saying, the child will often place a finger in each ear and make loud noises to drown out parental advice, admonishment, or even adoration. What do you do when others offer their advice, express dissatisfaction, or show affection?

Sometimes you may find it more comfortable to go through life deaf to words of wisdom, pearls of practical advice, or expressions of love. That's why a slogan like "Listen and learn" may be hard for you to follow. After all, isn't it sometimes easier to dump your problems on others or talk incessantly about all the things that are wrong with your life rather than hear advice about how you could solve your problems or make changes that could improve the quality of your life? Isn't it more comfortable to sit in judgment of others rather than accept criticism directed towards you? Don't you feel more protected by running away from intimacy than leaving yourself open to the possibility of being hurt?

Yet by opening your ears, you can open your mind and learn more about yourself through the words of others. So take the cotton out of your ears and be willing to accept that each person in your life has something important to share with you. What you listen to, can help you.

Can I listen to those around me? It doesn't matter whether the words are delivered eloquently, with humor, in sadness, or very simply. I'll learn from others—about their strength, hope, and experience—by listening to them.

The seven steps to stagnation: We've never done it that way; we're not ready for that; we are doing all right without trying that; we tried it once before; we don't have money for that; it's not our job; and, something like that can't work.

—Unknown

Dr. Patrick Thomas Malone, medical director of Mental Health Services at Northside Hospital in Atlanta, has invented the term "selficide" to describe a state of being where a person is unable to learn and grow from life's experiences. Common characteristics of people who are "selficiders" include: feeling that life is flat, not being able to enjoy intimate relationships, being out of touch with themselves, and not being able to find satisfaction in their world or themselves. In sum, a selficider is a stagnater.

To visualize how to change your feelings of selficide to feelings of self-satisfaction and pleasure, Dr. Malone uses the example of a baby. When babies first begin to explore their world, they crawl. But when they learn to walk, they stop crawling. When you're happy in your world, you walk from event to event, but when you're unhappy with yourself and your world, you resort to crawling. You react in old ways instead of responding in new ones.

From now on, end stagnation by being willing to dismiss the old ways you have of doing things. Be ready to respond in new ways—ways that express wants rather than shoulds, desires rather than daydreams, and hopes rather than regrets.

☆

Tonight I'll believe in the words of Karl Jaspers: "It is true that the whole world will not change if I change. But the change in myself is the premise of the greater change." To change my responses to the world, I'll change how *I respond.*

The only big ideas I've ever had have come from daydreaming, but modern life keeps people from daydreaming. Every moment of the day your mind is being occupied, controlled, by someone else—at school, at work, watching television. Getting away from all that is really important. You need to just kick back in a chair and let your mind daydream.
—Paul MacCready

The free moments you may have during a day rarely live up to their title. If you're like most people, you can't afford the luxury of physically or intellectually stepping away from work during your lunch hour, taking the required morning and afternoon break, or leaving work on time. If you're a full-time parent or student, then you know how every minute of the day is filled with some duty or obligation. Weekday nights are hectic; weekends are nonstop activity from Saturday morning to Sunday evening. Even vacations are replete with places to go and things to do. So when can you ever find time that's truly *free* time—time in which you can kick off your shoes, put your feet up, close your eyes, and let your mind take you to where *you'd* like to go?

Sometimes the best way to daydream is to set aside time during the day specifically for that purpose. By daydreaming on a regular basis, your nighttimes can be times in which you truly get away from it all!

Why continue to daydream about daydreaming when I can make it happen? From now on I'll set aside a half hour each day in which to daydream.

Look at that sunset, Howard. . . . It's like the daytime didn't want to end, isn't it? It's like the daytime is going to put up a big scrap, set the world on fire to keep the nighttime from creeping on.
> —Rosalind Russell watching the sunset
> with Arthur O'Connell in Picnic

There comes a time in every horror movie when you know something bad is going to happen. You can feel the tension mount as your heart starts pounding, and you may want to scream at the actors to alert them of the impending danger. But you can't, because it's only a movie.

You may feel that same type of fear whenever you see daylight fade and darkness approach. As the days grow shorter and the nights longer, you may feel like you're back in the movie theater experiencing the same sense of impending doom. Yet life isn't a horror movie where danger lurks around every corner and terrible things are out to get you. So what are you afraid of? The fears you have may spring from the shadows of the unknown.

Tonight, reflect on the words of an unknown spiritual advisor who said: "Getting rid of fear is not easy. When faced with a change I may slip back to my fear like the birds huddled on the wire. But more often I will welcome change like the geese do, with gratefulness for the sign from God that it is time to go in a new direction."

Tonight my life can be filled with safety, security, and harmony. I'll face my fears of the unknown so I can make changes in myself for the better.

*Ideals are like the stars: we never reach them, but like
the mariners of the sea, we chart our course by them.*
　　　　　　　　　　　　—Carl Schultz

The world's current ecological problems—pollution, acid
rain, destruction of the rain forests, and the depletion of the
ozone layer, to name a few—can remind you on a daily basis that you're part of a complex web of life. Major catastrophes such as oil spills or the release of harmful chemicals
into the atmosphere can impact everyone and everything,
from the bottom of the chain of life to the top.

Yet you may question the impact that you, as one person,
can make on healing the damages made by centuries of
civilization. While you may never be able to recreate the
ideal environment this night, this week, this year, or even
in your lifetime, you can take positive action every day.

American naturalist John Muir wrote that " . . . most
people are *on* the world, not in it—have no conscious sympathy or relationship to anything about them . . . ." His sense
of oneness with his environment led him to found the Sierra
Club, to campaign in Congress to preserve the wilderness,
and to establish Yosemite National Park.

What can you do? From now on, decide to do something
that will help preserve the environment. Plant a tree before
the ground freezes; set up a recycling area in your home for
plastics, glass, and newspapers; or join an organization dedicated to the preservation of sand dunes, conservation land,
or natural habitats.

☆

*Tonight I'll decide to do something to help preserve the environ-
ment. Whatever I do will be a lasting contribution I make—one
that'll be here a lot longer than I'll be.*

Habits are first cobwebs, then cables.
—Spanish proverb

To cope with stress, everyone has different ways of relaxing and unwinding at night. Some are healthy and pleasureable—taking a walk, having dinner with friends or family, or spending a quiet evening at home. Others, however, actually do little to relieve the pressure and can even create additional difficulties, health problems, or sleeping problems as well—smoking, drinking, overeating, fighting with family members, using tranquilizers or drugs, or withdrawing from people.

Frequent use of such unhealthy tension-reducing activities can put you in the worst possible condition at night to handle the day's stress. While an occasional drink or infrequent argument are probably not damaging, they can become habits that can undermine your health and, over time, make it hard for you to cope at night.

The key is to create balance. Any habit used to excess can add to your stress and further harm your health. So it's important that you take responsibility to modify or eliminate frequent unhealthy habits and replace them with ones that are more healthy. Instead of drinking alcohol, brew a cup of decaffeinated tea. Instead of going to bed angry at family members, seek resolution to conflict. Instead of cutting another piece of pie, eat a healthy snack. You're the only one responsible for breaking the hold a bad habit may have on you.

☆

Tonight I'll determine if my bad habits crop up frequently. I'll change the habit in the future by joining a support group, asking for help, or making the change myself.

To make a peach you need a winter, a summer, an autumn and a bee, so many nights and days and sun and rain, petals rosy with pollen—all that your mouth may know a few minutes of pleasure.

—Minon Drouet

In 1983 zoologist Alan Rabinowitz ventured into the rain forest of Belize, Central America, to study the jaguar in its natural habitat and to establish the world's first jaguar preserve. As he began his research, he discovered that the hours flew by with little work to show for the time. The villagers worked at a pace much slower than his and equipment took months to arrive or be repaired. As time plodded along, Rabinowitz started to lose faith in his mission. "It no big ting man," the villagers would tell him. "Saafly, saafly [softly, softly], tiger ketch monkey"—meaning that Rabinowitz would get what he wanted, eventually. It was only when he had become accustomed to the pace—"Whenever I wished to get something done that involved people other than myself, I would estimate the time it should take and multiply it by four"—that he was able to relax.

Tonight, recognize that when you expect others to work at your own pace or set out to do an incredible amount in a ridiculously short amount of time, you take away the pleasure of your tasks and replace it with pressure. From now on, strive to make accurate time estimates so you accomplish what you *can* do—and not all you *want* to do.

☆

Tonight I'll keep in mind that a peach can't ripen without a full season. With sufficient time, however, eating the fully ripened peach can bring me incredible pleasure.

A little thing comforts us because a little thing upsets us.
—Blaise Pascal

Are you sometimes hypersensitive at night—quick to take offense when none is meant or ready to shed tears at a sharp word or criticism—because your mind, body, and spirit are completely exhausted from the day's activities? When the little things start getting to you from the moment you arrive home from work or start to prepare dinner to the time you go to bed, then you're being given a warning signal. You need to pay more attention to taking care of yourself so such things don't throw you into a tailspin and ruin a good night's sleep.

Keep in mind that just as little things can upset you, so can little things restore your equilibrium. If you come home feeling out of sorts, don't let it destroy your evening or damage your interactions with others. Indulge in a simple pleasure. Take a hot bath, meditate, call a friend long-distance, or go to a movie by yourself. If you can bestow little kindnesses upon yourself, you may find that the annoyances and slights you overreact to lose their power to derail your serenity.

Tonight, respond to the normal inconveniences, slight criticisms, and minor upsets of life in calmer ways. Rather than plunge into anger or hurt, keep the little things in perspective and learn what you can from them.

☆

Everyone experiences daily annoyances and slights, but not everyone overreacts to them. Tonight I'll learn to roll with the punches and not allow small, insignificant events to throw me off balance.

*If you don't focus on strengths, you're playing a los-
ing game.*

—*Delores Caleagno*

Do you focus on your individual strengths and do things
that help build on them? Or are you more conscious of your
weaknesses and so concentrate your energy on trying to
eliminate them? One of the greatest mistakes you may make
in your development as an individual is trying to correct your
weaknesses *before* you capitalize on your strengths. What's
more beneficial to your growth is recalling your moments of
success rather than focusing on your times of failure.

Everyone is stronger when they have their successes
clearly in mind. The legendary coach of the Green Bay
Packers, Vince Lombardi, knew this. Before a game with
Green Bay's archrival, the Detroit Lions, Lombardi showed
films of only the successful running plays previously used
against the Lions. He believed that his team would be more
likely to take the field with confidence by ensuring that the
players had what worked—rather than what didn't—clearly
etched in their minds.

Ask, "When am I most confident?" Make a mental list of
such times, then consider how each time is, in reality, a
reflection of a strength. Use this mental exercise whenever
you find yourself focusing on your weaknesses. Then you allow your strengths to overpower your weaknesses, ultimately
making them irrelevant.

☆

*Can I soar with my strengths tonight, or will I let my weaknesses
ground me? If I can focus on what I do best, then success will
surely follow.*

*It's all right to hold a conversation, but you should let
go of it now and then.*
                                        —*Richard Armour*

When you're going through a difficult time, one of the best
ways to heal and recover is to talk about what's going on and
how it makes you feel. Talking to someone, either on the
telephone or in person, can help focus your attention on
yourself as well as provide an opportunity to listen to helpful or calming advice.

But late at night, when you can't sleep because of your
troubles and it's too late to call on a friend, you can still air
how you feel. Writing about a trauma, loss, or stressful circumstance in a journal can be just as helpful as discussing
it. In a study sponsored by the American Psychological Association, half of the members of a group of unemployed,
middle-aged professionals were asked to spend twenty
minutes a day for five days writing about their feelings surrounding the loss of their jobs. Eight months later, fifty-three
pecent of those who had regularly written about their experience not only felt more positive about themselves, but
had also found new jobs. Researchers summed up their find-
ings by saying: "Those who were able to express their feelings on paper were better able to confront their bitterness
and negative feelings, realistically appraise their situation,
and adopt a positive attitude towards the future."

☆

*I'll learn how to express myself in a journal. I'll be open and
honest about how I feel so I can work through the emotions I'm
experiencing. Writing can help me grow from an unpleasant
experience—and not stay stuck in it.*

I genuinely love what I do. Wouldn't it be great if everyone got to pursue a job they loved and if every- one applauded their efforts at the end of the day?
—*Diane Ford*

Comedienne Diane Ford has been featured as one of *The Hollywood Reporter*'s "10 Rising Comics," a "Star of 1989" in the *Los Angeles Times*, and a "Woman of the Night" on HBO. She has played "The Tonight Show." But, as is usually the case, it hasn't been easy. "When I was five years old I saw a guy on the 'Ed Sullivan Show' run into a wall. He got lots of laughs. So I did it. My brothers were hysterical so I kept doing it. The more I banged the more they laughed and the bloodier my head got. It's a great metaphor."

Do you often feel as if you're banging your head into a wall at work or at home, doing tasks for which you get little recog- nition, performing duties you often question the logic of, or asking for things you rarely get in return for your efforts? Few people get to pursue a job they love and earn the recogni- tion they deserve; most people feel that what they do every day lacks challenge and goes unnoticed.

From this moment on, strive to find meaningful challenge elsewhere in your life. Resolve to do something each day that you really love: play your favorite music, paint, go for a run, assemble a model train set, begin a complicated quilt, or meditate. By giving your full attention to something that fills you with a sense of purpose and enjoyment, you're less likely to lose sleep over another hopeless situation.

☆

Each morning I'll look in a mirror and tell myself some things I like about what I do. Giving myself approval and appreciation can help me build my self-esteem and increase my inner peace.

*If everything were to turn out just like I would want it
to, then I would never experience anything new; my
life would be an endless repetition of stale successes.*
—Hugh Prather

Actress, "Saturday Night Live" regular, and one-woman
show performer Gilda Radner, who lost a long battle with
cancer, kept her spirits up as her health failed by trying to
take things lightly. She even titled one of her books, *It's Always Something*—a phrase she often used to help her deal
with her difficult experience.

In your relationships, job, or life situations, there may inevitably be some turbulence that will hinder or prevent you
from achieving a desired goal. How you handle such rough
spots will determine whether you can set a new goal or try
again to achieve your old one—or whether you'll give up
making any further attempt. If you can believe in one of Radner's punch lines, "If it's not one thing, it's another," then
you're on your way to learning and growing in positive ways
from the experience.

Tonight, be prepared to respond to life's bumps in less serious, even more humorous ways—just as Gilda Radner did.
Some days and nights are going to be better—or worse—than
others. Be ready for such times with a funny story, a joke,
or a lighthearted attitude. As Allen Klein says, "Most of us
can laugh at the punch line of a joke, but few laugh at life's
punches."

☆

*Tonight I'll remember that just when I think I'm headed in one
direction, something can happen that'll take me on a whole
different path. How I handle this will determine whether I have
a defeatist attitude or a "succeedist" one.*

*One doesn't discover new lands without consenting to
lose sight of the shore for a very long time.*
—*André Gide*

Imagine the stress Christopher Columbus and his crew felt as they set sail from the safe shores of their homeland, knowing that they might fall off the edge of the world and never return home. But that didn't stop them from beginning their risky voyage.

Risk-taking means attempting something new, different, or unknown, without the comfort of knowing what the outcome will be. Sometimes you can take a risk and achieve positive results—for instance, you may ask your boss for a raise and get it. Or you can take a risk and feel you don't succeed—you may be turned down when you ask someone out on a date.

But whatever the outcome, it's important to take the risk. Being ready to take a risk doesn't mean you won't feel afraid. Fear is a natural reaction to the unknown. But fearing and *still taking the risk* is what risk-taking is all about. That's why the best risk-takers are the people who ask, "What do I have to lose?" They have the attitude that even if they don't succeed, they—like Columbus—are at least willing to try.

From now on, instead of thinking about a risk you'd like to take and what you might lose in the process, think about what you might gain. Keep the gains in mind—and take the risk!

☆

I'll work through my risk-taking fears by asking, "What's the worst possible thing that could happen if I take this risk?" Then I'll consider whether that's bad enough to stop me from taking the risk.

Buddha said the same thing about the good ox driver. The driver knows how much load the ox can carry, and he keeps the ox from being overloaded. You know your way and your state of mind. Do not carry too much.

—Zen philosophy

It can be very difficult to bring balance into all areas of your life. You may find it hard not to put in overtime at work. You may be compulsive about having the perfect yard or the perfect home. Or you may be so driven to live life differently from your parents that you may push yourself to live well—at any cost.

But becoming too absorbed in any area of your life can take time and attention away from other areas and make your entire life imbalanced. In your rise up the corporate ladder, you may be leaving your intimate relationship or children behind. In your mad pursuit to become physically fit, you may be forgetting to slow down and rest from time to time.

There's nothing wrong with focusing on one part of your life for a short time. But anything beyond that can negatively impact all the other areas of your life. To restore balance each night, think about letting go of an activity that has received a lot of time and attention lately. Reassign its time, or at least a portion of it, to other areas you've been ignoring. In doing so, you can gently and gradually begin to restore balance to *all* areas of your life.

☆

I'll imagine placing each activity in my life on a scale and weighing it to measure the focus I give it. I'll give less time and attention to those activities that weigh a lot.

Angels can fly because they take themselves lightly.
—*G.K. Chesterton*

Are you sometimes moved to hysteria over the smallest things? Are you unable to keep life's trials and tribulations in perspective? Are you too serious or too busy to laugh at yourself or life's ups and downs?

Taking life more lightly—and even humorously—can provide an enjoyable break from the tense moments caused by the not-so-funny things in your life. Humor can take you away from your problems and troubles, if only for a moment, and make them easier to bear. Yet humor is rarely recognized as a stress coping tool. After all, how can you laugh when you're feeling angry, worried, anxious, sad, tense, or struggling to be the perfect "angel"?

Laughter can provide a well-needed positive balance to negative feelings as well as benefit the body: a good, hearty laugh can give your heart, lungs, circulation, and muscles a rousing "inner workout."

When was the last time you experienced a real belly laugh—one that brought tears to your eyes, left you gasping for air, and made your sides hurt? Norman Cousins used laughter to help him battle a serious disease. He surrounded himself with "Candid Camera" videos, Marx Brothers films, and "Three Stooges" comedies. Then he had to check out of the hospital and into a motel because he was making too much noise healing himself!

☆

What makes me laugh? I'll discover what I think is funny and gravitate towards those situations, people, or resources that make me laugh the most.

The game of life is a game of boomerangs. Our thoughts, deeds, and words return to us sooner or later, with astounding accuracy.
—*Florence Scovel Shinn*

An old spiritual philosophy teaches that "What ye sow, so shall ye reap." This tells you that when you plant the seeds of goodness, serenity, and happiness, you'll often benefit by receiving such things in return. But when you scatter the seeds of criticism, discomfort, and unhappiness, you shouldn't be surprised when you experience the same things in your interactions with others. You teach others how to treat you by the thoughts, feelings, and actions you put out. So your energy can become their energy because *you have invited it*. You get your due because you've prearranged it.

Likewise, the energy of others can become your energy. A coworker who becomes angry or impatient with you can evoke similar feelings that you later exhibit towards your partner or children. But you can change this "game of boomerangs" by remembering that you're always in control of your behavior. You have the choice to pick up on the negative energy of others—or reject it.

From now on, become more aware of the energies around you. Make a decision to reject the negative energies. Say, "This is not my energy. I don't want it, so I'll let it go." Exhale the negative energy completely from your mind and body, then say, "I am now at peace."

☆

Sometimes when I feel an intensely negative energy around me, I make this energy my own. Tonight I'll mentally reject the negative energies of others so such things don't "pollute" my peace of mind.

*The evening star
is the most
beautiful of all stars.*
—Sappho

The first star in the evening sky shines with a special brilliance because it's the first. This star can be seen as an important symbol of a change in the day—evening is rapidly turning into night, the fall of the night curtain is signaling the closure to the day, and the day's performance is over, never again to be repeated.

The first of anything can be a symbol of something equally significant. Your first love, your first car, your child's first words or tiny steps, your first day of graduate school, your first job, or your first home are all profound signals of change. Each unique, never-to-be-repeated event becomes the first—and most special—moment. Even though it may be the first in a series of other loves, other cars, another child's growth, other degrees attained, other jobs, or other homes, the first usually has the greatest impact on your life. For the first not only touches you with its newness, but also signals a time of great excitement, adventure, discovery, and change.

Tonight, remember that when you can treat each new day, each new person, each new experience, each new goal you set, and each new change you make as though it were the first, your life can be touched by excitement every day.

☆

I'll make a wish upon the first star I see tonight. I'll wish to be attentive to receiving the special gifts of newness that can greet me each dusk and dawn of my life.

There are two days in the week about which and upon which I never worry. Two carefree days, kept sacredly free from fear and apprehension. One of the days is Yesterday. . . . And the other day I do not worry about is Tomorrow.
—Robert Jones Burdette

Worry is an energy-drainer. It can prevent you from living in the present as your mind wanders to what has already passed—an argument with a loved one or a missed deadline—or what has yet to come—whether you'll be laid off or how much longer your aging car will run repair-free.

How can you live each moment in the present and not somewhere in the past-present or future-present? The most effective cure for worry is to first distinguish between the facts and the fantasies of your worries. You may be worried that your partner will leave you because of your last argument, but you can ask yourself, "Is that a fact?" You may tell yourself that if you had managed your time better you could have met the deadline, but is that a fact? Whether you'll be laid off from work isn't a fact until you actually are, and the reality of your car's ability to run trouble-free can only be determined over time.

Learn to locate the facts in your worries. When you focus on the facts, you can then decide whether or not there's anything you can do about them right now, *based on the facts.* Then you can stop looking back or peering ahead and stay in the present moment—and enjoy it.

☆

Worry depletes my physical and mental energy. Tonight I'll conserve my energy by taking care of my present rather than worrying uselessly about the past or the future.

Some lucky souls sleep like babies, no matter what their age.

—*Judy Foreman*

For over 40 million American men and women, sleep disorders are a chronic misery; for 20 to 30 million, they're an occasional problem. It would be wonderful to think that, over time, such problems might work themselves out. But studies show that the older you get, the harder it becomes to sleep.

The underlying biological cause of increasing poor sleep as you mature in age is believed to be a result of the deterioration of the "clock" in your brain that controls when you sleep and when you wake up. This "aging clock" actually *speeds up* as you get older, pushing your body rhythms so you want to go to sleep earlier in the evening but then wake up much earlier in the morning.

How can you resolve this? Don't nap on and off throughout a day; if you need a nap, take only one that's no more than 45 minutes—preferably before three in the afternoon. Don't go to bed early in the evening because you feel lonely or you're bored. But *do* become more involved and interested in life. Of all the recommendations by sleep researchers, psychologist Peter Hauri says, " . . . the most important one is to have a reason for living. . . . If I can get that person involved in reading to the blind, or going traveling, or learning a new hobby, he or she will sleep better."

☆

Tonight I won't sit at home during the day, waiting for the evening to come, and then lie awake in bed at night waiting for the morning to come. I'll make my life interesting and exciting and get active so I can go to sleep when I'm good and tired.

"The question is," said Alice, "whether you can make words mean so many different things."
—*Lewis Carroll*, Alice Through the Looking-Glass

Read the following words slowly to yourself: *unhappy, gloomy, sullen, weepy, morose, frowning, hopeless, sorrowful, negative, bitter, miserable, despairing, suicidal.* Take a moment to reflect on how speaking and hearing the words makes you feel.

Now read the following list in the same way: *joyful, happy, joking, giggly, silly, delighted, inspired, carefree, sweet, jolly, cheery, pleasant, funny, chuckle, laughter, smiling, rosy, upbeat.* How do these words make you feel?

When a situation in your life causes you concern—the stability of your job, your relationship, or yourself—the way you talk or think about it can often determine how you feel about it. Words can have a major influence upon your feelings.

Author Vernon Howard once described a man who every day wrote down "beautiful words" in a small notebook. Each morning the man read aloud parts of his list. When an opportunity arose during the day, the man would use the words in conversation. To explain his habit, the man told a friend, "Because I looked at the world only through rose-colored words, I became rose-colored myself."

From now on, resolve to use positive, uplifting language in a conversation or journal entry as you describe an upsetting event, unpleasant person, or stressful situation. Use your language to influence your feelings.

☆

If I am what I think, then maybe I need to rethink myself. Starting now, I'll reprogram the language I use so I can become user friendly!

Relationships are only as alive as the people engaging in them.

—Donald B. Ardell

In any intimate relationship, there's often mutual work that needs to be done by both partners in order to identify, confront, and come up with solutions to issues that may affect the relationship.

But if you're unhappy with your relationship a good deal of the time or feel threatened by the interests and achievements of your partner, then you may need to do some work on yourself. The richness of any relationship depends upon two people who live their own lives in healthy and happy ways. So making personal changes in yourself such as dieting to improve your self-image, going to therapy, spending time alone, developing a new interest, or dealing with an addiction can bring about healthy changes in yourself that can positively affect your relationship.

The best relationships are those in which both people are happy with themselves first, and then with each other. So when you can abandon the desire to change your partner and how he or she lives life and focus instead on the changes you can make in yourself and how you live your own life, you may be amazed at how your relationship improves. Feeling good about yourself—alive to your individuality as well as your connection with yourself—can make you feel good with someone else.

Tonight I'll accept others for who they are, without trying to change them. I'll work on me instead so my relationship with myself and my partner can grow for the better.

I am ashamed of these tears. And yet
At the extreme of my misfortune
I am ashamed not to shed them.
                                    —Euripides

Nothing can rattle the nerves more than bottling up your feelings or feeling badly for even having them at all. Trying to keep your emotions under control, hidden from others, or ignoring them can be like trying to keep the lid on a pot of boiling water. Try as you might, the feelings just keep bubbling to the surface and threaten to blow the lid off at any moment.

While internalizing or not expressing feelings can be useful in some situations—for example, appearing calm under fire to show your boss you're a promotable employee or not crying in front of your children after an argument with your spouse—in the long run such things can create undue tension, unreleased stress, and negative feelings towards yourself.

The opposite of keeping feelings in is to let them out—freely, openly, and honestly. After all, they're part of what makes you—and everyone else—human; *everyone* has felt the way you do at one time or another. Why should you deny your feelings? Why should you feel badly about expressing them? Learn to be grateful for your feelings—not ashamed of them.

☆

Sometimes I'd rather not feel anything at all. But as long as I have a heart, I'm going to have feelings. I'll start to let my feelings out so I can feel more like a human being—and not a machine.

When God is doing something wonderful He begins with a difficulty. But when He is going to do something very wonderful He begins with an impossibility.

—*Anonymous*

How many times have you been discouraged at the immensity of a project or goal that faced you? Maybe it was the desire to lose several pounds or quit smoking. Perhaps it was doing something you felt was far beyond your capabilities. Maybe it was taking a risk that tapped into one of your biggest fears. Or perhaps it was doing something you've dreamed of doing, but always put off.

Feeling overwhelmed at the start of anything out of the ordinary or right before you undertake an incredible challenge is a common occurrence. Your insides may be screaming at you to walk away and just forget what you're about to do while outside you're responding by clenching your jaw, tightening your fists, sweating, and experiencing great anxiety.

That's when you need to tell yourself, "Maybe I'm experiencing such a strong response to what I'm about to do because I don't know how I'll handle *succeeding* at it." You may be facing one of the greatest adventures of your life, getting ready to make your wildest dream come true, or beginning the process of turning your life around.

So from now on tell yourself, "Nothing is impossible." Instead of being overwhelmed by what's facing you, break it down into manageable steps. Tackle them one at a time— and you'll make possible the impossible!

☆

With faith, persistence, and a refusal to use the label "impossible," I can do whatever I set my mind to do. I'll start to be a schemer as well as a dreamer!

A soft answer turneth away wrath but grievous words stir up anger.

—Proverbs

The guests on a popular talk show were twins who had cut off contact from one another. One guest tearfully related how her brother hadn't talked to her for two years, even though they lived two miles from each other and often passed on the street. When they were reunited on the show, the man told his sister why he hadn't talked to her for so long. "Because I was mad at you," he said. "I wanted you to apologize to me and you didn't. So I knew I couldn't talk to you without blowing up."

Staying angry at family members, while it may not end the relationships, can severely damage your ability to connect with them. A disinherited son is still your child, but he may never come back through your door and give you a hug. An abusive parent is still your parent, even though you may not be able to let go of your anger over past hurt.

While you can't change the actions or behaviors of others that may have caused your anger, what you can do is strive to reconcile the past with acceptance and forgiveness in the present. One way to do so is to ask, "What can I do to let go of my anger?" It may be helpful to write a letter you don't mail, in which you vent your feelings, or to identify some of the good qualities of the person you're mad at. Such things can help you release your anger so you can speak to this person again with a soft voice.

☆

I'll believe in what Indira Ghandi once said—"You cannot shake hands with a clenched fist." I'll strive to extend my hand to another family member in reconciliation so we can once again communicate.

Everything's got a moral, if you can only find it.
—Lewis Carroll

President Eisenhower once told a story to the National Press Club about a boyhood experience while growing up on a Kansas farm. An old farmer had a cow his family wanted to buy. So young Dwight and his father went to the farmer and asked about the cow's pedigree. The old farmer didn't know what pedigree meant. So Dwight's father asked about the cow's butterfat production. The farmer told them he had no idea. Dwight's father asked the farmer if he knew how many pounds of milk the cow produced each year. The farmer once again shook his head. Exasperated, Dwight's father took his son's hand and began to walk away from the farmer. It was then that the farmer said, "I don't know the answers to all your questions. But I do know that she's an honest old cow and she'll give you all the milk she has!" Without hesitation, Dwight's father purchased the cow.

How proud are you tonight of the morals you lived by this day? Were you honest? Forthright? Forgiving? Patient? Kind? Ready to offer assistance? The morals that guide the way you treat yourself and others can fill your life with positive energy or reflect distrust, dishonesty, impatience, and selfishness.

Tonight, know that inner peace comes from living life in ways that show to yourself and others your very best. Like the old farmer's cow, be proud to display your morals. Be honest, and give everything you have!

☆

Each evening I'll conduct a private review of my day so I can see the standard of morals I lived up to. Then I'll be an honest critic who can provide me with moral guidelines to live by tomorrow.

Hating people is like burning down your house to get rid of a rat.

—*Harry Emerson Fosdick*

Hatred is an all-too-common emotion. Oftentimes you may feel it towards people you barely know: the stranger who cuts you off in traffic, the person in front of you at the grocery checkout who unloads a cart filled with more than the "express line" limit, the child who treats your own child badly, the cold-blooded killer, or a corporate bigwig who initiated cutbacks and layoffs in your company.

Yet do you realize that when you hate someone, you're the one who actually suffers? The person you hate is often totally unaware of your feelings and is likely to be unaffected by the negative energy you're sending. Rather, you destroy your emotional serenity by obsessing over this person as you continually refuel the fires of your intense feelings; you endanger your physical health by skipping meals because you're too tense to eat, by smoking or drinking more, or by losing sleep because of your anger; you disrupt your spiritual connection by harboring resentments and allowing your anger to grow, by fantasizing revengeful actions or wishing ill will towards the person, or refusing to let go and forgive.

Tonight, before you let hatred consume you, remember that it's a chain-reaction feeling. All it takes to stop it is to remove one link in the chain. When you hate, you suffer; when you release hate, you prosper.

☆

Hatred not only consumes me, but also interferes with my relationship with my Higher Power. From now on I'll realize the destructive potential of hatred and begin to deal with the person and situation that caused my hatred more rationally and logically.

I thought I was frightened the other day, but today when I—when I saw the light beginning to fail and night coming nearer and nearer, I felt my fingertips getting cold and I knew for the first time what real terror was.
  —Rosalind Russell *warning Dame May Whitty in* Night Must Fall

Sometimes when the day is over, your terror may grow and you may feel that you can't distinguish between what's real and what's unreal. Your imagination may run wild. You may begin to suspect that anything can happen. You don't feel safe. You don't feel certain. You don't trust that all is well.

At times like this you may see your life as a dance between trust and fear. In the daylight, when your trust level is high, you may feel more capable of handling any minor or major difficulties that come your way. But at night, when you feel afraid and unsure, you may want to "flee" from dealing with even the most insignificant inconveniences. "Wake me when it's daylight," may be your way of coping with nighttime anxiety.

While it would be wonderful if everything you approached could be based on the trust that you may feel in the light of day, the truth is that *everyone* experiences some level of edginess from time to time at night. Even the most confident people can have lingering doubts and insecurity in darkness.

Tonight, deal with your nighttime edginess by saying, "I trust that I can get through my fears. I will simply do the best that I can and trust that this is all right."

☆

Tonight I'll recognize that the more trust I have in the supportive people and familiar surroundings in my life, the less fear I'll feel at night.

Look well into thyself; there is a source of strength which will always spring up if thou wilt always look there.

—Marcus Aurelius

Where does your sense of security and emotional well-being come from? Your profession or the company you work for? Your parents? Your children? Your partner? Your friends? A twelve-step support group? Your connection with a Higher Power? Your service to your community?

While each of these areas can provide you with some degree of security, approval, and prestige, depending on others to *fulfill* your inner needs is unhealthy. Emotional dependency, like any other addiction, requires that you lose yourself so something or someone else can reclaim you. When this happens, instead of being your own person, you become the creation of someone else—in their own image. By thinking, feeling, dressing, walking, and talking as others want you to, you become a person behind a mask rather than your own person.

Tonight, accept that by decreasing your dependence on others and increasing your dependence upon yourself, you gain independence. If you're always looking at yourself through the eyes of others, then you'll only see what they want you to see. But by looking at yourself through your own eyes, you'll see who you really are. Look *at* yourself and *to* yourself for security, approval, and prestige. Then you can become a more healthy and whole person.

☆

Most of my life I may have listened to what others told me, and so I thought "the problem" was me. But tonight I realize that the problem isn't me, but that I can't see me.

The beginning of love is to let those we love be perfectly themselves, and not to twist them to fit our own image. Otherwise we love only the reflection of ourselves we find in them.

—*Thomas Merton*

How would you write "I love you" to someone you love in twenty-five words or less? There's just one catch to this challenge. You can't use the words, "I love you."

Love is not always an easy emotion to feel. It may be easier to say those three words than to try to put into words why you feel them. Sometimes it can be difficult to look at the qualities, gifts, and uniqueness of someone you love. You may wind up making comparisons—"He's more successful than I am" or "She's much better with the kids." You may, in making your comparisons, be confronted by your weaknesses and question why someone would even love you. You may be a negative thinker who has a hard time focusing on the good qualities you have and instead can only find the things you don't like—"I love you, but not when you don't listen to me" or "I love you, but I wish you'd learn to dress differently." You may be a rational person who has a tendency to think about your emotions rather than feel them.

But love shouldn't be based on a "me-you" comparison or a "things-that-displease-me-and-things-that-please-me" checklist. Love is simply seeing and accepting someone for who he or she is.

☆

I can compose an "I love you" essay to my partner. In my essay, I'll focus on the good qualities in this person and think about how nice our love feels.

I have always known that at last I would take this road, but yesterday I did not know it would be today.
—*Narihira*

As much as you might like to know what's going to happen to you from day to day, week to week, month to month, or even year to year, sometimes it's quite impossible to plan ahead. The one conclusion you may reach in trying to predict what might happen to you at the next turn in the road is that you're not psychic. Rarely have your predictions come true or happened in the way you've wanted them to; rather, the events have unfolded in the way they were intended. Because of this, you may hesitate to make a change, try something new, or take steps towards a dream you've always had. You may spend more of your time wondering, "What if . . . ?" instead of "Why not?"

But it has been said that "Every tomorrow has two handles. We can take hold of it with the handle of anxiety or the handle of faith." Every day, don't put off doing something or taking a different turn in the road because you're unsure of the outcome. Hug the person you've been meaning to hug. Pursue a sport you've always wanted to try. Try out a new recipe. Send for graduate school catalogs. Apply for a new job or promotion. Watch a video of the movie that has always moved you. Then go to bed content and fulfilled that you've achieved what you set out to do. Practice this on a daily basis, and you'll never have any regrets about your life.

☆

Each day I'll let my travels on the road of life lead me to be more spontaneous and take more risks. I'll worry and obsess less about outcomes as I ask, "Why not give it a try?"

Genuine beginnings begin with us, even when they are brought to our attention by external opportunities.
—William Bridges

Consider this following list of difficulties you may encounter in your life: You've lost your job. You've been in a car accident. Your marriage has ended. You've just retired. You're having financial troubles. Do you consider such things tragedies or opportunities?

Now consider this list: You've been offered a job in a new business. Your insurance company and parents have provided you with enough money to buy your first luxury car. Your best friend has introduced you to someone with whom you have a lot in common. You and your partner have decided to sell the house, buy a mobile home, and drive around the country for a few years. Do you consider such things merely strokes of good luck or opportunities?

Frederick Phillips says, "It is often hard to distinguish between the hard knocks in life and those of opportunity." Yet, if you think about it, some of the most beneficial changes you have made in yourself and your life may have been the result of painful circumstances as well as golden opportunities.

What things were handed to you today that you can see as blessings? Whether they were enjoyable or not, each can be perceived as "nudges" that can push you and encourage you to use them as positive tools for self-transformation.

☆

Sometimes it may be hard for me to look a gift horse in the mouth as well as to be kicked from behind by the same horse. But each event can point to change—and out of change can come opportunity.

You just have to learn not to care about the dust-mice under the beds.

—Margaret Mead

A joke about two cockroaches who meet for dinner one night goes like this. As they were munching on their meal, one said to the other, "You wouldn't believe where I tried to eat last night. The house was spotless. Whoever lived there had to be a cleanaholic. Everything was shiny. Everything was sparkling. There wasn't even a crumb on the floor."

At that moment the other cockroach stopped eating and looked up at the other with annoyance. "Say, do you have to talk like that while I'm eating?"

This joke about cockroaches can also apply to you if you're someone who can't go to bed at night until your house is impeccably spotless. If you're frequently up late at night doing laundry, mopping floors, ironing, or straightening cabinets, drawers, and closets, then you may find little in your life to enjoy. In your struggle to have everything "just so," you may wind up exhausted.

Tonight, learn from the Japanese. They believe that perfect order destroys the imagination and individual experience. When planning their gardens, they place the plants asymmetrically so the uneven areas stimulate viewers to complete the picture in their own minds.

☆

Tonight I'll remind myself that a little clutter, a little disorganization, and a little dust never killed anyone. I don't have to dress impeccably, have a spotless house, or look like a fashion model in order to enjoy life.

*It is my retreat and resting place from the wars. I try
to keep this corner as a haven against the tempest outside, as I do another corner in my soul.*
　　　　　　　　　　—Michel Eyquem de Montaigne

Just as you provide for others, do for others, please others,
and give to others each day, so too must you take self-
focused actions to provide, do, please, and give to yourself.
One area of self-focus in which you need to take action involves your spiritual health and well-being. You owe yourself space for privacy of thought, prayer, and meditation. In
order to develop your inner resources and strengthen your
relationship with your Higher Power, you need to set aside
some peaceful time in a quiet space that's away from outside
pressures.

You don't need to go to church every Sunday to find this
time and space. As Laurence J. Peter says, "Going to church
doesn't make you a Christian any more than going to a
garage makes you a car." So many people seek a spiritual
connection with nature because they feel a certain sense of
faith and trust in it.

From now on, each evening, appreciate nature and connect with it in some way. Take a walk, breathe in the chill
October night air, and survey the starry heavens above you.
In this quiet space you can forget your problems and difficulties for a short time, open your mind and heart to new
experiences, and take in the wonder of something greater
than you.

☆

*At night I'll lose myself in the natural beauty around me. With
an appreciation of nature I'll trust that there isn't a problem that
can't be solved or a weary body that can't be spiritually renewed.*

Peace is when time doesn't matter when it passes by.
—Maria Schell

Do you see time as an enemy—a heartless bandit that steals your valuable jewels of seconds, minutes, and hours and hides them so well that you can never retrieve them? "Where did the time go?" you may frantically question. "I can't believe the day's nearly over!"

"Time bandits" have existed since the beginning of life. But their thefts have only recently become more evident because the pace of living has increased, thereby making time that much more precious. But trying to hold onto time, wishing there were more hours in a day, pushing yourself to do everything just a bit faster, or purchasing gadgets designed to save time can never get you more time. Time can't be protected, set aside for later, watched over, or hoarded.

But you can outwit the time bandits. Don't let your life be run by time. From now on, stop wearing a watch, glancing at the clock every five minutes, or agonizing over the passage of time. Focus on what it is that you need or want to do, then tell yourself, "I'll get it done when I can—and not one minute sooner!"

Time's going to move on; there's nothing you can do about that. When you no longer feel imprisoned by time, you can learn to use it to your advantage. You can feel free to enjoy it as much as you can—or to simply disregard it.

☆

I'll stop focusing on the clock and turn my attention to the pleasurable activities that lie before me. How well I enjoy getting them done matters much more than when I get them done.

NOVEMBER 1

Make yourself necessary to someone.
　　　　　　　　　　　—*Ralph Waldo Emerson*

Creation can be seen as interdependent. That means that you may often find yourself in the position—not always by chance and sometimes by design—to involve yourself in many different ways in the world around you. Within the context of your home, your job, your partner, your family, your friends, and others with whom you have contact, there are hundreds of experiences that can create opportunities for you to reach out to others—to make yourself necessary to them.

How can you be necessary? By contributing your best efforts and talents to the situations that involve you. By creating a balance of giving and receiving. By providing comfort and support to others who share your journey. By valuing yourself and assigning a similar value to others. By offering what you've learned from the lessons of life as well as by paying attention to the lessons you're being given in return.

Because every person is necessary to the completion of the whole portrait of your existence, the gift of life obligates you to extend yourself to others. Each day, make yourself necessary to others. Be there for them and be grateful for their existence in your life. For, as François Mauriac says, "No love, no friendship can cross the path of our destiny without leaving some mark on it forever."

From now on I won't doubt my value nor the value of others in my life. Each of us is necessary to the other one. We are all here in each other's lives by design.

If you want to kill time, why not try working it to death.

—*O. A. Battista*

Do you realize that "this very instant" is all the time you really have? Although you may plan for the near or distant future, look forward to tomorrow morning, start to get ready for your next task tonight, or invoke memories of the past, right now is all you have. So to learn how to be in the now and act in the moment at hand is critical; after all, *you haven't any other time.* The only time that's truly "your time" is what exists right now. So what do you want to do with this time?

Because each moment is yours, to make as beautiful or as painful as you choose, you can either lose touch with your present time and make its passage dull, humdrum, or filled with tension, or you can truly be in the moment and make each second of it fun, dazzling, fabulous, or totally unpredictable.

If you choose to use your nighttimes to obsess or worry, to push yourself beyond your limits, to lose touch with the things that are important to you, or to strive to hurry the passage of time, then you're not enjoying time—you're killing it. But if you can believe in the words of Louise Bogan, that "Perhaps this very instant is your time . . . your own, your peculiar, your promised and presaged moment, out of all moments forever," then this time will become precious.

☆

Am I using the time I've been given constructively or destructively? I'll become more conscious of the way I use my present moments so I can create a more positive passage of time.

What makes people despair is that they try to find a universal meaning to the whole of life . . .
—Anais Nin

The only universal meaning to life that holds true for everyone is that no one's ever going to get out of it alive! So rather than waste your time and energy trying to understand why you're here, where you're going, or why you have to face the trials you do, perhaps the best approach to life is to simply enjoy it for as long as you can. Or, as Dr. Robert William Smith advises, ". . . learn to spend your days in the proper way."

Some view "the proper way" as a combination of discipline and adventure—doing things you have to do to fulfill your responsibilities, but then doing other things for stimulation and inspiration. Would you enjoy life more if you added a meaningful challenge that would bring adventure to it? Then sign up for snowboarding instruction or go winter camping. Would you enjoy life more if you were more playful? Then build a snowfort during the next snowstorm or spend an evening bowling. Would your life be more enjoyable if you had more opportunities to get in touch with yourself? Then look at your calendar and plan to spend a weekend at home alone or make reservations at another location. Would you enjoy spending more time with friends? Then plan a dinner party or make time to be with your friends. The enjoyment of life can involve many different things. What you do is up to you.

☆

I'll make up my mind to stop trying to figure out the "whys" of my existence or life's circumstances. Instead, I'll view each day as a challenge and an adventure.

*Oh, I ain't worried, Miss. Gave myself up for dead
back where we started.*
> —*Humphrey Bogart, being chipper about
> the dangers ahead for him and
> Katherine Hepburn in* The African Queen

Once there was a king of a magnificent kingdom. One day,
as he was surveying his domain with his nobles, he stopped
at a scenic spot and cried out, "To think that one day I must
die and leave all this behind! Wouldn't it be wonderful if we
could live forever? Then we would always be able to enjoy
what we have."

All the nobles except one nodded their heads in agree-
ment. "Not me, sire," the one noble said. "I wouldn't want
life to be everlasting. And neither would you!"

The nobles gasped at the audacity of the direct contradic-
tion to the king's wishes. The king replied in an icy tone, "Do
tell, noble, why you know this would be so."

"Well, sire," the noble began, "if life were everlasting then
the first king would still be among us—the one who was so
horrible—as would all of his terrible nobles. And I would still
be a rice planter and you, sire, would be a clerk."

The king thought a moment about the noble's words, then
smiled. "I am foolish to even think about living forever," he
said. "For you have shown me, wise noble, that although the
good can't last forever, neither will the bad. For that lesson,
I am forever in your debt."

☆

*I may not want all the difficulties in my life that make me feel
sometimes as if I'm hanging onto life by a thread. But even in
my darkest times, I can look around me and find something that
can make me feel better.*

A man that studieth revenge keeps his own wounds green.

— *Francis Bacon*

Past incidents that still arouse your anger can prevent you from living a healthy and happy life today. Hurt experienced in a former marriage or relationship can prevent you from having a warm and loving relationship today. Or anger at an alcoholic parent may prohibit making a connection with that parent today, even if the parent has stopped drinking.

How can you learn to let go of deep-rooted anger from the past so you can get on with living in the present? First recognize that your anger is often a response to feelings you didn't express at the time you experienced them in your childhood, in a former intimate relationship, or during an incident that happened years ago. Because you didn't express them, they remained "alive" and grew into the anger you feel tonight.

Then let go of your anger by completing the following sentence: "I felt anger when _____, and I'm still angry about it." As you bring up the past memory and its feelings, you may feel hurt, anxious, fearful, or even sad. Such responses are normal and, like the past anger, should be acknowledged rather than suppressed. By recognizing past hurtful feelings, you can begin to put your anger behind you rather than carry it with you in the present.

My hope for a good life is proportionate to my forgiving heart. Tonight I'll let forgiveness heal my soul so I can let go of someone or something that hurt me in the past.

God has given each one of us approximately 25,000 to 26,000 days on this earth. I truly believe He (or She) has something very specific in mind; 8,300 days to sleep, 8,300 to work, and 8,300 to give, live, play, pray and love one another.

—Quincy Jones

Musician Quincy Jones survived a brain aneurysm and two brain operations in 1974. Since that time the highly successful and driven record producer, composer, and musician has renewed his belief in the importance of having a balance in his life. No matter how busy his schedule, he sets aside time for enjoying life to the fullest and for listening to the voice that comes from "divine guidance."

Many people believe that peace of mind comes from material success or financial security. So they devote the majority of their days and nights on earth to working hard to achieve such things. But true peace of mind comes not from what you can *get* from your efforts, but from what you can *give* to others, from how well you can live each day, from how often you allow yourself to play, from your ability to reach out to a Higher Power in prayer, and from your desire to love others.

To find this true peace of mind resolve to give, live, play, pray, and love another every day. Do something kind for your partner. Enjoy the beauty of the autumn. Play a game with your kids. Pray for riches in your life that money can't buy. And express your love to a family member.

☆

Peace of mind, like the restless need to always be achieving and doing, is a habit. I can either nurture it or destroy it through my actions.

And I watch and I listen and I think about what I have seen and heard. . . . Yes, that is what I do. The really frightening thing in life, I think, lies in our capacity for inattentiveness to it.

—Edith Konecky

How aware are you of the world around you? How often do you take time to smell the outside air on a fall night, notice the shadows the branches of the trees make in the moonlight, distinguish the sounds of morning songbirds from evening songbirds, taste a snowflake, or look up at the sky— no matter what the weather or what time of day or night?

Too often people think their reason for being here is to stay active until they can't be active anymore. They become so caught up in activity that they equate rushing here and there with being alive. Yet there's a difference between being alive and living. Being alive means you're breathing and functional. But living means you're part of *everything* that's breathing and functional.

Unless you take the time to pay attention to what's around you, you'll never have a sense of connection to the world and the people in it. You won't be able to notice the vastness, beauty, and marvels of nature, nor the fascinating differences between people. Living means seeing everything and ignoring nothing. So from now on open your senses—sight, sound, taste, touch, and smell—to the world around you.

☆

What haven't I noticed before? Tonight I'll take a few minutes before I go to sleep to pay attention to the world around me so I can experience something in a way I haven't.

An optimist expects his dreams to come true; a pessimist expects his nightmares to.

—Laurence J. Peter

It has been estimated that today *ten times* as many people suffer from severe depression as fifty years ago. But is that such a surprising statistic? With businesses failing, inflation rising, unemployment lines growing, unrest at home and abroad, and the number of violent crimes soaring, it's often hard to find positive people and uplifting topics of conversation. Pessimism is all around you, while optimism is suspect.

Think about conversations you have with people. Do you prefer to talk about the problems and hassles in your life, or do you focus on personal achievements and light-hearted, entertaining anecdotes? Do you find yourself drawn to listen to those who discuss tragic topics and personal crises, or do you prefer to listen to those who make you laugh or who have something interesting and exciting to share?

The other side of nightmares are dreams; the other side of pessimism is optimism. Optimism, although not "in vogue," has been known to fight depression, assist personal achievement, ease the symptoms of stress, and result in better physical, emotional, and spiritual health. Tonight you have a choice. Can you stop looking for the dark side of life? Can you switch to a more positive outlook? *Will you be a pessimist or an optimist?*

☆

When I'm a pessimist, I'm living a life of fear. But when I'm an optimist, I may be pleasantly surprised at the more positive outcomes there are to the things I desire.

A man sentenced to death obtained a reprieve by assuring the king he would teach his majesty's horse to fly within the year. . . . "Within a year," the man explained, "the king may die, or I may die, or the horse may die. Furthermore, in a year, who knows? Maybe the horse will learn to fly."

—Leonard Lyons

Never giving up, despite the odds or obstacles, is not only a test of belief in yourself and what you can do, but it's also a symbol of how you approach life. When confronted by impending defeat, failure, disappointment, frustration, or rejection, it may be far easier to simply give up. But such action can shape the attitude you then bring into every situation of your life. And that attitude can spell the difference between long-term success and satisfaction or a series of defeats.

When Thomas Edison's manufacturing facilities were heavily damaged by fire in 1914, Edison lost nearly one million dollars worth of equipment and all the records he had kept. But the next morning, as the inventor surveyed the charred embers, he said: "There is value in disaster. All our mistakes are burned up. Now we can start anew."

Imagine what your world would be like today if Edison hadn't continued his work after the fire. His positive approach to personal disaster reflected a "can-do" philosophy rather than a "can't-do" one. From now on, strive to foster the same philosophy by eliminating "I can't" from your vocabulary and saying instead, "I'll try."

☆

A positive, tough-minded approach can turn certain failure into assured success. Tonight I'll keep in mind that failure or success rests in my attitude.

Not in a perturbed mind does wisdom spring.
—*Wisdom of Kapila*

Although problems constitute a normal part of life, it's possible to solve most problems rather than let them upset you. The key to doing so lies in the way you approach any difficult or perplexing situation. If you believe a problem will get the better of you, it will. But if you believe there's a solution to every problem, then you'll be able to find it.

To become an effective problem solver, first don't respond to your problem right away. Ineffective problem solvers tend to be impulsive, impatient, and quick to give up if a solution isn't immediately apparent. Then they become angry when their problem isn't solved after their first ineffectual try. So follow the words of advice spoken by Joseph Cotton in the film *Gaslight*: "In the morning when the sun rises, sometimes it's hard to believe there ever was a night. You'll find that, too."

Then tomorrow follow the Number One rule for effective problem-solving: A good problem solver is able to first identify what the *real* problem is. Perhaps it's not related to a present situation—such as not being able to sleep, but something else, like yesterday's confrontation with your boss.

Once you identify the real problem, think of as many ideas as you can to solve it. The greater the number of solutions, the greater the likelihood of your being able to find the best solution.

☆

The real problem isn't what's done or not done, how it happened, or why it happened. The real problem is how I respond. From now on I'll be a positive, rather than a frustrated, problem solver.

Shoot for the moon. If you miss it, you'll still land among the stars.

—*Les Brown*

Are you willing to take chances, or does the thought of taking a risk scare you?

The experimental pilots who were the inspiration for the book *The Right Stuff* were well-known for their lack of fear and their desire to challenge both the limits of man and the boundaries of space. They were unafraid to fly higher, to travel faster, and to push themselves and their jets to the edge.

Within you is that same "edge," which defines the boundary of your "comfort zone." When you do things that are comfortable and familiar to you, you're operating *within* your comfort zone. But when you seek to transcend past performances, explore new capabilities, take chances, and risk failure, then you're operating close to the edge of your comfort zone.

How can you expand the edges of your comfort zone so you can take greater risks and try more new things? Begin by taking small risks and achieving them first before you try to tackle bigger risks. Rather than quit your job to start your own business, for example, talk to other small business owners about their own experiences. Preparing yourself to take a risk, rather than taking it right away, can help build confidence so you can conquer your fears.

☆

It has been said that "All life is an experiment." I won't be too timid or too frightened to take a risk. I'll reach for the stars to see what I can achieve.

Fasten your seatbelts. It's going to be a bumpy night.
—Bette Davis bracing for a rocky
party in All About Eve

In less than two weeks, the holiday season will kickoff with the annual Thanksgiving dinner gathering and then will progress rapidly towards the Christmas and Hanukkah celebrations. Does this thought make you happy or tense?

The reason many people become stressed out around the holidays is they feel they're not in control of the family situation. Your out-of-control feeling may come from a dysfunctional childhood, an alcoholic parent, fault-finding relatives, or siblings that act like oil and water. How can you stop holiday family gatherings from driving you crazy?

First, remember that you're an adult. Just because you're getting together with your family doesn't mean you have to think, act, or be your parents' child all over again. You decide when, where, and how you want to get together with your relatives. You're in control.

Second, let the past go. Don't dwell on old grudges, past hurt and pain, or unresolved confrontations or arguments. Make sure that the holiday you're getting together to celebrate is this year's—not last year's, the one a few years ago, or the one over a decade in the past.

Finally, remember that you can limit the time you're going to spend with family members. Tell yourself you'll spend only as much time as you can handle—and then leave.

☆

Tonight I'll use positive tools to handle my tension over the up-coming holidays. Rather than focus on anticipated strife with family members, I'll come up with ways to avoid the strife so I can have a happy holiday.

In three words, I can sum up everything I've learned about life: It goes on.

—Robert Frost

Have you ever dug into an ant's nest? Their first reaction to your unintended intrusion is to do everything possible to save their lives, their nest, and its contents. So the ants immediately *act*. They scurry around, moving the larvae into a safer underground chamber. Exposed contents of the nest are relocated to unseen passages. The hill of grains of dirt is rebuilt. In a matter of minutes, the ants are again safely underground and ready to resume the normal flow of their daily routines.

How do you react when some catastrophe or unplanned event occurs? Do you want to crawl under a rock and escape having to deal with change, or are you as resilent as the ants—ready to take positive action? Instead of moaning over postponed plans or the loss of something in your life, you can try to be like the ants and learn how to best work *with* the circumstances that come your way.

Tonight, remember that life doesn't stop, try to make everything better for you, or give you time to simply lick your wounds. Hours pass, you grow older, and nature continues. Every event is part of life's cycle. So you need to meet each event head-on, adjust to its ebb and flow, and keep on keeping on.

☆

Tonight I'll look at an unplanned event in my life as simply part of life's cycle. Then I'll trust that life will go on.

Great trouble comes
From not knowing what is enough.
Great conflict arises from wanting too much.
When we know when enough is enough,
There will always be enough.

—Tao

A young college graduate recently landed a new job in a city far from her hometown. She rented a small studio apartment, bought a few affordable pieces of furniture, and started her job.

After a few weeks she called her father, a successful businessman, and asked, "How does it feel, Dad, to have everything you've ever wanted? You can buy anything. You have a beautiful house with lovely furniture, a new car, and you take lots of trips. It'll be years before I can have those things. You must feel great!

The father was silent for a moment. Then he replied, "You know, some of the best memories I have are from the days when I lived in a small apartment like yours. I furnished it with orange crates scavenged from the trash. I was pretty happy back then. I have a lot today, but, well, the days of the orange crates were fun, too."

From now on, rather than wish you had it all, be realistic about what you can reasonably have. It's far better to accept that while you may lack in some areas, you may have enough—or even be rich—in others.

☆

It's a pervasive cultural misconception that teaches I can have it all—money, success, a happy family, a beautiful home, grand vacations, and so on—and at the same time. I'll be content that what I have right now is enough.

*I have had responsibilities and work, dangers and
pleasures, good friends, and a world without walls to
live in. . . . I sit there in the firelight and see them all.*
—Beryl Markham

Peter Lynch, the investment superstar who built the Fidelity Magellan mutual fund into a thirteen million dollar behemoth, stunned Wall Street when he decided to give up his prestigious position and hefty salary. Even though he had everything he had always wanted, he realized he wasn't happy. So he went from picking stock to packing lunches for his daughters because "I don't know anyone who wished on his deathbed that he had spent more time at the office."

Many people believe happiness is measured in material terms—a house, money, lots of clothes. Others insist it's found in enjoyable moments—a sunset, dinner with friends, a walk in the woods. Still others equate happiness with personal victory—achieving something they've worked hard to attain such as a promotion, a degree, or a home.

Imagine sitting in the warm glow of a crackling fire. As you peer into the flames, recall moments in your life that brought you happiness. What do you see? A personal victory? Great friends? A wonderful relationship with a parent? A risk you took? A passionate romance? A trip to a country you'd always dreamed of visiting?

Take a moment to reflect on the things in your life that have brought you great pleasure. Remember them as keys to your happiness tonight.

*Have my yesterdays been good? Have I found happiness in my
life? Tonight will be a time for reflection on the joys and pleasures I've been so fortunate to experience.*

Better to ask twice than to lose your way once.
—*Danish proverb*

How many people do you communicate with in an average day? Probably dozens—and hundreds in a week and thousands in a year. But are you communicating effectively? Effective communication happens when you not only speak and impart information or share how you feel, but also when you hear what others are imparting and sharing. If you find yourself not catching every word of what's being said to you—and then not bothering to ask for anything to be repeated—then you're only half-listening. You need to become a better listener.

Walter Lippmann says, "While the right to talk may be the beginning of freedom, the necessity of listening is what makes that right important." Active listening involves focusing on *everything* a person is saying without jumping in with reactions, retorts, defenses, justifications, or distracted "uh-huhs." It means allowing others to express everything they need to say without concentrating on other people, places, or things.

How can you become an active listener? Make sure you have the time to really listen. If you only have a few minutes before your favorite television show begins, make sure this is known. Set aside a time in which you won't be distracted, then *listen*. Active listening means making the time and exerting the energy to hear wholly, not partially, what others have to say.

☆

From now on I'll put aside my own problems or concerns, unfinished business, or the desire to second guess; I'll just listen to what's being said to me. Then I won't miss words that are spoken or have to ask for anything to be repeated.

. . . for in every adult there lurks a child—an eternal child, something that is always becoming, is never completed, calls for unceasing care, attention, and education. That is the part of the human personality that wants to develop and become whole.

—Carl Jung

When you were growing up, did you imagine living a way of life different from that of your parents? Are you struggling today to make this happen in your own life—as a needy, unhappy child in the body of an adult?

The more severe the influences are from your past, the more determined you may be today to strive to achieve a different life—one in which your childhood needs are met in a way they weren't in the past. Rising above poverty, limited education, dysfunctional behaviors, language barriers, prejudice, divorce, or death can make you hungry for a life that's free from all those things. Even if you were raised in a home of wealth, unlimited educational opportunities, and healthy parents, you may still feel the need to live life different from theirs.

While the phrase, "Never forget where you came from" is an apt thought to keep in mind from time to time, it doesn't have to be the pervading influence that makes you always honor your inner child first and yourself last. While you can't make up for your childhood years tonight, you can start now to simply be kind, protective, patient, and gentle to both the child and the adult in yourself.

☆

My neglected inner self doesn't have to behave like a demanding, spoiled child. Tonight I can simply start paying attention to it by being a wise and loving parent to the child who lives in me.

Within you there is a stillness and sanctuary to which you can retreat at anytime and be yourself.
—Hermann Hesse

Have you ever seen the ocean in a storm? The water is in constant, frightening motion, capable of sinking boats, eroding shorelines, and sweeping away entire homes. Yet below the churning surface is a stillness that enables the tiniest fish to dart gently to and fro.

Within you is a similar "center"—a part of you that's capable of being calm and still in the most nerve-racking and restless moments. Being centered is like being a tree in a storm: while wind, rain, and lightning may affect you on the outside, your roots hold you fast and firm in the ground.

How long has it been since you felt the sensation of having your feet "planted" firmly on the ground? Aikido masters who teach their students to maintain their centers claim it can generate incredible personal force that enables one to withstand the power of many. To gain your center at any time, stand with your feet about a foot apart. Keep your spine straight. Bend your knees slightly. Hold your hands in front of you with your elbows bent, slightly above waist level. Now inhale deeply. Imagine the energy rising up through your feet. Then exhale, feeling the energy flow out through your hands. Repeat three times, continuing to center and strengthen yourself.

☆

Whenever I feel stress or the stress of others moving me away from my center, I'll do my standing centering meditation. I'll become as firmly rooted as a tree as I stand my ground.

*If time be of all things most precious, wasting time
must be the greatest prodigality, since lost time is never
found again.*

—Benjamin Franklin

Do you feel as if you waste a great deal of time each
evening—time that takes you away from doing responsible
as well as recreational activities?

Starting tonight, you can think about making more time.
You can assess how much time each night you spend watching the biggest time-killer of all—television. Think about cutting out a half hour to hour of television-watching each night
or use a videocassette recorder to record your favorite shows.
Then watch them at another time, fast-forwarding through
commercials.

Second, you can throw away all the mail you possibly can
when you get home by simply scanning it and then tossing
it. Third, you can incorporate "planning" time with time you
spend doing other things. For example, plan a dinner party
while you vacuum or write down Christmas gift ideas for
friends and family members while you're waiting for dinner
to cook.

Finally, block off the "escape routes" that lead you to waste
time: daydreaming, puttering aimlessly around the house, so-
cializing on the telephone, doing tiny and unimportant tasks
rather than big and important ones, or running out for a dessert treat rather than face the things you need to do. Then
make the most of the time you have left!

☆

*From now on I'll make up my mind to just get things done. I'll
stop wasting my time doing mindless or procrastinating activities.*

Like the body that is made up of different limbs and organs, all mortal creatures exist depending on one another.

—*Hindu proverb*

How often do you use the phrase, "I'll take care of it"? You may believe that you—and only you—are the one who should handle your problems and satisfy your own needs.

Certainly there are some things that only you can do for yourself. For example, only you can eat right, exercise, get plenty of rest, and connect with a Higher Power. Yet there are other things that you may not always be able to take care of alone: working through a crisis, solving business or personal problems, comforting yourself, developing intimacy with others, or feeling loved and cared for. These are things that need to come from others.

Imagine how dependent you would be if you lost your eyesight, hearing, or mobility. But just because you don't have a physical handicap doesn't mean you can't ask for help.

Have you ever stopped to consider the people in your life you can turn to for friendship, problem solving, fun and relaxation, or advice? Make a mental list of such people and identify the value they bring to your life. Whether one person provides you with many things or many people perform several functions, the support of others is an important factor in surviving everyday stress and strain.

From now on, instead of saying, "I'll take care of it," I'll ask someone, "Will you help me?"

We are only as sick as the secrets we keep.
—Anonymous

Not letting others know who you really are—your thoughts, your feelings, your dreams, your goals, your background, and your wants and needs—is like spending hours preparing a fancy new dish and then not being able to taste it. While finding the recipe, shopping for the ingredients, and preparing the dish might be enjoyable, not being able to sample its flavor deprives you of truly being able to experience it.

While risking full openness with others—even close friends or a life partner—isn't always easy, the discomfort and pain that can often accompany secret-keeping far outweighs your potentially being uncomfortable with self-revelation. The pain of alienation can diminish you as you lose your sense of equality, similarity, and attachment to others.

The act of complete honesty, however, is a gift. It can help you discover that you're like others, foster greater intimacy in your relationships, build trust, and nurture healthy personal growth.

Think about why you may be keeping a secret from a friend, family member, or loved one. Then consider the words of Flora Whittemore: "The doors we open and close each day decide the lives we live."

☆

Hiding nothing can convince me that I have nothing to hide. Tonight I'll remember that my burdens are only as heavy as the secrets I choose to hang on to.

Tomorrow doesn't matter for I have lived today.
—Horace

Have you ever observed a child watching a nighttime winter storm? The child may be thinking, "I wish it would hurry up and snow more. I don't want to go to school. I want to build a snowman. I want to go sledding." As you watch the same storm, you may be thinking, "Look at all that snow I'll have to shovel in the morning. The roads are going to be treacherous. If school's cancelled I'll have to find someone to stay with the kids."

Looking ahead, whether in youth or adulthood, can prevent you from enjoying the moment. You don't see the beauty of the glistening snow, hear the stillness of the sounds muted by the snow, or feel the warmth of your home. You only see what lies ahead.

Tonight, imagine how your life could be different if, for every minute that passed, you stayed focused on that particular minute and all the events and people in it. That may sound pretty easy to do, but are you even aware of how often your mind strays from the present? Have you been able to read every word of this meditation without losing your concentration?

To stay in the present, whenever your thoughts stray to some future time ask, "What can I do about this right now?" Your response can serve as a reminder to keep your thoughts in the present moment so you can appreciate it more.

☆

Everything in life happens one minute at a time. If I don't stay focused on each minute, I may miss some wonderful things. Tonight I'll enjoy each moment without concerning myself about the future.

Life is terribly deficient in form. Its catastrophes happen in the wrong way and to the wrong people.
—*Oscar Wilde*

In the fantasy world of movies and fiction, villains get punished and the heroes triumph. In "real life," however, that's not always the case. Those who break the law are sometimes allowed to go free. Unjust events happen that cause children to die, airplanes to crash, and rivers to flood. Those who wish to lead people so they can live in peace and harmony are imprisoned or murdered while those who preach supremacy and bigotry gain power. Crime claims the innocent and unarmed while the guilty often get their way.

In the tapestry of life, the strands of right and wrong and good and bad are interwoven; there's no untangling them. The world contains starvation and abundance, violence and gentleness, harmony and discord in its pattern. To have faith that good will triumph over evil isn't hopeless, but it also isn't realistic. Yet neither is it worthwhile to believe that catastrophe will always strike.

Tonight, remember that every day holds brand new possibilities. Some will be good and beneficial; others will be destructive and harmful. Yet hanging onto only the potential in disaster multiplies its effects. Believe in good things to come, and your life can become one of triumph, reward, and hanging in there for possibilities.

☆

When a catastrophe strikes, it may be hard for me to find any good in it. But tonight I need to remember that if I can accept the bad, then I can also accept the good.

To me, the imagination is a place all by itself. A separate country. Now, you've heard of the French nation, the British nation—well, this is the imagination. A wonderful place.
> —Edmund Gwenn opening up new worlds to
> Natalie Wood in Miracle on 34th Street

When was the last time you played "Let's pretend . . ."? Have you ever made snowballs in the winter and stored them in your freezer so you could have them in the summertime? Have you ever seen a flock of geese flying south and wished you could be up there with them, holding a place in the V? When was the last time you watched a movie and imagined yourself to be one of the heroes on the screen?

Cathy Better says, "Life is raw material. We are artisans. We can sculpt our existence into something beautiful, or debase it into ugliness." No matter what happened earlier today or what will happen tomorrow, each night is like a blank canvas on which you can create whatever picture you want. All you have to do is use your imagination.

What do you want your nights to be like? You can draw a picture that's peaceful and relaxing, black and somber, or chaotic and busy. Visualize your night now. What colors do you see? What objects are pictured? What feeling does it produce? Keeping this picture in mind, step joyfully into a peaceful sleep tonight.

☆

It's very simple to use my imagination. All I have to do is just pretend how I'd like things to be. Tonight I'll not only be creative, but also enjoy what my mind creates.

*We do not weary of eating and sleeping every day, for
hunger and sleepiness recur. Without that we should
weary of them. So, without the hunger for spiritual
things, we weary of them.*

—Blaise Pascal

When you finish your enormous Thanksgiving meal, do
you feel that your hunger is truly satisfied? Or are you left
with an empty feeling inside—a restless, unsettled feeling
that may come from trying to fill your emptiness with con-
sumable goods rather than by selfless giving to others?

On Thanksgiving night, you can celebrate the holiday in
ways that can satisfy your physical hunger as well as your
spiritual hunger. Call an old school chum you haven't seen
for years and reminisce about old times. Take the weekend
off from work and home responsibilities and, with friends or
family, together learn about the city you live in or near. Approach the city as you would a visitor; go to a museum, walk
through a park, explore some unique stores, and sample the
nightlife. Contact friends and relatives you know will be
alone this Christmas or Hanukkah and invite them to join
you for the holidays. Organize an event for seniors at a local nursing home. Arrange in advance to donate a portion
of your Thanksgiving meal to a local homeless shelter. Or,
before you go to sleep, be thankful for all you've been given.

☆

*I'll never be able to fully nourish my spirit by concentrating only
on satisfying myself and my needs. Tonight I'll learn how to give
freely to others so I can be more at peace in my world.*

I have plumbed the depths of despair and have found them not bottomless.

—Thomas Hardy

Sometimes the most significant personal achievements can come out of the greatest pain, sadness, or depression. An alcoholic who hits bottom and then reaches out to Alcoholics Anonymous can find a new way of life without the bottle. A grief-stricken spouse can discover wonderful friendships from those who are there for her in time of need. Numerous rejections from employers can lead someone to become a more assertive interviewee who eventually lands a job.

Sometimes it takes reaching your lowest point to become ready to make a change or to see the same situation through a different perspective. Just when you may feel that you can fall no lower or that your situation is hopeless, what you may find is that some transformation happens—either in yourself or in your circumstance—that can help you see your way out of your predicament.

A Sufi aphorism states: "When the heart weeps for what it has lost, the spirit laughs for what it has found." Tonight, rather than bemoan whatever difficult circumstances are in your life, remain open to new possibilities. Tell yourself, "I won't let _____ get me down." Then rest assured that all will soon be well.

☆

Tonight I can look at my opportunities and options, or I can focus only on my stress and strife. Can I remember that I can always find a positive way out of any predicament?

We're overwhelmed with so much information, our circuits are overloaded. We're overstimulated. Everybody is screaming for our immediate attention. Everything has become urgent.

—*Jeffrey J. Mayer*

Think about a lightbulb. It has an average life of thousands of hours, so it can shine brightly for months. But eventually it's going to burn out.

Human burnout is like a gradual dimming of what once was bright. You experience burnout when you lose the excitement and energy you once felt for a job, a cause you once believed in, a way of life, or a relationship. Burnout is the overwhelming sense of fatigue and frustration you feel when you don't get what you want or expect from the things in your life, you don't know how to get what you want, or you feel trapped or pressured to stay in unsatisfying or unrewarding situations.

You can ask, "What in my life is wearing me down?" Perhaps your job isn't as challenging as it used to be, going back to school isn't holding your interest, or a relationship isn't as exciting as it once was. You can then think about what it might take to feel excited again. A simple change such as taking on a new project, joining a study group, or having a candlelit dinner with a loved one may be all you need to brighten your motivation and interest.

☆

Avoiding burnout is like installing a new lightbulb. Tonight I'll think about ways I can renew and recharge the interest I once had in some areas of my life.

When you look at relationships that make it, the people are good friends and treat each other with respect; they have shared values and they trust one another. Trust is the foundation. Without it, you don't feel safe. If you don't feel safe, you can't be vulnerable. If you're not vulnerable, you can't be intimate.
                                                —*Lonnie Barbach*

Are there times when you can't seem to get along with your partner, no matter what you do? It may seem that everything said becomes the topic of a heated debate, any comment made is misconstrued as criticism, and all facial expressions and body movements are interpreted as silent judgments.

At times like this you may wonder, "Whatever happened to the person who's also my best friend—who I can trust with all my secrets and with whom I can share anything and feel safe?" Yet instead of voicing this question, you may instead snap, "Oh, why can't we just get along?" You focus not on the strength of the relationship you've already established, but on the weakness created by an argument, disagreement, difference of opinion, or sour mood.

Sometimes the reasons for a disagreement or disconnection can never be found. From now on, instead of trying to get to the bottom of friction, you can say, "No matter how this started, it won't stop the love I feel for you. What can we do to move beyond this point and get back to being good friends and great lovers?"

☆

It has been said that "Nothing can keep an argument going like two persons who aren't sure what they're arguing about." From now on I'll concentrate on the reasons I'm with my partner instead of the cause of a temporary rift.

There is something infinitely healing in the repeated refrains of nature—the assurance that dawn comes after night, and spring after the winter.
—Rachel Carson

Time brings summer to a close as well as winter to an end. Time ages the brilliant petals of flowers as well as prepares the new buds. Time advances moments in order to bring about change. Time brings the end to a life as well as the beginning to another. Because of this continuum, you can trust that time will bring the good to you as well as take away the bad.

Yet sometimes it may seem as though time speeds up during the fun-filled, enjoyable hours and slows down during times of boredom, misery, or pain. But time always will proceed at its same steady, unchanging pace. Because of this, you can be assured that with every minute that passes there can be new hope. Bad times will end with the great healer—time.

Today may have been a trying time—one filled with stress, tension, pain, heartache, loneliness, rejection, and dejection. But rest assured tonight that tomorrow will dawn; along with that dawn will come renewed hope. You can always trust in the constancy of this: that time will always move forward, taking you away from the old and gently guiding you towards the new.

☆

Time is always on my side, taking me ever closer to new moments that are fresh and untouched. Tonight I'll trust that tomorrow will always bring me what I need.

. . . one could be carried out to sea and drowned while asleep, and the fact that one had been unconscious and unaware would not cancel out the fact that one had, indeed, drowned.

—Felice Holman

"Dear World . . . I am leaving because I am bored," wrote George Sanders on April 25, 1972. The actor, who had to his credit more than 90 film appearances and an Oscar for his performance as a cynical drama critic in *All About Eve*, found life too dull. So he swallowed five bottles of Nembutal and penned his infamous suicide note as a farewell to a world that bored him to death.

How often are you bored? What do you do about it? Too often people complain that they're bored, but don't do anything more than that. That's why it's up to *you* to change your feelings of boredom into feelings of interest. If you're bored sitting in front of the television every night, then turn it off and pick up a book or go for a walk. If you're bored with your work, then scan the classified ads for a more interesting job or enlist the help of a career counselor. If you're bored in your intimate relationship, then do something out of the ordinary—make reservations at a bed-and-breakfast inn or prepare a special dinner. If you're bored in general, renew an interest in the arts—rent a classic film, enroll in a painting class, or listen to some old records or tapes. Rather than be bored to death, you can become more interested in life.

☆

It's my responsibility to overcome the boredom in my life. From this moment on I'll take the initiative and explore what's available to capture my interest.

*Old folks—and here I'm talking about myself—need
more than anything else to feel they are needed, that
they have a purpose in life.*

—*Ruth Youngdahl Nelson*

Everyone needs to believe that they count in the lives of
others. No matter what your age, you need to know that
others need you and appreciate your contributions in the
workplace, in the classroom, in the community, and in the
home. Although you have no control over the advancement
of time and your eventual aging, what you do have control
over is the attitude you bring to growing old. If you believe,
for example, that turning sixty-five means your life is over,
then you'll probably communicate this to others so that they,
too, believe you don't matter anymore. But if you think, "I
still want to be jogging when I'm seventy" or "I'm as young
as I feel—and I feel peppy and alive," then others will be
scrambling to keep up with you.

Whether you're young, middle-aged, or old, your involve-
ment in life can have meaning—but only if you have the
right attitude. Get in touch with your attitude by picturing
your "older self." What do you look like? What do you do?

Then go to sleep with an image in mind of a vital, active,
lively, attractive, worthwhile older self who will be aging
gracefully over time.

☆

*As I look ahead to my "golden years," how do I see myself? Am
I fragile and slow or strong and spry? Tonight I'll visualize that
I'm a valuable contributor to my life and the lives of others.*

*Sometimes I go about pitying myself and all the time
I am being carried on great winds across the sky.*
—Indian saying

Do you remember the story of the man who thought God had deserted him during a most troubling time because he only saw one set of footprints along the difficult path he had just walked? When he asked God why He wasn't with him when he needed Him the most, God told him that he had only seen one set of footprints because He had been carrying him.

Whether you realize it or not, the seeds of God—your faith, belief, and trust in the process of being able to make it through troubling times—are always with you. All it takes is for you to plant them, tend to them, and let them grow.

The bird that sings before the sun has risen has planted God seeds because it trusts that the sky will soon lighten, the sun will rise, and the world will come alive. It's when the bird doesn't sing that it loses its God seeds—and its faith.

To plant your God seeds, tonight keep in mind that things *will* get better. There isn't a problem that can't be solved, a teardrop that won't be dried by a smile, and a weary soul who won't be energized again. Tend to your God seeds— nurture them through your prayers and meditation—so you can strengthen the faith you need to get you through the difficult times.

☆

Tonight I'll trust the guiding Voice within me so I can have faith that all things change, all wounds heal, and all is eased through the passage of time.

If you find your inner conversation running along negative lines, you have the power to change the subject, to think along different lines.

—Martha Smock

Do you carry on an inner dialogue in which you continually comment on subjects such as your appearance, a piece of work you've just completed, or your capabilities to handle a new challenge in your life? If you were to listen closely to this inner dialogue and then categorize whether your self-talk is positive or negative, where would most of the minutes of dialogue fall?

What you may discover is that very few moments of your ongoing "Self-talk Show" are filled with words of support, praise, or encouragement. Rather, you—as the Host of your own program—may see fit to criticize, judge, blame, and negatively label yourself. In fact, you may even verbally abuse yourself!

You're under no one's power but your own when you decide to listen in to such negative thinking. Yet what's the payoff for wanting to "tune in" to such insensitive negative programming? *You become the person your sentiments tell you you are.* From this moment on, make up your mind that it's time to switch the programming dial whenever you need to "listen in" to more positive self-talk. You'll have a much better night's sleep when you can end each day "hearing" good about yourself.

☆

If I want to find greater peace and happiness in my life, then I have to tell myself I'm a good person. Tonight I'll be a positive self-talker as I identify three positive things about myself.

I also had nightmares. Somehow all the feelings I didn't feel when each thing had actually happened to me I did feel when I slept.

—Andrea Dworkin

Dreams are the messages you send yourself about the people, places, and things in your daily life for which you may have strong, often unexpressed feelings. When certain situations in your life impact on you, you may numb yourself so you don't feel the pain, fear, hurt, anger, tension, or sadness that such things evoke. During your waking hours, your numbing may be quite successful. But while you're sleeping, your dreams "know" these feelings and sometimes resurrect them so you have to confront them.

In your dreams may be scenes from the day's events that made you feel anxious or tense. You may view a collage of images that convey your fears. Or you may get to reexperience wonderful feelings you shared with someone you loved—and lost.

Although your dreams may sometimes turn into frightening nightmares, it's important to recognize that they're simply outlets for feelings that you yourself are not expressing. Tonight, when a dream rouses you from your sleep or touches your emotions, remember that if you're honest with yourself you can probably figure out what the dream is about. By understanding the dream, you can then learn what feelings you need to express in your waking moments.

☆

My dreams are my gentle emotional guides. I don't have to interpret every last detail in them in order to understand what they're about. But what I do with my interpretation is most important.

. . . the journey begins by quieting one's insides, making room, leaving time to hear and to notice . . . the practice of spiritual growth has as its core the practice of silence.

—*John Fortunato*

The ancient Chinese taught that it was wise to emulate the tortoise, a creature that knew when to withdraw into itself to restore its inner energy. Are you like the tortoise? Do you know when it's right to withdraw from conflicts, pressures, and energy drains? Are you able to step back from difficult or painful situations so you can become less confused and more centered?

Whenever you're confused and uncentered, you project your own inner conflicts into the world around you. So rather than resolve situations that already exist, your being unsettled serves to escalate them. But when you're at peace with yourself—when you're able to "go within" so you can restore your energy—then you become more capable of seeing disruptive situations clearly so you can act more definitively. You restore peace to the world around you because you have restored peace in yourself.

Cultivating inner peace can involve deep breathing to slow the mind and restore the body to a relaxed state, periods of silence in which to quietly reflect without interruption, or listening to a guided meditation tape.

But no matter what form of spiritual exercise you choose, practice it every night. It's a simple, two-step process: calm the mind and listen.

One by one, from the top of my head to the bottom of my feet, I'll relax each of my muscle groups. I'll breathe deeply to take in calming energy and expel tension, noise, and discomfort.

DECEMBER 6

Why do so many houses turn into . . . "homework hell" every evening around 7 o'clock?
—Barbara F. Meltz

While doing homework is a child's responsibility, the child's desire to avoid it or put it off in favor of participating in other activities can create argument and pressure that can impact on your relaxing evening at home. After a long, tiring day, the last thing you may want to do is get into a "homework hell" argument with a child who refuses to take responsibility for schoolwork. Each time such arguments occur, it makes it hard for you to relax and have a good night's sleep.

The dilemma you face when you try to help your child do homework is that if you *don't* say anything, chances are the work won't get done. But if you *do* attempt to set parameters or make rules governing homework, you end up assuming some of the responsibility that belongs to the child. Either way, you lose!

How can you ensure your child gets the most out of homework without inhibiting your child's decision-making skills and accountability? From now on, think of yourself as a manager and your child as an employee. Hold a "planning" meeting with your child to discuss "workload" (homework) and "time management" (how to budget the time needed to complete the work). If you can think of yourself as a guide or mentor rather than a disciplinarian or dictator, then both you and your child can benefit in the long run. You can turn a "homework hell" evening into a good night for everyone!

☆

I'll show my child, through my experience, how to get things done in a timely fashion. I'll be a teacher first and a parent later as I satisfy our need to have a relaxing, tension-free night.

*There is no royal road to anything. One thing at a
time, all things in succession. That which grows fast
withers as rapidly; that which grows slowly endures.*
—Josiah Gilbert Holland

During winter you can walk through a grocery store and
see an array of fresh vegetables and fruits on display as if it
were summer. You may select a tomato for a dinner salad
that took only a few weeks to grow in a climate-controlled,
enriched environment while a snowstorm howled outside.

But a winter tomato grown in haste will rarely compare to
the one that grew to fruition over months in the natural sun
and soil. And so it is with the things you desire. Instant anything is like instant breakfast—it's quick and stills your hunger, but is rarely satisfying in the long run.

It may seem that many things you want move at a snail's
pace—finding a job, saving for a home, having a healthy relationship, making changes in yourself, getting all your holiday shopping done. But these things can't be speeded up by
temperatures, soil conditions, or trying to force them to fruition. They will happen through a combination of your efforts and the passage of time.

The best you can do tonight about all the things you want
to have by tomorrow is to simply let them happen in their
own time. Keep in mind the effort you need to put into them,
trust that you're doing the best you can, then let things stand
the test of time.

☆

*Tonight I'll slow down my desires and try not to push things to
move more quickly. I'll accept the pace of the world—not my
own pace—and trust that everything will happen in its own time.*

DECEMBER 8

The soul is dyed the color of its thoughts.
—Marcus Aurelius

If you give a group of children paper and crayons and ask them to draw a self-portrait, you'll see that their choice of colors will communicate how they feel about themselves. Pastel colors can convey happiness and contentment; bright colors can reveal strong feelings; black or blue can mean sadness or pain.

Students of Eastern philosophy say that everyone is a walking rainbow. That's because you have within you seven chakras, or energy centers, running through your body. They range from the emotionally passionate lower centers of red and orange to the yellow solar plexus, the green heart chakra, upwards to the cool colors of blue for the throat chakra, indigo for the third eye, and violet for the crown chakra at the top of the head.

Oftentimes, when you dress in the morning, you unconciously choose colors that harmonize with the energy level in your chakras at that moment. So tonight, think briefly about the colors you'd like to wear tomorrow. Do you want to harmonize with your usual morning feelings, or do you want to try to modify the feelings? You can change your mood simply by your choice of colors. Just as an interior decorator would select colors that would not only complement the furniture in a room, but also create "the mood" of the room, so too can you choose colors that will convey your mood to the world.

☆

What colors will I wear tomorrow? Red and orange are energetic colors, yellow stimulates the intellect, green has a calming effect, and pale blue or violet stimulates creativity and serenity.

*Sometimes I feel mad at her. Feel like I could scratch
her hair right off her head. But then I think [she] got
a right to live too. . . . Just cause I love her don't take
away none of her rights.*
— *Alice Walker,* The Color Purple

You might not mind being in love if the other person
would stop hurting you. Sometimes it seems to be done
deliberately: coming home late for dinner, forgetting an appointment or special event, or falling asleep when you want
to be intimate.

Fighting with an intimate partner is like stepping into the
boxing ring with a familiar sparring partner. You may be so
used to how the other person behaves or treats you that what
you each say and do may seem choreographed. So while the
actual cause of the hostility stays untouched, your "dance of
disagreement" begins: walking away when one person is
talking, rebuffing physical intimacy, maintaining feigned po-
liteness, blaming, or name calling.

But don't you sometimes come home late for dinner, forget an important date, or are too tired to express intimacy?
If those are your rights, then shouldn't they also be the rights
for someone else? Conflict and confrontation can be healthy
when dealt with in ways in which room is given for both
people to be able to make mistakes, to distinguish between
what's personally right or wrong for them, to express needs,
and to have room to grow as individuals.

☆

*In any disagreement with a loved one, I'll make sure that what
I'm complaining about isn't a behavior that I'm allowed to
express. I'll give the same space to my partner that I want to
be given.*

*You who are letting miserable misunderstandings run
on from year to year, meaning to clear them up some
day . . . if you could only know and see and feel all
of a sudden that time is short, how it would break the
spell!*

—*Phillips Brooks*

Anger doesn't always appear as temper tantrums or obvi-
ous hostile behavior. Rather, anger can be a very carefully
suppressed response to irritations, annoyances, unresolved
conflicts, frustrations, and hurts that pile up from day to day,
week to week, month to month—even year to year. Even
though you may think you're managing your anger by not
expressing it, unexpressed anger can disrupt your life in
many ways. It can ruin your relationships with others. It can
produce serious physical problems, including hypertension,
headaches, overeating, and excessive drinking. It can be an
underlying source of unhappiness and depression.

As the end of the year draws near, take time to seriously
evaluate whether your physical, emotional, or spiritual
health shows the symptoms of unexpressed anger. Then, as
a goal for next year, decide to transform this anger into ɛ
positive force. Begin to try to understand what makes you
angry. Then make it your goal that, starting now, you won't
let angry feelings escalate. Communicate your anger by
speaking and acting in ways that show others—as well as
yourself—that you want a positive outcome.

☆

*Tonight, I'll live by the words of Aristotle: "Anyone can become
angry—that's easy, but to be angry with the right person, to the
right degree, at the right time, for the right purpose, and in the
right way—that is not easy."*

People who suffer a trauma . . . must reinvent their lives.

—*Dr. Kathryn D. Cramer*

If you've lost your job, had an accident, been through a divorce, had to take out a loan to pay your bills, ended a relationship, or are in the midst of some other major life change such as a move, illness, or retirement, then you know how stressful such times can be. Even though you may feel exhausted, you may be so wound-up thinking about your difficulties that you can't get a good night's sleep.

Some people approach traumatic life events with the attitude of a passive, helpless victim who moans, "Nothing ever works out for me!" Others become angry, resentful, or full of blame or threats as they say things like, "I'll show my boss he can't lay me off—I'll take him to court!" or "I hope my ex gets dumped really badly!" Still others become negative, depressed, or apathetic about life, adopting attitudes such as, "I don't care anymore" or "Nothing I do matters."

But there's a much better way to deal with traumatic life events. From now on, look at the ways the experience is *helpful* to your life. For instance, an illness can encourage you to take better care of yourself; a divorce can give you the opportunity to focus on your own needs; a layoff can help get you out of a rut and pursue another career. Traumatic life events can be beneficial when you can see them as opportunities to reinvent the way you live your life.

☆

Sometimes the events in my life can be devastating. But I can start to look at each event as an opportunity to learn, grow, and change as I develop a more positive attitude.

Nothing is more seductive, and at the same time more deceitful than wealth. It is extremely troublesome to acquire, to keep, to spend and to lose.

—Hindu saying

Money is the number one cause of arguments between couples. Even couples who don't fight about anything else may fight about money; couples who have lots of money still argue about it. Now that the annual holiday spending season is in full swing, you may have noticed that you and your partner are having more than your share of money-based arguments.

Money is such a volatile issue because it symbolizes many different things to people—love, power, security, dependency, freedom, control, and self-worth. Because of this, it's important that you and your partner communicate your individual views on spending money at this time of year.

For example, are you a bargain shopper who loves to buy all your gifts when they're on sale while your partner searches for the perfect gift and pays full price? Are you someone who wants to pool your money so you can buy gifts from the two of you while your partner prefers to purchase gifts separately? Consider discussing your views on money with your partner in the near future. But, for tonight, reflect on the words of Seneca, who advised: "It is not the man who has too little who is poor, but the one who craves more."

☆

Sometime soon I'll let my partner know my views on spending money to facilitate an understanding about how I choose to use my money. Such an understanding can help ease tensions between us.

Tomorrow is the most important thing in life. Comes in to us at midnight very clean. It's perfect when it arrives and it puts itself in our hands and hopes we've learnt something from yesterday.

—*John Wayne*

Do you always see each day as a new beginning—one that's fresh and clean and full of possibilities for the future—or do you sometimes begin a day by looking back at the previous day and thinking about all the things you could have or should have done differently?

Beginning a new day with thoughts about a day gone by is like writing on a chalkboard that hasn't been washed since the start of a school year. Your new message is going to be hard to distinguish among all the other faded messages on the dusty surface. Chalky, ghostly images of minutes, hours, and days gone by make it hard to focus on the activities of the present time or to look ahead to see your future—whether that future is one minute from now or one year from now.

The best way to start tomorrow is to treat tonight like it's a clean slate. Tell yourself, "There's nothing I can do right now that will change the course of today." Then feel yourself in the present—comforted in your bed, ready to lay your head on your pillow and fall fast asleep.

☆

I have no idea now what's in store for tomorrow. Rather than try to anticipate what will happen, I'll rest assured so I can awake tomorrow refreshed and renewed.

Experience is what you get when you don't get what you want.

—Dan Stanford

There's a story about a little boy who always wanted the biggest of everything because he thought it was the best. Once he was invited to dinner at a friend's house. He took the biggest piece of meat, but found it tough and gristly. He took the biggest baked potato, but discovered it was uncooked in the middle. He grabbed the biggest piece of chocolate cake, but it was bitter and stale. The moral of the story: What you want isn't always what you get.

How many times have you longed for something only to discover that it wasn't quite what you expected? Perhaps the second job you picked up after Thanksgiving isn't giving you as much extra money as you thought. Maybe the decision to stay with your spouse through the holidays for the sake of the children is creating more tension than you thought. Perhaps plans to bring the entire family together over the holidays isn't working out. Or maybe your goal to spend less money this season isn't being achieved.

How you react to things that disappoint you or fall short of your expectations will tell you how adaptable you are to dealing with dashed hopes and desires. From now on, resolve to learn from such experiences. Once you find out what *doesn't* give you what you want, you can then strive to discover what *will*.

☆

What I ask for may not always be given to me right away. Can I revise my goals or lower my expectations so I can find satisfaction rather than dissatisfaction?

We all got one, don't we, tucked away somewhere in a fold of our brain, a torn and frayed-around-the-edges picture of the ideal family. Admit it. Whether it's the Cleavers, the Bradys, or the Huxtables, visions of a functional group different from our own family dance in our heads. It's part of the American Dream.
                                            —Elisabeth Nonas

If you could be granted one wish for the get-togethers you'll attend with your family of origin this holiday season, what would it be? Not to argue? To have everyone get along? To have things be better?

Denise Lang, author of the book *How to Stop Your Relatives from Driving You Crazy*, says: "If you think this time, for the first time, you're going to get everything right, that Mom and Dad aren't going to fight, that nobody's going to drink too much, that everybody's going to be happy, then you're bound to be disappointed."

How can you make your family get-togethers more bearable, keeping in mind who your relatives are, their behaviors, and the fact that such things aren't going to miraculously change overnight? From this moment on, think about trying to view your relatives more objectively when you get together with them. Distancing yourself from difficult family members by not reacting subjectively can help you to emotionally detach so you can interact with them in more positive ways.

☆

I'll close my eyes and imagine I'm the writer of a new television comedy show. The storyline focuses on a holiday family get-together. Can I laugh at the behaviors of the "characters" in my show?

Imagine how little good music there would be if . . . a conductor refused to play Beethoven's Fifth Symphony *on the ground that his audience may have heard it before.*

—A. P. Herbert

Are there routines you perform night after night that have become so tedious they make you tense to even think about them? "I'm so tired of this!" you might scream as you pick up your children's toys, open the refrigerator door and stare at its contents as you ponder what to make for dinner, or sit in bed with office paperwork scattered around you.

While some things at night will always stay the same—for example, you have to eat dinner or else you'll go to bed hungry—what you can change is the way you *do* them. Mundane tasks can take on new meaning when you let go of the desire that they change or you revise your attitude toward them. Just as it can be fun to sing along with an old, familiar song so, too, can you make some of the routine tasks in your life more pleasurable.

Instead of feeling frustrated with scattered toys, for instance, you can make up a game you play with your child as you return toys to the box—green toys first, blue toys next, and so on. You can prepare and exchange a "mystery dinner" with a coworker or neighbor. Or you can listen to your favorite classical tape while you make your way through a pile of routine paperwork. Sometimes just a simple change can make your evening less routine—and much more pleasant!

☆

Can I live in the solution, not in the problem? Tonight I'll follow the philosophy of Francis Bacon, who says: "He that will not apply new remedies must expect new evils . . ."

I seriously thought about suicide. I had a bottle of pills the doctor had given me because I was so nervous. Killing myself seemed like the only way out. . . . I was in a panic, but a small part of me didn't want to die.
　　　　　　　　　　　　　　　　　　—Marcia

The stress and anxiety presented by the holiday season are enough to send even the most positive, upbeat person into a tailspin of unhappiness, confusion, and dejection. But if the strains of the holiday season are also combined with your feelings of pain, loneliness, and hopelessness, you may be experiencing suicidal depression.

Suicidal thoughts should never be ignored. They are like brilliant red flags, alerting you to the seriousness of your hopeless, desperate, feelings. Perhaps you're feeling suicidal because there's no immediate family in the area or still living with whom you can share the holidays. Maybe you're feeling desperate because of the financial burden placed on your dwindling bank account in purchasing extravagant gifts for family and friends. Perhaps you and your partner are contemplating separation or have just ended your relationship. Or maybe you want to escape any interaction with parents who abused you when you were a child.

If you're feeling suicidal, get help! Call a close friend, a suicide hot line number (listed in the telephone book), a spiritual advisor, or a therapist or counselor. Ignoring your need for connection will only make you feel worse, while asking for help can make your life better.

☆

Tonight I'll make a call to a hot line or make my feelings known to a friend. Just opening up to someone else can provide me with the immediate comfort I need.

The higher the flame has leaped, the colder and deader the ashes.

—Olive Schreiner

The camp counselor was showing the campers how to cook a marshmallow over a campfire. "First you have to find a green stick and slide your marshmallow onto it. Then you hold it a few inches above the fire like so."

"But how do you know when it's done?" asked a camper.

"Well, uh, you just know," the counselor replied. "You see, it's not ready now because it's only a light brown color." A few seconds passed. "And it's not ready now because it's not quite a golden brown color." A few more seconds passed. "And it's not ready now because it hasn't started to puff up yet." A few more seconds passed. Then the marshmallow suddenly burst into flame.

"Is it done now?" asked the camper.

The counselor held up the blackened treat. "No. *Now* it's ruined."

Trying to do "just a little bit more" before you go to bed—work, errands, chores around the house, holiday planning, or other things—can leave you short-changed on your sleep time. So stop what you're doing now and say, "Enough is enough. I'm ready to go to sleep." Rather than get burned out, extinguish your high-energy fire now so you have ample time to unwind before tomorrow.

☆

Before I'm as done-in as an overcooked marshmallow, I'll stop whatever I'm doing and go to bed. I'll read this book, meditate for a few minutes, then shut off the lights and go to bed early.

I've done the research, and I hate to tell you, but everybody dies—lovers, joggers, vegetarians and nonsmokers. I'm telling you this so that some of you who jog at 5 A.M. and eat vegetables will occasionally sleep late and have an ice-cream cone.

—Dr. Bernie S. Siegel

How do you approach life? Do you constantly push yourself beyond your limitations? Do you take on everything that needs to be done—and then volunteer for more? Do you feel as if everything has to be done now?

"Type A" behavior involves feeling as if you have to take on every project, do everything yourself, and constantly be in control of everything and everybody. You may feel that if you don't do these things—if you release your control for even an instant as you relax or take a breather—then everything will remain unfixed, unchanged, or uncompleted.

The best method for changing Type A behaviors is to learn how to let go of the controlling grip you have on at least one area of your life: your desire to work a certain amount of hours each week, your wish to have things in your home a certain way, your expectations of how your intimate relationship should be, or your rigid diet or exercise plan. But changing from Type A to a Type A minus doesn't happen overnight! You must ease yourself gradually into this new behavior. Just become willing to let go from time to time—go to bed earlier or sleep in once in a while or throw calories to the wind with a double scoop cone.

☆

Can I tell myself, "I don't have to do everything"? From now on, I'll try to let go of an area which I feel I must handle and put it off for another time.

When you finally go back to your old hometown, you find it wasn't the old home you missed but your childhood.

—Sam Ewing

Holidays focus on families. Because of this, it may be hard to escape from old hurts or unhappy childhood memories when you interact with your parents. It may be hard not to want to try once more to get from them the love, attention, support, validation, or apologies you may not have gotten when you were growing up.

It may be futile to try to get from your parents this holiday season what you didn't get when you were growing up. But that doesn't mean you can't strive as an adult to reconnect with them in the present so you can have a good relationship now—and possibly in the future.

To do so, keep in mind that your relationship today isn't parent to child—it's adult to adult. Instead of making demands on aging and perhaps still dysfunctional parents, expect less from them. Rather than carry old grudges and hurts with you when you go home for the holidays or your parents visit you, take a moment to think about all the things you do appreciate about your parents. Even though it may be hard to find things that are wonderful and warm, at least there may be little things they've done for you that you may discover mean a lot to you right now.

☆

Tonight I'll anticipate some of the anxiety and tension I might feel over the holidays by imagining returning to my hometown as an adult and not as a child. I'll focus on ways my parents help me now rather than on how they may have hurt me in the past.

[To] take something from yourself, to give to another, that is humane and gentle and never takes away as much comfort as it brings again.

—*Thomas More*

Perhaps the most wonderous gift is that given to a child so young that it only knows the pure joy of receiving. The child isn't bothered by knowing who gave the gift, why it was given, or whether something needs to be given in return.

But in adulthood, gift-giving can take on a different meaning. When adults exchange gifts, their pleasure may be tinged with anxiety: "Did I give more than I got? Did I get more than I gave? Was my present more or less expensive than the present I received?" Or there may be the expressed or unexpressed implication of having to get something in return from what was given: "He'll always remember where he got that shirt" or "She owes me something now for that expensive jacket I gave her."

While the gifts you give to others may reflect many things—prosperity, a desire for love or approval, or recognition of another's likes—the best gifts you can always give are the ones that bring you pleasure in their giving.

This holiday season, perhaps your greatest gift can be a gift that comes from your heart, not your wallet. Volunteer your time at a shelter for homeless people, make a donation to a worthwhile charity, give blood, or provide a home for an animal from a shelter. Such a gift may give *you* the greatest joy!

☆

I'll remember that a gift of myself this season—one that's selfless in nature—can actually be a gift I give to myself.

*It usually happened . . . particularly at the beginning
of a holiday. Then, when I was hoping for nothing but
sleep and peace, the chattering echoes of recent concerns would race through my head, and the more I
sought rest the more I could not find it.*

—Joanne Field

Stress and anxiety are especially dominant before and during the holidays. The upcoming family events, shopping,
cooking, preparing for guests, and the scheduling of activities may seem to take precedence over everything else in
your life—sleep included—as you lie awake at night and toss
and turn in worry and anticipation.

Yet there are ways to seek out calmness, peace, and
serenity amidst all the hustle and bustle. Instead of lying in
bed at night focusing on all the things that put pressure on
you this holiday, focus instead on things that are positive and
hold enjoyment for you. You might think, "I'm looking forward to eating a great meal with all my favorite dishes," "I
can hardly wait for time off from work," "It'll be wonderful
to see my cousins again," or "I especially like watching the
parades and football games on T.V."

Then, with those positive images in mind, pick up a book
you've been meaning to read or rent one of your favorite
holiday videos and watch or read until you're sleepy. By putting holiday enjoyment first in your mind, you can get the
physical, mental, and spiritual rest you need.

☆

*This holiday, I don't have to be rest-less. Tonight will be a night
for rest, relaxation, and restoration of my peace of mind so I can
face the hustle and bustle of tomorrow.*

When we hear ourselves raise our voices to our children, or see or hear ourselves through their eyes and ears, we meet the ghosts of our own young parents.
—*Richard Louv*

Comedian Dom DeLuise talks about a time when nothing made him laugh: "Everything was wrong—life was hopeless and I was feeling useless." When his young son asked what he wanted for Christmas, DeLuise replied with a snap in his voice, "Happiness—and you can't give it to me." But on Christmas day his son handed him a piece of paper with the word HAPPINESS printed on it in bright colors. The boy declared, "See, Dad, I can give you happiness!"

As a parent, you have a choice. You can treat your children the way you may have been treated when you were growing up, or you can see them as a valuable resource when you feel hopeless, helpless, unhappy, or overburdened. Children look at the world differently than adults; to them, everything's a game and the world's one huge playground. As Conrad Hyers says about children, they ". . . refuse to appreciate the gravity of our monumental concerns, while we forget that if we were to become more like children our concerns might not be so monumental."

Tonight keep in mind that your children can also be your buddies. Resolve to make time to play with them so your larger upsets seem smaller and so they can learn to see that the adult world can sometimes be fun.

☆

Play can expand my limited picture, get me to see more than my problems or pressures, and help me to understand that sometimes solutions can be quite simple. If I want happiness, sometimes all I have to do is print it on a piece of paper!

Intimacy happens in moments. The mistake we make is in wanting it all the time.

—JoAnn Magdoff

Wouldn't it be nice if the warm glow, loving feelings, and laughter and lightness you felt with your loved ones tonight was like an eternal flame? So, from this moment on, no matter what circumstances occurred, how difficult times became, or how much time passed, the flame of intimacy would always burn bright.

Close your eyes and remember looking at your loved ones earlier in the evening. See them gathered together in peace and harmony, but keep this thought in mind: "This is what the holidays are all about." That doesn't mean that from now on, conflicts will be easier to handle or loving feelings will predominate. What it does mean is that for one night, there was a respite from the tension of the day-to-day or year-to-year struggle to get along. And that respite can be enjoyed for as long as it lasts and then released, without a struggle, when—or if—it ends.

You can delight in the shared laughter, relax with the ease of casual chatter, and be excited by a physical touch or embrace. But rather than strive to light an eternal flame from this evening's intimacy, seek out the glow of a simple candle. Although from time to time the glow may be extinguished, it can always be relit.

☆

Tonight I'll remember that intimacy, like everything else, changes. I'll enjoy each intimate moment when it occurs and then be willing to release it when it lessens or goes away.

When you feel grateful for something others have done for you, why not tell them about it?

—Anonymous

It's one thing to express gratitude to your Higher Power at the end of a day for the wonderful Christmas you just spent with friends, your childhood family, or your own family. But to be able to go one step further and express gratitude directly to the people who have helped you to feel grateful is one of the best ways to show them love, kindness, and respect.

How do you define gratitude? Is it the thanks you give to those who have given you gifts today? Is it the pat on the back you gave to the person who helped you prepare the meal, clear the table, or do the dishes? Is it the smile you flashed at the homeless stranger who held up a plate for you to fill? Is it the hug you gave to your parents after making a long journey to their home?

You can enlarge the one-way Gratitude Avenue that connects you to your Higher Power by widening it into a two-lane Gratitude Road that welcomes those into your heart who have given to you in many ways today. From now on, express your gratitude directly to those who have given you wonderful gifts today. Once you do, you may find that you want to travel Gratitude Road more often—both to give to others and then to give thanks for what you receive.

☆

Is there someone to whom I can express my gratitude tonight? I'll take some time soon to write a thank you note, make a telephone call, or personally express my gratitude to a loved one.

*Action may not always bring happiness, but there is
no happiness without action.*

—Benjamin Disraeli

Wishing problems away doesn't solve them. Neither does avoiding them, walking away, or denying them. While it's human nature to delay doing anything painful or difficult, procrastination only keeps problems temporarily at bay. Facing problems is the most effective way of dealing with them. Talking through a disagreement, making a difficult decision, asking for help when you're stuck, or letting your feelings out can help you get through trying situations.

But knowing you must face a situation and actually facing it are two very different things. One way to gently ease into the process of confronting a difficult situation is to write about it in a journal. A journal can help you explore why you're having such a hard time facing a particular situation. Then, when you're finished writing, you can reread your thoughts; see how you express yourself, and ask: "Am I stating my needs clearly? Is my tone too harsh, argumentative, blaming, or defensive?"

By first writing out how you feel and then going through a mental "rehearsal," you may be able to face the difficult situations in your life with a little less anxiety and a little more confidence and clarity.

☆

*I often feel overwhelmed at the thought of having to work
through a difficult situation in my life. But I can start a journal
soon so I can focus on one difficulty and work out ways to
handle it.*

Life is tough. It takes up a lot of your time, all of your weekends, and what do you get at the end of it? . . . Death, a great reward.

—Mark Twain

Have you ever thought, "If I only knew back then what I know now?" Imagine how you would've handled hard times you may have had in high school. Now you might think, "So what if I wasn't the greatest athlete, the brightest student, or the most popular kid in the class? It might have mattered then. But look at me now. I did okay." Or think about where you might be in your life right now if you could use today's knowledge to help you years ago. Would you still want to marry when you did? Would you have opted for a degree instead of a job? How might your life be different today?

Mark Twain once composed an essay that proposed that the life cycle is backwards. He wrote that everyone should ". . . die first, get it out of the way, then live twenty years in an old age home. You get kicked out when you're too young, you get a gold watch, you go to work. You work forty years until you're young enough to enjoy your retirement."

Tonight, you don't have to despair over yesterday's decisions. Although the past is gone, you have the power now to change your life whenever you'd like. Even though time marches on, you can determine what direction you'll take.

☆

There are some things I'd like to do that I've never had a chance to do before. I'll make up my mind to ensure that such opportunities happen in the new year.

The greatest success is not in never falling, but rising each time you fall.

—Vince Lombardi

When Thomas Edison and his assistants had finished an improved prototype of the first electric lightbulb, Edison handed the bulb to a young helper. As the boy nervously carried the fragile bulb up the stairs, he dropped it. Hours more work had to be put into producing another lightbulb. When it was finished, Edison handed it once more to the boy who had dropped the first one, who gingerly carried it safely to the other room.

In that simple gesture, Edison may have changed the boy's self-image from one of failure and incompetence to success and confidence. Rather than let his young worker wallow in a mistake, by giving him another chance Edison taught the boy that he could rise above his failure.

Being unable to rise above failure can prevent you from getting up when you've been knocked down. But failure can be a learning experience. From now on, look upon your mistakes or failures of the day as valuable teachers. Instead of saying, "I blew it," ask, "What can I learn from this?" And then, "How can I use what I learn so I can try again?" Your capacity to learn from your mistakes and move on will be key to your ultimate success and achievement—as well as to a secure, serene self-image.

☆

Some of the greatest thinkers used their errors to discover medical cures, time-saving inventions, or scientific theories. The errors of today can become the stepping stones I can use to cross the river of life tomorrow.

*So I close in saying that I might have had a bad break,
but I have an awful lot to live for.*

—Lou Gehrig

Who has had a sadder break in life than Lou Gehrig, the
major league baseball player who had to give up his career
because of amyotrophic lateral sclerosis, or "Lou Gehrig's
Disease." Who knows what pressures and stresses Gehrig
faced as he lived through each day, knowing his body was
weakening while he was powerless to do anything about it?
Time couldn't heal his wounds. Nor could patience or a positive attitude cease the spread of his illness. Yet Gehrig coped
with pride and dignity and drew on the strength of those who
supported and cared for him. In his farewell speech he was
able to proclaim: "I consider myself the luckiest man on the
face of this earth."

What inner strengths do you call on to help you through
troubling times? Do you use the support of nurturing friends
or the love of family members? Do you rely upon the comfort of spiritual reading, meditation, or prayer? Does the
ocean, a walk through the woods, or watching the snow fall
restore your strength so you can make it through times of
darkness?

Now, not later, is the time to create and strengthen your
sources of support. Tonight, think of the ways you consider
yourself lucky—lucky because of the people, places, or beliefs you have to lean on when you need them.

☆

*Who or what would I turn to if I needed help and support some
time soon? Tonight I'll think about the people or things I consider
resources for comfort.*

*It is good to have an end to journey towards; but it is
the journey that matters, in the end.*
  —*Ursula K. LeGuin*

Your goals lend direction to your life. Without them you
might flounder, uncertain of who you are and where you're
going. Goals can provide you with a source of confidence,
motivate you, and give you something to look forward to.

Yet at some point you need to sit back and simply enjoy
the goals you've accomplished. After all, what's the good of
losing weight if you can't buy new clothes that will show
your new body off? What's the point of learning how to ski
if you can't take off on a long weekend to a ski resort so you
can enjoy your new skill? What fun is it to save money unless you can spend some of it on something you want?

It may be far easier to set more goals than it is to take some
time out to appreciate a goal's end. Goal setting and achieving can keep you so occupied and active with the many
steps, the myriad activities, and the trials and errors that you
may feel that the process—not the goal—is what gives your
life true meaning.

Tonight remember that setting your sights on a goal's end
is a way of accomplishing your goal. But looking around you
at the place you reach is a way of giving your goal meaning.
Appreciating a journey's end—as well as the journey itself—is
what really matters.

☆

*Tonight I'll remember this lesson: A goal is never really accom-
plished until it's fully appreciated. I won't be able to experience
the full joy of living if my sights are set on my next goal.*

Little story now concluded, but history of world un-
finished. Lovely ladies, kind gentlemen: go home to
ponder. What was true at beginning remains true.
Play make man think. Thought make man wise. And
wisdom make life endurable.

> —Marlon Brando delivering the closing remarks
> *in* The Teahouse of the August Moon

The first step in your search for inner peace begins with words from the *Tao:* "A journey of a thousand miles starts with a single step." The remaining steps in your journey bring you closer to the courage you need to follow the principles of truth and morality, the serenity you need to function in harmony with all of nature, and the maturity you need to look for the lessons of life.

The journey to inner peace is different for everyone— where you go is not necessarily where others will also go. And, for the most part, your journey will lead you into unknown territory. You sometimes must leave well-traveled paths to those less traveled, step from well-lit stairs to ones shrouded in darkness, or follow trails made difficult from the tangles of weeds and rocks that sometimes block your passage. Yet your journey is always one of progress.

Tonight, persevere on the path of life into the new year. Be strong, yet yielding. Be open to all things, yet let nothing disrupt your center. Be compassionate and kind. Seek harmony with nature and within yourself. Then surely peace will fill your life.

☆

Tonight, before the new year begins, I'll recite the following af-
firmation: "I'll always remember that my life is a process. I'll
respect myself and this process. And I'll look forward to the
progress I make in this process. Happy New Year!"

INDEX